Francis Vinton Greene

Sketches of Army Life in Russia

Francis Vinton Greene

Sketches of Army Life in Russia

ISBN/EAN: 9783337299187

Printed in Europe, USA, Canada, Australia, Japan

Cover: Foto ©ninafisch / pixelio.de

More available books at **www.hansebooks.com**

SKETCHES

OF

ARMY LIFE IN RUSSIA

BY

F. V. GREENE

Lieutenant of Engineers, U. S. Army

LATE MILITARY ATTACHÉ TO THE U. S. LEGATION IN ST. PETERSBURG AND AUTHOR OF "THE RUSSIAN ARMY AND ITS CAMPAIGNS IN TURKEY IN 1877-78."

LONDON:
W. H. ALLEN & CO., 13, WATERLOO PLACE.

1881

PREFACE.

A YEAR ago, in "The Russian Army and its Campaigns in Turkey in 1877-78," I endeavored to explain to military readers the organization of the Russian army, to narrate the events of the war I had been sent to observe, and to state certain professional conclusions which that war justified.

In the following pages I have attempted to give a few sketches, which, crude and imperfect as they are, may yet serve to give some idea of the soul which animates the Russian military machine, and tell what manner of man the Russian soldier is, and how he lives and moves and has his being.

To analyse the characteristics of a large body of men is always a difficult matter, and, moreover, in writing publicly of a people from whom the greatest kindness and hospitality have been received, one runs the risk either of offending those who have bestowed this kindness, by giving too great prominence to unpleasant truths, or else of being false to the public which is addressed, by stating only the virtues of the people described. I have certainly had no intention of limiting myself to the latter, and I hope I have not been indiscreet in stating the former. Should these sketches ever come to the notice of those who treated me as one of themselves during the campaign in Turkey, I feel sure they will see that whatever I have written in criticism of their countrymen is wholly free from malice, and is only what I have often said to them and they to me in friendly conversation; and they need have no fear of having it made public. If I have not shown the Russian soldier to be above all manly, generous, and warm-hearted, then I have certainly failed to transcribe the picture of him which remains in my own mind, and have done injustice to a people whose hospitality to individual Americans is no less conspicuous than their unvarying friendship for the United States as a nation.

F. V. G.

WASHINGTON, *June*, 1880.

CONTENTS.

CHAPTER		PAGE
I.	THE TSAR	1
II.	THE RUSSIAN SOLDIER	16
III.	SHIPKA PASS	36
IV.	PLEVNA	53
V.	THE WINTER CAMPAIGN	88
VI.	RUSSIAN GENERALS	126
VII.	WAR CORRESPONDENTS	152
VIII.	CONSTANTINOPLE	168
IX.	ST. PETERSBURG	205
X.	THE EASTERN QUESTION	251

SKETCHES

OF

ARMY LIFE IN RUSSIA.

CHAPTER I.

THE TSAR.

In attempting to give any description of the characteristics of the Russian Army, one naturally begins with the Tsar, who is at once the head and the object of the whole organization. It is in Russia alone, of all civilized countries, that at this day we find the idea of personal allegiance existing in its primitive purity, undisturbed by the tendencies of modern representative government. This personal allegiance is the corner-stone of the whole fabric of society in Russia, and it has been strengthened rather than weakened by the changes which have taken place in the development of the country since the time of Peter the Great. In other countries the soldier fights for his country, for the idea that is so clearly crystallized in the German motto "Für Gott und *Vaterland;*" but the Russian soldier fights for God and the *Tsar*. To his mind the Tsar is specially appointed by God as his Viceroy to govern that large portion of the earth called Russia, and devotion to the Tsar includes all that we understand in the word patriotism.

I arrived at the little Bulgarian village of Biela, where the Emperor was then quartered, on the afternoon of August 5, 1877. Winding my way through the crooked little streets I inquired for the Emperor's headquarters, and finally reached a court-yard surrounded by a fence in front of whose entrance two sentinels were pacing. I addressed an officer in the yard whom I supposed to be the aide-de-camp on duty, stating my name and position, and asking him to send my card in to the Minister of War. He politely invited me to enter the yard, took my card, and quickly returned to say that the minister would be out in a few minutes, and would present me to the Emperor before dinner which was about to be served. I was covered with the dust of a ride of twenty-four consecutive hours across the parched plains of Roumania in a telega,* and I was somewhat appalled at the idea of being presented in such a condition; but, on asking if it were not possible for me to wash my hands and face, I was assured with a good-natured laugh that there

---

* A small Russian postchaise on four wheels without springs.

would not be time, but I need give myself no uneasiness as it was a daily occurrence for some aide-de-camp or other officer to arrive covered with dirt just at dinner time. Wiping off a part of the dust from my face with a handkerchief, I looked about the place where the Emperor of Russia was quartered. It was a plain little courtyard, about a hundred feet across, on one side of which was a small one-story house built partly of wood and partly of mud, in which the Minister of War and his office were quartered. Opposite this was an immense tent, formed of three hospital tents joined end to end, in which were tables set for dinner. At one side, partly concealed by a little hedge, were two ordinary officers' tents in which the Emperor lived. In the courtyard, officers of various ranks, ministers, generals, aide-de-camps, officers of the escort, etc., were beginning to assemble. I was introduced to a number of them, and presently to the Minister of War, with whom I was talking when the Emperor appeared. Every one stopped, faced in the direction of the Emperor's tents, cracked his heels together, and carried his hands to his cap to salute. The Emperor was dressed in an ordinary general's undress uniform without the sword. He walked slowly, coming from behind the hedge in front of his tents, stopped to say something to the men composing the band of music, who replied with a simultaneous shout, and then came among the officers, bowing in return to their salutes and extending his hand to some of them, who acknowledged the favor by loyally kissing his shoulder. I was immediately taken up by the Minister of War and presented. The Emperor asked a few questions concerning my journey, etc., and then motioned to dinner. In accordance with the invariable Russian custom, there was a side table containing Vodka and other brandies and whiskies, cheese, caviare, small fishes fried in oil, and other appetizers. After partaking of this preliminary meal, known as "zakooska," we went into the dining tent where there were two long tables containing about eighty places. The Emperor sat at the middle of one of these; on his right a white-headed veteran, General Suwaroff, Prince Italiisky, grandson of the famous one whose deeds at Ismail are familiar to all readers of Byron; on his left General Milutin, Minister of War, and on either side of them other generals in the order of their rank. Opposite the Emperor sat General Von Werder, Military Agent of Germany, and on either side of him a Roumanian officer just arrived, and myself—the only three foreign officers present—and beyond us other Russian officers. As we sat down the band struck up an air outside the tent, and continued playing at intervals throughout the dinner. The service was of silver, the cups lined with gold, and each piece bore the imperial cipher and the letter N. It evidently was not new, and had in fact seen service in the war of 1828 with the Emperor Nicholas. The servants wore the crown livery of dark blue coats, bordered with gold fringe, covered with double-headed eagles embroidered in black silk, but otherwise the surroundings of the table were of the plainest. The dinner was simple, soup, joint, entrée, *compôte* and coffee, and a small allowance of the light wines of France and Germany. Conversation was general and unrestrained, principally concerning the incidents of Gourko's first passage of the Balkans from which one or two aides had just returned. Just after the *compôte* (preserved peaches or some other fruit) was finished there seemed to be a silence, when the Emperor said something in Russian and the whole company responded with one loud simultaneous shout. I looked up startled and saw the Emperor staring at me and laughing very heartily at my confusion. He explained that it was the signal for smoking, and that I must learn to answer with the others. The words were *Vweenemai pah-h-h-* to which every one answered *tronn; vweenemai patronn* being the Russian command "Take cartridges." After this little pleasantry every one produced from his pocket his silver cigarette case, lighted a cigarette, and smoked, and sipped his coffee. Candles were then lighted, and a large package was brought and placed before a gray-headed old courtier, Count Adlerberg, the Minister of the Court, who immediately began reading the comments of the various newspapers of London, Paris, Berlin and Vienna upon the progress of the war. These were articles which had been carefully selected by an official of the Foreign office present at headquarters, from the files of papers brought the previous day by a courier. They had all been translated into French, and were read off in a monotonous tone. Occasionally there was an interjection at some opinion favorable or unfavorable to the Russian cause, and a slight discussion at the termination of some of the articles, but most of them were received in silence though listened to with attention.

It seemed to me, fresh from the bustling rough and ready world of America, where people read their own newspapers, a strange scene.

The autocratic ruler of eighty-seven millions of people, scattered over a territory comprising one-fifth of the inhabited portion of the entire surface of the earth, sitting here in a tent in a rude village of a foreign land, whither he had come to free his fellow christians from the yoke of bondage to their hereditary enemies, surrounded by his ministers and generals, and listening to the news from the outside world and the opinions formed in the editorial rooms of newspaper offices! We had news from England, then from Austria, from Germany, from France. I almost wondered whether I was really in the midst of the every-day bustling life of the 19th century, or whether I was not assisting at some slightly varied rehearsal of one of Shakspeare's plays, so thoroughly medieval did the scene appear to me. After the news had all been read there was a little conversation, and then the Emperor rose to leave the table. Every one stood up to salute him, and he passed along saying a word or two to this or that person. As he passed me he stopped and said he supposed I wished to join the army and see the active operations. I replied that such was my desire, with his permission. He then said with a certain emphasis that his brother had the entire command of the army, he himself being only a spectator; that his brother was expected here in a few days, and that I could then make arrangements to return with him to the army headquarters proper.

After the Emperor passed out the officers gradually dispersed to their tents or quarters. I found that my baggage had been directed to a deserted Turkish house, a few hundred yards off, and installed there, and I was informed by the aide-de-camp on duty that by the Emperor's invitation I would be expected at his table so long as I remained at his headquarters, and that coffee was served at eight in the morning, breakfast at noon, dinner at six, and a cup of tea for those who desired it, at nine in the evening.

The dinner was the principal gathering of the day at the Emperor's headquarters, and varied but little from that just described, except that the reading of newspaper articles only took place on the days following the arrival of a courier. The Emperor ordinarily rose between seven and eight in the morning, took coffee in his own tent, and was busily engaged with his ministers until noon, when he came to breakfast with his suite; this meal was short, and he then went out for a drive in an open barouche with one of his family, if any were present, if not, with Prince Suwarof or some other general; in his drive he always included a visit to the hospitals, if any were near, or to some of the troops; returning to his tent, he devoted three or four hours to work, then dined, and after dinner, if before sunset, took a short walk, and then retired to his tent, where none but the most intimate of his followers were admitted. His life varied but little from this throughout the whole campaign. He was with the army at Kishineff at the time of the declaration of war, April 24th, but returned to St. Petersburg a week later. A month afterward, however, he came back to the army again, reaching Ploiesti, in Roumania, on the 8th of May. For the next seven months—until after Plevna had fallen on December 10th—he remained continually with the army, not commanding it, though he was advised as to all its affairs, but sharing in more than the proportion of a sovereign its hardships and dangers, animating it by his presence, and extending to those who reaped its misfortunes in wounds and sickness his sympathy and his aid.

The Minister of War, the Minister of the Court, and the Chief of the "Third Section," or Secret Police, were always with him. Prince Gortschakoff's age prevented him from coming to camp, but he established himself at Bucharest, the nearest town. Communication with St. Petersburg was kept up by incessant telegraphing and by means of special couriers leaving each place three times per week, and, traveling without rest by rail and post, accomplishing the journey in four to five days.

During the greater part of the time the Emperor was in the possession of good health, although suffering at times from bilious fevers, particularly during the autumn rains. His headquarters were shifted from one village to another, to be as near as possible to the most important operations of the troops. During the summer he lived with comparative comfort in a tent, but as the cold autumnal rains came on he was forced to seek such shelter as the miserable huts of the villages afforded. His manner was always the same—dignified, courteous, and apparently calm; yet even a casual observer could detect the weight of care and responsibility which seemed to rest so heavily upon him. The expression of his face grew still sadder as the summer and autumn wore on and Plevna held fast, and he gradually lost flesh—more than thirty pounds—giving him a gaunt look. Only once he broke down, and, as I was told, could not restrain his tears as the list of killed in his guard at the battle of Gorni-Dubnik was read out to him—every name being as familiar to him as his own, and comprising those who had grown up about him from boyhood. Just after this battle he rode over one Sunday to thank the troops who had taken part in it. I was then at General Gourko's headquarters, who commanded these troops, and rode out with him to meet the Emperor and his suite. They arrived about noon—the more important officers in carriages, and the others and the escort of cossacks on horseback. Leaving his carriage and mounting his horse the Emperor rode forward, followed by his suite, toward the men who were drawn up for parade. As he rode down the lines, saluting the men with "Good morning," and they answering back in long shouts—stopping now and then to talk with some of the officers or distribute crosses to the men—the men followed him with eyes stretched to their utmost, and with awe and veneration depicted on their faces. Studying their intent expressions one got some insight into the thoughts of these simple-minded, faithful creatures, and saw that it still was possible in this sceptical age for men to look up to another man with personal adoration. The enthusiasm was not forced—nowhere was there an indifferent face—every man fastened his eyes on the Emperor, and kept them there so long as he was near him. For a moment they seemed to forget every one else but the Tsar who actually was before them in the flesh. Their expression was not so much one of joy as of absent-minded, wondering veneration. I have never seen a similar look on men's faces elsewhere, and at other reviews of the same troops by generals or princes the same sort of ceremony was gone through, but the men never had the same thoughts written on their faces as they had when they saw the Tsar.

After the troops had all been visited an open air mass was held. One division of about ten thousand men was drawn up on the plain west of Plevna, and about two miles from the high range of hills on which the Turkish batteries stood; the division was formed on three sides of a square, with a few squadrons of cavalry on each flank. In the centre stood the Emperor, alone and bareheaded, slightly in advance of his suite; in front of him was the priest in gorgeous robes, with a golden crucifix and the Bible laid on a pile of drums which answered for an altar; a short distance to one side was a choir consisting of twenty or thirty soldiers, with fine musical voices. Every one uncovered his head, and the service began in that slow, sad chant which is peculiar to the Greek church; at the name of Jesus every one of the vast crowd crossed himself. On the opposite hills, as the service went on, could be seen large numbers of Turks congregating in wonder at the assembly of this large number of men. Finally came the prayer for the repose of those who had died in the battle a few days before; the Emperor knelt on the ground, resting his head on the hilt of his sword, every one followed his example, and the whole division knelt there with their guns in one hand, crossing themselves with the other, and following in a subdued voice the words of the chant.

Nothing could give a clearer perception of the relations between the Tsar and his men than this strangely impressive scene; the *Gosudar Imperator* (Our Lord the Emperor), surrounded by his people, with arms in their hands, facing their hereditary enemies in religion and politics, and chanting in slow monotone, whose periods were marked by the booming of distant cannon, the requiem for their dead comrades. The Russian people have no fewer daily sins to answer for than other people, but the feeling which binds the lower classes to their Tsar is one of purely religious enthusiasm and veneration, which finds no counterpart elsewhere in these latter days. The west of Europe and America have succeeded, without substituting anything better for it, in destroying that faith which constitutes the poetry of the Christian religion; in Russia, on the other hand, we find only primitive faith—or else nihilism—among the middle and lower classes; modern scepticism, which discards religion but respects good government and morals, has taken no root among them. With them the divine right of kings is still a living principle.

It would be idle to pretend that the upper classes, which travel widely, speak many languages, habituate Paris, and lose their distinctive national traits in cosmopolitan intercourse, have much of the reality of this religious feeling; they attend the church services with great regularity, and make the sign of the cross at the proper moments; but they do it in a perfunctory way, and with many signs of weariness on their faces. But to the class from which the soldiers come, the religion of miracles and ceremonies which they are taught, is the most real thing of their lives, and on earth it all centers in the Tsar.

No one who saw the Emperor at any time during these long months that he remained with the army could doubt his honesty, or his firm conviction of right in the cause he had espoused. He is a man who lacks the iron will and energy of his great progenitor Peter, or even of his own father Nicholas, but he is endowed with a greatness and tenderness of heart which few autocratic rulers have possessed; he began his reign with an act of justice (in freeing the serfs) the greatness of which as the individual act of one man is equalled but by one other—the emancipation by Abraham Lincoln—in our times; he is closing it by another act of justice only less great—the effort to free his co-religionists from the intolerable oppression of the Turk. No more generous or holy crusade was ever undertaken on the part of a strong race to befriend a weak one. So all true Russians believe; so even a sceptical foreigner is forced to admit after seeing and appreciating the sacrifices which the effort entails, the enthusiasm with which these sacrifices are endured, and the small returns which it brings in material benefits. The strong sense of right is his only support; no mere ambition could suffice to sustain him in the terrible trials and responsibilities which his acts have brought upon him. The reorganization of the landed system and of the administration of justice, and the other radical reforms of the early part of his reign, called forth the opposition of the nobles to such an extent as nearly to cost him his throne; and while this opposition is hardly yet dead, these very reforms have given rise to the most chimerical aspirations and the most bitter disappointments; to-day in his later years (he is the longest-lived by two years of all his race) his life is in constant danger from those on whom he has conferred such great benefits, while his efforts in behalf of the Bulgarians have excited the suspicion, jealousy and hatred of half the nations of Europe. Weighed down with the deepest sense of the responsibility of his acts, keenly alive to the ingratitude of a portion of his own people, and to the taunts and suspicions of foreigners, his only consolation must be in his profound conviction of right, and his belief that the God of Justice is on his side and will not let his labors go for naught, but will in His own good time give peace to his own people, and happiness to those of his own creed whom he has striven to befriend.

CHAPTER II.

THE RUSSIAN SOLDIER.

THE peasant class—or *moozhiks*—which supplies the great body of Russian soldiers, ever ready to do battle for God and the Tsar, leads a hard life. The peasant is born in a little village composed of several hundred log huts of one story each and thatched with straw, containing but one room in which a family of five or six persons live, eat, and sleep, and a large part of whose space is occupied by an enormous flat stove, on top of which most of the family pass the winter's nights. The only building in the village which has any pretence to good appearance—the only one which to a person passing in a railway train in winter denotes the existence of a village at all—is the village church, a large white structure with bright green roof and gilded cupolas; within it is a mass of pictures, heavily gilded and bejewelled altar-pieces, and swinging censers—an interior calculated to overawe the imagination by contrast with the poverty of view of the rest of the village. The surrounding country is a rolling plain unbroken in any direction by peak or mountain and usually destitute of trees, wrapped in an endless mantle of snow for half the year, and bright with green grass or yellow wheat for the other half. The railroads are few in number and invariably leave the villages several miles on either side ; the post roads are equally few and the post infrequent. There is no bustling activity in the villages, nor are there striking features in the landscape to develop the imagination or engender habits of daring or self-reliance. Everything is on a dead level, benumbing the senses; the sky during the greater part of the year is of a dull leaden color, and seems to bear upon the spirits with all the weight of lead.

In this depressing atmosphere the peasant grows up, attending schools in the winter months, doing his share of the farming of the commune during the summer, listening to superstitious tales in the winter's evenings, imbibing a religion of forms and ceremonies, miracles and superstitions, and, knowing little of the outside world except that he lives in a land governed by a ruler of unlimited greatness called the Tsar. On attaining the age of twenty, his name is placed in the urn to be drawn for military service, and if the lot falls upon him, he leaves his village and is but little heard of for the next six years; at the end of this period (if no war is on hand) he returns to his village on permanent furlough for the remaining nine years of his military service, but liable to be called up at any moment to rejoin his regiment. At the age of thirty-five his military service is over, he receives his share of the commune's property to work, marries, builds himself a hut like the others, breeds a family, works through his life, and dies.

His disposition, character, and habits are determined by these dull, sombre surroundings, a cheerless climate, monotonous village life, and a superstitious religion. He is sallow in complexion, lank in figure, has straight yellow hair, and a heavy expression of face; he wears high boots at all seasons of the year, and dark cloth trowsers tucked into them; above this, in summer, a bright red shirt worn outside his trowsers and gathered in at the waist by a belt; on his head a slouchy cap with a peaked visor. In winter, he is wrapped, both day and night, in a long "*shuba*" or pelisse, of sheep skin, with the wool on the inside, reaching from his neck to his heels, and his head is enveloped in a woolen "*bashlik*" or muffler.

His personal habits are to a certain extent cleanly, since they include a steam bath once a week, but, on the other hand, the bath by no means involves a change of linen, and his greasy sheep-skin pelisse is worn half a lifetime. The sanitary condition of his village is at once primitive and filthy, and but for the cold winters would generate diseases which would depopulate whole districts.

His diet is as monotonous as his life; once a week, or twice at the most, he has meat, fresh beef or mutton, made into a soup or a stew. Of vegetables he has a variety, but cares little for any of them except cabbage and onions. His great staple article of food is a gruel made of unbolted buckwheat, called "*kahsha*," his taste for which never diminishes. With this and an abundance of heavy black bread, and an occasional taste of fish or meat, he is abundantly satisfied. His disposition is gentle and good-natured, even his brawls being of the maudlin and foolish and not of the fighting character; he is as incapable of taking care of himself as a child; all his important actions are determined for him by the village commune, whose open-air meetings are full of noisy arguments, but from whose decision no appeal is ever thought of. The whole nature of his communistic village life precludes the idea of striking out on his own responsibility to make himself independent in fortune; he has the benefit of his own labor on the land allotted to him, but otherwise his individuality is completely destroyed. He is very gregarious, fond of singing and of reciting or listening to long stories, and with all his sombreness of character, he has a latent fund of mirth and humor peculiarly his own.

He leads a sober, temperate life for months, but celebrates the great religious festivals, such as Christmas and Easter, by a prolonged drunk, undertaken apparently to relieve the monotony of his existence, and infuse some ray of cheerfulness or at least of excitement into his unvaried life. The liquor is the native *vodka*, a pure rye brandy, which does him but little harm, and when the celebrating is over he returns contentedly to his work.

I do not know of anything which so pithily illustrates the submissiveness and dependence of the character of the Russian peasant as the following anecdote, related by Leroy-Beaulieu in a recent number of the *Revue des Deux Mondes*, and which I reproduce in full.

A satirical novelette, called "Two Generals on an Island," was read to some peasants one evening by the village schoolmaster. A synopsis of the story was as follows: "Two generals awake on a desert island; they know not what is to become of them, when suddenly they perceive a *moozhik* asleep. 'Come on, you lazy fellow,' they cry to him, 'what are you doing lying there? Jump up and get us some dinner.' The peasant obeys, catches a hare, cooks it and serves it for dinner. 'Well,' say the generals, 'there is no house here. Are we going to live in the open air like savages? Come, you idiot (*doorak*), make us a house,' and the peasant takes his axe and makes them a wooden house. Although lodged and fed the generals tire of this isolated life. 'Well-bred people cannot live like this on a desert island. Come, you loafer, take your axe and make us a boat.' The peasant, always scolded and beaten, makes a boat, and, taking the oars, rows the two generals back to St. Petersburg, where they give him a rouble for his pains."

Beaulieu continues: "The schoolmaster was asked what did the peasants say of this story. 'They laughed a great deal, and were greatly flattered that generals should have need of one of their like; it made them very proud.' That was all the impression that the story made upon them."

The character thus formed by his village life and surroundings the peasant carries with him into the army, there to be slightly modified by his new career.

The first thing he learns is unquestioning obedience and respect to his superiors. He never meets or addresses an officer without standing at "attention," with his hand at his cap through the whole conversation, and until the officer has passed. He does not even answer a question with a direct "Yes, sir," or "No, sir," but with "Quite so" (*Tak t'otchen*), or "Not exactly so" (*ne kak nyet*). He always addresses an officer by his title, "Your Excellency" for generals, "Your Illustriousness" for princes and counts, "Your High Nobility" for field officers, "Your Nobility" for company officers (all officers of the Russian army belong ex-officio to the nobility). Would that the officers always requited this never-failing respect with the courtesy which should be its never-failing complement; but, unfortunately, it is not so. There is a strong trace of that meanness which a division into insuperable classes often engenders, and which leads every class to kick the one just below it. I have only too often heard officers, particularly of the lower grades, call a soldier on slight provocation a fool, an idiot, a dog, a pig, and follow it up with blows. I have even seen the first sergeant knocked down and cursed by one of the company officers in front of the whole company in line, for some slight misunderstanding of his instructions. Such cases are, of course, rare exceptions, but one of them leaves an impression on the memory not easily eradicated; and the deed is all the more flagrant because an instance of a soldier striking his officer is, so far as I know, wholly unheard of.

Yet in spite of this humility in outward forms, it cannot be said that the soldier degenerates into being servile. Side by side with this unbending discipline, there exists a peculiar feeling of good-fellowship and mutual dependence between the officers and men. The men are jovial and good-natured among themselves, and have their own glee songs and dances, in which the officers are daily spectators. They freely discuss the movements of the campaign, and try to reason out—often arriving at a very just appreciation—the causes and effects of their marches and battles. The officers, when in good humor, are always offering some banter or jest, and receiving in turn quite as good as they give—the answers being never disrespectful, but often framed with very great cleverness and wit, and so aptly pointed as to bring down shouts of laughter from the' men at the officer's expense. As a specimen of this sort of humorous banter, I may cite the following incident. I was in the habit of passing from one portion of the army to another, accompanied only by a Russian dragoon, who had been detailed to me as an orderly. One night we stopped with some troops bivouacked in a village, and the officer with whom I lodged asked me how I managed to make myself understood. "Oh!" I replied, "I know a few Russian words and phrases—enough to pick my way about." The officer then turned to the dragoon and asked him how he managed to understand me. The dragoon put his head on one side, with the air of a modest school-boy possessed of great knowledge, and answered, "*Nemnoshko gavariou˘ pa Amerikansky*" (Oh! I speak a little American)!!

Whenever a commanding officer—captain, colonel, general, field-marshal, or emperor—meets the troops under his own command for the first time during the day, his first act is to wish them " Good morning" (*Zdarova, Kazansky, Uralsky*, or whatever be the name of the regiment), to which the men reply with one long rolling shout, *Zdravie zhelaiem, vass imperatorsky vweesochestvoe*, " Your good health, Your Imperial Majesty (Excellency, or Nobility, as the case may be). When a general meets some troops under his orders whose regiment he cannot at once distinguish, he salutes them with "Good morning, brothers!" (*Zdarova bratzie*.)* When a general first meets his troops on the conclusion of a battle, after wishing them good morning, he shouts, "*Otsebo vam!*" (I thank you,) to which the men answer that they are glad to serve him.

As a soldier, the Russian is most strong in all the staying qualities, and weak in the vivacious ones.

---

* The origin of this habit of addressing the troops as brothers was once told to me as coming from Peter the Great, whose address to his troops on the eve of the battle of Pultowa was somewhat as follows: "*Brothers!* Know that in the battle of to-morrow your Tsar fights among you, and watches you, but that the life of Peter, like your own, is as nothing compared with the welfare of the country which we serve in common." I imagine, however, that the custom could be traced back still further than that, and is merely a peculiarity of the Slav character. I noticed that the Bulgarians were constantly in the habit of speaking of themselves or the Russians as brothers.

In this he is the exact opposite of the French soldier; the latter depends on his *élan*, and the aid which his imagination gives to his courage, but once his cohesion is lost his imagination only serves to destroy his discipline, and turns everything into a wild panic. The Russian, on the other hand, has none of this sort of *élan;* he goes into battle enthusiastically and with lively energy, but not quite vivaciously; there is more of a grim solemnity in his manner as he marches forward singing lustily the national hymn, and thoughtless of his fate. He is at first dull and slow in initiative and self-reliance; and it is only after he has passed through several battles that he learns by terrible experience the knack of looking out for himself—of taking advantage of every shelter, of quickly protecting himself by intrenching, and all the other little tricks of battle which may save a man's life without impairing his efficiency or detracting from his courage. He instinctively looks for orders, and obeys them with a blind instinct, without stopping to question their merit; left to his own resources, he is almost helpless, and will often get killed from sheer stupidity in standing still and waiting for an order when every one is dead who has the right to give one. But these same qualities, which are so different from those of our own quick-witted volunteers, have their good side. The Russian soldier's patience is boundless; his endurance, his good-humor under hardship, his capacity for fighting on an empty stomach and under difficulties, are beyond all praise, and will enable a general who appreciates these qualities to work wonders with them; and he is probably the steadiest of all soldiers under defeat and adversity. Deprived of their officers, a body of Russian soldiers may degenerate into a helpless, inert mass, and be slaughtered by means of their very cohesiveness, but they will never take a panic; their history affords none of those examples in which a mass of crazy fugitives *fly with a cry of "*Sauve qui peut*" from a danger conjured up by the imagination and exaggerated and inflamed by the senseless cries of others.

His faith is simple and childlike; in the one phrase of "God and the Tsar" is summed up nearly all his religion and his philosophy of life. God will take care of him hereafter and the Tsar so long as he lives. When his battles result in defeats, when his biscuits are full of maggots, when his clothing is made of shoddy, when his boots drop to pieces, he reasons it out slowly, and can only come to the conclusion, so pathetic in its simple faith, "Ah! if the Tsar only knew!" Every one within his reach he freely discusses, criticizes and blames; he half suspects that his generals may be fools, and he is sure that his commissaries are rascals, but no thought of censure ever crosses his mind against the Tsar. He never for an instant doubts that the Tsar is his best friend, and would correct all these evils if only he knew of them. But alas! he reasons, the Tsar cannot know everything, and so there is no help for him; he goes on doing his duty faithfully, bravely and patiently, hoping that at some day and in some way, he knows not how, things will go better.

The regimental and company officers possess many of the solid stubborn qualities of the soldiers, but in the great mass of the army they are deficient in the higher attainments necessary to direct these qualities in such a way as to derive the full benefit of them. In the regiments of the guard the officers are gentlemen of polished address, familiar with the life of courts and capitals gained in constant travel through Europe, speaking several languages fluently, and are possessed of a wide variety of knowledge if none of it is profound. In the regiments of the line—the great body of the army—this superficial elegance and smattering of knowledge is quite lacking, though it is partly made up by a greater familiarity with the technical duties of their profession. It is no wonder that, in an army requiring over 25,000 officers, and in a country where education as a science has only just begun to flourish, it should be difficult to find enough men possessing what we are accustomed to look upon as the necessary qualifications for an officer. The lack of initiative, which forms no great demerit among soldiers if their officers are equal to every emergency, is a terrible defect among the officers themselves. The ready grasp of a new problem, the energy and "enterprise" which are so common in America, particularly where it is fostered as in the western States by life in a new country and habits of independence and resource, find no counterpart in Russia; and hence we see their officers when placed in a novel situation letting things take their own course, regardless of consequences, until they at last learn how to deal with it. If 40,000 prisoners are thrown suddenly on their hands, as at the surrender of Plevna, no better expedient presents itself than to herd them out in the snow in great flocks like sheep, and let three days pass before they get anything to eat, and twelve days before measures are perfected for marching them to the Danube, only twenty miles off—the prisoners meanwhile perishing by hundreds every night. If a bridge forming part of the main line of communication of a great army is constructed across a large river, one end of it leading into a miserable little town with streets so narrow that two vehicles can not pass, you do not find the lines of opposing travel so clearly marked out that there can be no divergence from them, and men stationed at every corner to compel vehicles to take a certain direction, but you see two long lines of small supply wagons gradually approaching each other until they become jammed and blocked in the middle of the town, and several hours and even a day or more are occupied in unloading a half a mile of wagons and dragging them out backwards in order to re-open the communication; and these are things which do not occur only during the first days or weeks but throughout a whole campaign of months.

The essential characteristic of the whole class of Russian officials or "Tchinovniks" is their clumsiness, joined to a centralization whose multiplicity of reports and papers defies all belief or comprehension and supplemented only too often by the most petty tyranny. Instead of straightening things out by his own ready wit on his own responsibility, the official is either content to let them take their course, shrugging his shoulders with an air of *laissez-faire* and satisfied that the responsibility rests not with himself but with the official next above him, or else wasting the time that should be devoted to action in an excited discussion with one of his subordinates as to what should be done or how things came to be in such a condition.

Any large army must always represent with very considerable fidelity, the nation from which it is drawn, and Russia's geographical position, backwardness in mechanical invention, and the dense ignorance which still in spite of all the efforts towards education pervades the peasant class, constitute difficulties in her way as a military nation which it is impossible to overcome by any amount of numbers, mutual organization, or bravery. Its only remedy lies in time and the advance in civilization.

At the close of a long conversation about America, a Russian officer—an ardent admirer of our country like many of his compatriots—said with a sigh, "Ah! my friend, you fortunate people have not the middle ages at your back." The middle ages are close to Russia, and she finds it hard to separate herself from them.

Peter the Great was the first Tsar who broke with the traditions of the past, and the key of his whole system is found in his saying that he built his town of St. Petersburg "as a window to let in the light of Europe." Many of his successors, with minds only less great and wills almost as indomitable as his own, have struggled to bring their people forward, but usually on the same principle as Peter's, of introducing and adapting foreign ideas rather than of stimulating the development of native ones; at one time French ideas have predominated, at another time German, and although in the present reign the development has been more of a pure Russian type, yet at all times the progressive reforms have been forced upon the people from above downward, instead of springing from their own wants and necessities, and spreading upwards. In this respect, the progress of Russia has been exactly the opposite of our own in America. Starting from a small but self-thinking and self-dependent sect in the highest civilization of their day, and absolutely rejecting everything in that civilization which could not maintain itself as specially adapted to our own wants, we have gradually evolved a form of national life and habits peculiarly our own, and peculiarly adapted to our requirements, and have constructed a government which at once gives the widest scope to individual action, and the greatest average measure of comfort, knowledge, and happiness to every one, without pre-eminent examples of learning, science or art, on the one hand, or of pauperism and degradation on the other.

In Russia, on the contrary, the classes are separated by immense gulfs, and above them all is the Tsar, attempting the herculean task of dragging eighty millions of people forward, rather against their will than with their assistance, and in the manner which he considers best for them, without asking them to think much about it for themselves.

Among the numerous dissertations incident to the recent twenty-fifth anniversary of the present Emperor's accession to the throne, the following appeared in the *Golos*, one of the most thoroughly representative of Russian newspapers, and one which, far from being a court journal or government organ, has suffered greatly from the penalties inflicted by the censorship. It says: "Strangers have trouble in understanding the bond which unites the Tsar to Russia; it comes from the fact that our national life has been developed under different conditions from those in the west of Europe. With us the sovereign is venerated as the anointed of the Lord, in the biblical sense of this term, and the statute itself takes care to impose on all his subjects the obligation 'to obey him not only from fear but from a sense of conscientious duty.' While in western Europe the Church has often been in conflict with the State, with us the orthodox religion is closely united to the Emperor. Finally, whereas in the west all the great political reforms have been conquered by the people from the secular power; with us, on the contrary, all the reforms have emanated from the sovereign power. It is the Emperor who has always guided the nation on the path of progress; which explains why the Russian people have never ceased to regard the Tsar as a father, attentive to the welfare of his children. It is in this collection of ideas that the love of the people for their sovereign takes its origin. There are no sacrifices which the nation will not cheerfully undergo at the command of the well-beloved monarch. The people rejoice in the joys of their Emperor; they weep in his sorrows; they have with him but one thought, one sentiment, and one will."

The above is a perfectly accurate analysis of the national life of Russia, and the relations between the Tsar and his subjects. I am well aware that recent events seem to contradict it *in toto*, but the contradiction is apparent and not real. It is entirely foreign to my subject to attempt to give any account of Nihilism, even were it possible—which I doubt—for any foreigner to thoroughly explain it. It springs from the peculiar nature of Russian development; from certain moody, visionary traits of character, with which the readers of Tourguénieff's novels are familiar; from the general unsettling of ideas, caused by the vast social changes made in the present reign, and from some concrete, well-founded grievances against the high-handed tyranny of the political secret police, or "Third Section." But although the Nihilists are recruited from every section of the upper and middle classes, yet the most extravagant estimate which has ever been formed of their numbers does not place them at more than a third of one per cent. of the entire population. They no more represent Russian society at large than the Socialists represent Germany, the Communists France, or Kearneyites America. They have not changed in any manner whatever the opinions or character of the mass of the Russian people of all classes, and they have achieved a noisy prominence only by reason of their desperate deeds and of the inability of these same police of the "Third Section" to cope with them.

But the point to which I would call particular attention is that in Russia "all the reforms have emanated from the sovereign power." It is in this way that not only has the country been developed, but the character of its people been formed; and we find them to-day docile, obedient, strong in endurance, lacking in initiative and individuality, receptive rather than creative; their very thoughts are furnished to them, and they expect to be told what they need, instead of reasoning it out for themselves; their capacity for individual thought is repressed not stimulated, and they must read only what is deemed good for them; as the Tsar is their father, so are they in very truth children, and the sturdy, self-reliant manhood which is developed by the responsibility of self-government is unknown in their midst. The great mass of the Russians of all classes thus remain in easy-going, contented tranquility of mind, following in the path which has been marked out for them, and not desiring to deviate from it; while from time to time certain restless spirits, finding no legitimate outlet possible for their activity, imbibing certain western ideas, but incapable of practically testing them, because of their own inexperience and of the system of repression which forbids their ideas from being made public, brood in secret only to bring forth those miserable outbreaks which have nothing better to propose than anarchy, murder, and nihilism or nothingness. They strike at the Tsar, not from personal animosity as against a tyrant, but because he is the head of society; and they have nothing to propose but the annihilation of all the existing forms of society because the great body of the people is unalterably attached to them.

Were their ideas exposed to the cold analysis of the public they would be combatted and overthrown; were the people treated more as full-grown men, responsible for their opinions, these ideas would never come into existence, for they are the offspring of minds distorted and inflamed by the command not to think—under pain of punishment; but, paradoxical as it appears to us, it is none the less a fact that the great body of Russians cling to this system of repression more tenaciously than the Tsar himself. They do not desire to have it changed except as he deems fit, and in the manner which he judges most expedient.

CHAPTER III.

SHIPKA PASS.

As soon as I had had time to return to Bucharest, and purchase certain articles which were necessary for my camp outfit, I availed myself of the permission tendered by the Emperor and joined the headquarters of the Grand Duke Nicholas, Commander-in-chief of the Russian Forces in Bulgaria. Both the Emperor and the Grand Duke then had their headquarters in the same village (Gorni-Studen), on opposite sides of a ravine. The Grand Duke lived in much the same style as the Emperor, although somewhat plainer; his suite was smaller, his table more meager, and his service made of iron lined with porcelain instead of silver lined with gold.

I had been there but two days, when at dinner in the evening, a message was brought in to the Grand Duke which caused him to break off a jovial conversation, and hastily write something in pencil for the chief of staff, who immediately left the table. The Grand Duke is of an entirely different temperament from his brother, the Emperor; responsibility seemed to rest as light as air upon his broad shoulders. He was ever jovial, ever in good humor. Throughout the whole campaign this was the one occasion when he manifested anxiety. But there was no doubt he was very anxious now. The hum of conversation of the fifty or sixty officers present at dinner ceased, and there was a painful silence— every one waiting to hear what the news was. In a few minutes, to relieve the suspense, the Grand Duke read out the despatch in Russian; it was translated for me by my neighbor at table, and was to the effect that the troops in Shipka Pass, consisting of only 2,000 Russians and 3,000 Bulgarian Militia, had been fighting all that day (August 21st) with the Turkish army of Suleiman Pasha, numbering about 30,000; that so far they had held their own, defeating the Turkish assaults, but the battle was still going on and its issue was at least doubtful.

The dinner soon broke up, and the Grand Duke with his chief of staff retired at once to his tent, instead of walking about as usual, chatting with the officers and listening to the music of the band. Returning to my own tent I found that my neighbor, Major Von Liegnitz, the military attaché of Germany, was preparing to start for Shipka in the morning. It needed but a moment's reflection for me to determine to do likewise. I went back to headquarters to ask the Grand Duke's permission, got an order for a Cossack to accompany me as an orderly, came back and packed a few necessary articles in my saddle bag and went to sleep. We were off before five o'clock the next morning, and took the most direct, but not the main road, to Shipka Pass, distant nearly eighty miles. Liegnitz was familiar with the country from having passed over it during the previous month with Gourko. The heat was excessive, absolutely compelling us to lie over for a couple of hours at noon.

The portion of Bulgaria through which our route lay is as lovely a bit of agricultural land as the earth affords. Gently rolling hills, separated by brooks or small streams of pure cold water, and covered with corn, wheat, barley, or vines, with bunches of dark elms and oaks interspersed here and there, and patches of grass with flocks of sheep grazing on them—it was everywhere as gentle and pastoral a scene as could be imagined. The huts of the inhabitants were congregated in little villages, three or four miles apart, there being no isolated houses except now and then a "tchiftlik," or country place of some Bey, with so many buildings around it as to form almost a village in itself. In the fields the men were reaping and gathering the grain; in the villages the women, in bright picturesque clothing, were occupied in threshing. This was being done according to the methods current in the time of Moses. In the yard of each hut was a smooth, well-beaten and baked floor of earth, with a post in the center. To this post a half dozen little ponies without shoes were attached by a cord, and were driven round and round through the pile of grain. In another yard, a rickety old cart without tires on the wheels, loaded with weights and drawn by a pair of oxen, replaced the ponies as threshers; in another the threshed grain was being thrown into the air with a wooden shovel, the wind blowing away the chaff as the grain fell.

As I stood watching these primitive and primeval operations, my mind wandered back to California, and my imagination tried to conjure up what would be the expression of one of these heavy-faced peasants if transplanted to the San Juaquin valley, and brought face to face with a six-horse mower-reaper-and-thresher, moving over an immense field of standing grain, loading its bins with the same grain ready for sacking, and accomplishing more, with the same animal power, in a day, than these people in two months.

We passed the night in one of these villages, sleeping on the porch of the "Starshina," or elder of the village. Although ready to pay for everything with good gold and silver, it was only by dint of threats and blows that we obtained food for our horses. There was everywhere the cunning of affected stupidity, which answers all questions with other questions, finally ending in the reply of "don't know." Every man watched his neighbor, every one ready, no doubt, to betray his neighbor should the fortune of war bring the Turks into the village, and every one fearing the arrival of this fortune and betrayal. A more uninviting race on casual acquaintance than the Bulgarian peasants can hardly exist; centuries of oppression, extortion, misrule, and injustice, have apparently deadened every sense of manly independence and straightforward courage, and replaced them with the low cunning and duplicity, which are commonly attributed to the Jews.

On the morning of the second day we reached the edge of the Balkans, joined the main road, and passed through miles of artillery and supply wagons and troops, hastening forward as re-enforcements, alternating with other miles of fugitives, fleeing across the mountains from before the Turkish advance. The latter formed a motley collection, old and young, men, women, children and babes, carts and wagons, buffaloes, oxen, horses and jackasses, pieces of bedding, tables or other household furniture, gathered together in every variety of form—stopping, gypsy fashion, in a field along side the road to rest, or moving on in a long caravan they knew not whither, but certain that every step widened the distance between them and the dreaded, hated Turk.

In the afternoon, we came within sound of the guns booming away upon the mountain, and as we crossed a ridge, saw the smoke curling up through the trees in the distance. Then we descended into a valley and reached the town of Gabrova, where the peasants were stolidly standing about the corners or in the coffee shops, staring at the troops as they marched past, or at some mounted messenger striving to make good speed over the slippery broken pavement of the crooked little streets. Here we met a Cossack officer with his squadron, which had been in the fight the day before; he had an acquaintance with Liegnitz, and gave us two horses in place of our own, which were exhausted and were left behind with our Cossack orderlies. With our fresh mounts, and the insufferable Cossack saddles, we pushed on rapidly up the mountain, and reached the field about four o'clock.

Shipka Pass is not a pass at all, or at least not a gorge or defile. It is a long, gently sloping cross spur of the Balkans, up and over which a fine high road has been built, passing its highest point at an altitude of nearly five thousand feet above sea-level. On either side of the spur are deep, precipitous valleys, heading at the base of the main range, and beyond them are other parallel spurs. The Russians were on a few knolls at the top of the road on the central spur; the Turks were in front of them and overlapping them on either side along the parallel spurs, and completely commanding their position from three directions. We wound along the road up the hill, passing batteries of artillery with double teams striving to pull up the guns; alternating with these were battalions of infantry, many a man of whom had but a few hours to live, but whose only thought now seemed to be the intense heat and the fatigue of the climb. Then we came to a collection of immense soup-kettles which had just arrived, and were being set up on the side of the road to cook some supper for the men; the cooks were busy with their preparations, or standing about in their shirtsleeves, joking with the troops as they passed. Half a mile further on were the temporary hospitals, three or four tents pitched on the side of the road, sending forth painful groans or screams; a line of stretchers supplying the patients on one side, and a line of ambulances on the other, carrying them down the mountain after their wounds had been dressed or operated upon. From here on, the sharp, incessant rattle of the musketry was plainly distinguishable among the more intermittent booms of cannons, and from the lines of smoke curling up through the trees we began to make out the positions of the opposing troops. We soon arrived among the Russians, and Liegnitz advised dismounting and leaving our horses behind the shelter of a little knoll, while we made our way forward on foot. From this knoll we turned into some bushes and met two officers making their way back, and telling us not to go ahead, we could not pass there. We kept on quietly, and in a few yards came out of the bushes into the open, on a narrow bit of road completely commanded by a cross-fire from the Turks. Along this road was the only way to reach the main Russian position in advance of us. We walked along rapidly, the bullets singing and whistling about our ears and scattering the dust on our feet; I "ducked" my head at the sharpest whistles, as one instinctively does until he finally learns by experience that there is no use of dodging, for the bullet whose sound you hear has already passed you, and you will never hear the whiz of the one that strikes. This little piece of open road was not over three hundred yards long, and we were across it in half that number of seconds. Once passed, we came under the shelter of a little knoll or ridge about fifteen feet high, along the base of which ran the road, and on the crest of which was a line of Russians blazing away with all their might at the Turks a few hundred yards in front of them. It was the third day of the hard, unequal fight. Just here, a few hours before, the Russians had grown discouraged with the great odds against them, and the exhaustion incident to sixty hours of fighting, almost without food or water; their officers had been nearly all killed, and, mistaking a large number of wounded making to the rear for a general retreat, they had begun gradually to turn back, when they were stopped by the determined energy and courage of a certain Colonel Lipinsky; and, as good fortune would have it, were just rallying when the vanguard of the re-enforcements came trotting up the road on Cossack horses, and dismounting and joining them, succeeded in driving back the Turks, who had nearly reached the crest of this little hill. The hot fight at this particular place had been going on for a couple of hours, and had now turned definitely in favor of the Russians, and the Turks were rapidly retreating across the little valley in front of them. In half an hour's time the firing began to lull, except the long-range shots of the Turks from the woods in the opposite spur, whose bullets went whistling away over our heads, but doing no harm.

We sat down on the reverse slope of this little hill, and learned from the commanding general the details of the fighting of this and the preceding days. We were soon joined by General Radetzky, the commander of the Eighth Corps, who had arrived on the field a few minutes before us, and had been engaged in that preliminary survey of the ground. By virtue of his seniority he assumed command of all the troops present.

Meanwhile a few troops continued arriving as re-enforcements. They were huddled together as compactly as possible under the slight shelter afforded by the little hill, until the arrival of night, when they could be moved forward into other positions.

The desultory firing continued, and an hour or more later the sun went down behind the mountains on the west, and simultaneously a grand full moon came over the peaks in the east. It was one of those scenes which print themselves indelibly on the memory. A rugged chain of mountains, covered with deep forests tinged with the peculiar greenish tint of the moonlight, and surrounded by deep gorges, across which the shadow of some projecting rock was thrown with startling clearness of outline; a cloudless sky, warm summer air, and the stillness of mountain solitude, interrupted at intervals by a momentary pop-pop of some sharpshooter across the ravine, or by the rumble of artillery wheels, or the groan of some sufferer nearer at hand—it had all the elements of striking contrast necessary for the highest artistic effect.

All the troops having arrived which might be expected before morning, they were roused from the fragmentary slumber which they were seizing in the midst of the road, unmindful of the wheels which passed hardly a foot from their heads, and were led forward quietly around the point of our little hill, and along the open road toward the advanced Russian position on another rocky hill called St. Nicholas.

The moon betrayed us at once, and immediately the two Turkish hills on either side were all ablaze with little lines and specks of fire as in an exhibition of fire-works; the long, sharp rattle of the muskets alternated with the occasional deeper boom of a field-piece, quickly followed by the peculiar rushing scream of pieces of shrapnel; and all these sounds went echoing and reverberating down the gorges, while along the woods on either side sharp lines of transitory flame were darting about like meteors. It was a beautiful sight—beautiful in the sense that a terrible storm at sea on a bright sunny day is beautiful, when one stands near the stern and watches the rich green bend of the wave just before it breaks, then the snowy foam, and the angry snarl of the water as it surges past the rudder—the deck pointing one minute into the very base of a mountain of water, and the next into the sky itself; and then a sudden thud and tremor, when the mind wonders whether this pigmy of a ship will hold her own against the mighty forces of nature. It was beautiful, as all strong sensations, unmixed with vice, are beautiful, and particularly when surrounded with strange unusual effects of nature.

It was an hour or more before the troops had all been posted; then Liegnitz and myself quietly walked back to find our horses and pick out some place to sleep. No troops being in sight, the Turks were perfectly quiet; hardly a shot was fired as we walked back along the whole position for about two miles; the stillness was almost oppressive, and the bright light of the moon was most weird. We found our horses, shoved their noses into a pile of hay belonging to an artillery battery, feeling sure that they would not move before morning, and we were soon in a profound slumber on the side of the road.

I was awakened by Major Liegnitz tugging at my clothing and exclaiming, " *Voilà! l'affaire recommence*." The sun was just visible, rising above the woody tops of the mountains toward a cloudless sky, and the Turks had saluted its appearance by a rousing fusillade from all sides. It was an animated reveille. The whole mountain sides were enveloped in smoke, through which, but not so distinctly as in the moonlight of the evening, the lines of flame marking the muzzles could just be seen. We got up and crossed the road to a little clump of rocks from which, with our glasses, a large part of the mountains could be seen, and there we watched the beautiful sunrise and its strange attendant surroundings. Nothing developed itself, however. The Turks were merely giving a morning salute from behind their woods, firing across the ravines at the Russian positions in general, but at nothing in particular. An hour or two later a battalion of infantry came marching along the road, and turning into a little open space near us, it stacked arms. It was the advance guard of the Fourteenth Infantry Division, the troops who had led in the passage of the Danube, and the rest of the division was not far behind them on the road. With this battalion came General Dragomiroff, the commander of the division, a stout person wearing spectacles and having the general appearance of a German professor, although very quiet and undemonstrative in manner. He sat down with us on the rocks, and Liegnitz, who had been with him at the passage of the river and formed his acquaintance there, explained to him the position of the troops, the events of the past three days, and the general condition of affairs. In this way a considerable time was passed, during which a few more of his troops continued to arrive. He then made certain dispositions of them—sending a portion across the ravine on our right, and leading the rest forward to the hills where we had been the previous day—first, however, relieving our personal anxiety concerning food by sharing with us a large piece of cold mutton, some white bread, and a flask of brandy.

The troops fell in, took their arms, and moved out in column of fours along the road; Liegnitz was asked to pilot the head of the column in order to avoid as much as possible of the ugly open space of road so exposed to the Turks; the General with his staff and myself rode at the rear of the column. Just after the leading portion of the column had turned a clump of rocks and came out in the open, the Turks discovered them and let go their fire. It was very nearly a volley of about two thousand or more pieces (nearly all, fortunately, aimed a little too high), and the number of bullets was so great that the individual whistle of each was swallowed up in a general rushing sound as of a sudden gust of wind just preceding a shower. The effect on the men was most comical; they all toppled in succession like a pile of bricks towards the rocks whose shelter they had just passed. The General and other officers sung out to them something like " What are you about, you geese ? " and the men recovered themselves, looked at each other and grinned as men do on an escape from danger, and turning again in the direction of the advance, moved forward without the slightest further deviation, though a very considerable number were hit before we got across to the shelter of the hill. Arrived there, the men were massed under the reverse slope to await further orders, while General Dragomiroff was met by General Darozhinsky, who invited him to come up to the eastern point of the little hill, whence he could show him a good bird's eye view of the whole position. In dismounting, Liegnitz and myself had a little trouble in inducing the Cossack orderly to hold our horses, he having already nearly as many as he could attend to. In this way we were delayed two or three minutes; we then began climbing the hill towards the point where the others were standing in a group, fifty or sixty yards in front of us. Just then we saw two of the group stagger, and running forward we met General Dragomiroff and his chief of staff, both of whom had been hit only a moment after they showed themselves on the point of the hill. Dragomiroff was shot in the knee, and the other in the upper part of the thigh. Boots were cut off, a stretcher hailed, tourniquets applied to stanch the bleeding, both smiled with an effort and said they felt comfortable, and then moved off on their stretchers to the field hospital—one to die the next day, and the other to endure the torture of a journey of thousands of miles swung on his back, and to hobble through life with a crooked knee and a heavy cane. It was all an affair of so few minutes, and yet so decisive to them individually. It represented fairly the touch-and-go nature of war and of a soldier's life, and the lack of melodramatic elements (as a rule) in modern war since the invention of long range muskets. A man lives to the age of forty-five years, and the grade of Major General, without ever being under fire. He then commands the advance guard at the passage of a river, and with success. In his second fight he arrives quietly on the field, goes to take a view of the position, and is immediately knocked over. There is no charging, no close combat, no hot blooded excitement, every one is as cool as if we were a party of tourists, taking a first look at a fine bit of mountain scenery. It is an affair of a minute, and for the rest of his days there is no more battle, no more commanding troops in action, of which he has been thinking these twenty-five years, no more *active* practice of his profession (as a lawyer's practice is active when he argues a great cause, or a merchant's when he does a great stroke of business), nothing but hobbling through life and teaching military science to junior officers. And it happened all by such a chance!

Such scenes are every-day scenes in war; they are as old as war itself; they are the essential characteristic of any one's experience in war—but they sharpen one's wits, and, during them, minutes count as years of ordinary existence in developing the faculities.

As the two stretchers moved down the hill and we turned to watch the fighting again, poor General Darozhinsky was much troubled in his mind; he had invited them to the position where they had been hit, and in a measure felt responsible for their misfortune. He little imagined that he would be dead before either of them. A dozen rods from the same spot, the next morning about sunrise he was sitting on the ground, drinking a glass of tea, and fancying himself under shelter. A plunging bullet entered his left side, and he was dead before the tea fell from his hands. Such is war, and yet soldiers, like other people, fancy that they have some share in shaping their own lives and directing their fate.

We watched the battle throughout the greater part of the day. There was a short but vigorous assault on the Russian left at Mount St. Nicholas about noon, but for the rest of the time the firing was desultory. The Turks had wasted their strength in ineffectual assaults, and the first part of the four months' fighting around these mountain tops was over. Liegnitz and myself hastened back to headquarters in order to be in time for the grand affair at Plevna, which was daily expected.

CHAPTER IV.

PLEVNA.

THE name of Plevna has ground itself into history. Full twenty thousand men died fighting on the pretty vine-clad hills which surround the little town, and nearly three times that number there found wounds, the effects of which they will carry through the rest of their shortened lives. It was the scene of one of the great sieges of history, accompanied with many bloody battles, and it is almost the synonym of the latest and fiercest of the many wars, incident to the settlement of the Eastern question.

The town is made up of about a thousand houses, situated on wandering, crooked little streets, such as only a Turkish town affords. Seen from the hills from which we watched it so long, it was a little clump of red-tiled roofs and whitewashed walls, with half a dozen staring white minarets raised above the surrounding roofs, and in the suburbs a large Christian church, with much green paint on the roof and a collection of gilded crosses above the cupolas. It nestles in a little valley at the junction of two meandering brooks, which unite at its lower end, and after a couple of miles discharge into a river about three feet deep and two hundred feet wide at ordinary seasons. On the west of this river, as seen from the bluffs on its eastern bank, the eye discovers nothing but a treeless plain, although in traveling over it it is found to be undulating; on the east the hills rise abruptly to the height of seven or eight hundred feet, and their crest at this altitude surrounds the town in a radius of five to six miles, the surface of this circle being broken into deep ravines by the brooks above-mentioned and their branches.

The place has no military importance beyond that belonging to any junction of two high-roads and a few smaller ones. At the declaration of war it was an ordinary agricultural town; the surrounding hills were planted in corn and wheat and vines, and the inhabitants led that life of comparative peace—waiting for the opportunity to arrive when their smouldering hate should break out into violence against each other—which is characteristic of all mixed Mohammedan and Christian towns in Turkey. The events of the war brought a Turkish army to the place and forced it to defend it to the last extremity; this, in turn, forced the Russians to concentrate their whole energy upon its capture; and both sides followed out their necessities to the bitter end. Three times in the space of seven weeks the Russians attempted to take it by the brute force of an open assault, only to be each time defeated with ever-increasing slaughter. Then they turned their efforts to hermetically sealing it up from the outside world, and finally starved it out. The third and most bloody of these assaults—that of September 11th—I witnessed from the batteries which contributed their share towards it, and it is of this one that I shall try to give a sketch.

On the 4th of September the headquarters of the Ninth Corps, commanded by General Krudener, with whom I was sojourning, were moved from one little village to another about ten miles east of Plevna. Then a halt was made, the preparations for the advance not yet being completed, and the whole of the 5th and of the 6th were passed in the nervous inaction of awaiting the development of events. They were cold, rainy days; nobody had more than the shelter of a tent-fly, and few had that; the sutlers moved about from point to point doing a thriving business; the officers ate prodigiously and drank freely; there was everywhere a forced but boisterous gayety. At sunset on the evening of the 6th the troops were formed and moved forward. They had only a few miles to go, but the night was dark and the road obstructed. The troops marched short distances only to halt for long intervals and lie down in the road for a nap, while the officers sat nodding on their horses. After a while the general and his staff rode forward to the head of the column. Some five hundred men were here working silently but most vigorously with their picks and spades, while others were placing gabions, fascines, and platforms in position. A regiment had been thrown forward about half a mile in advance as skirmishers and pickets to cover the construction of the battery, and the ear listened nervously to hear their first shot. But, save the hurried, muffled noise of the spades and earth, no sound was audible. Soon after midnight the battery was completed, the eight siege-guns hauled into position, the ammunition stored in some sort of bomb-proofs, the troops disposed on either flank, and everything was ready for the morning. The general rode back a few hundred yards, and we dismounted and dozed there till daylight. As the day broke the whole Turkish position was in front of us, a couple of miles away. On our right was a high, rounded hill, whose green slopes culminated in a low, brownish mound, which we knew at once to be the great Krishin redoubt. Curving from this as an apex, on either side of the town, the lines of fortifications could be dimly made out in the twilight of dawn. Not a soul seemed to be stirring. The sun rose in a clear sky, and the lines became plainly distinguishable, and off on our left, on the brow of the Radishevo ridge, was also seen the freshly-turned earth of the Russian batteries. At six o'clock there was an explosion from the battery in front of us, followed by the vibrating scream of the shell, the sound of which gradually diminished in the distance; eleven seconds afterwards a cloud of dust was thrown up from the Krishin parapet, and greeted by a loud hurrah from the Russian troops. Immediately the parapet was lined with black dots, a hundred or more men jumping up to see what had happened, and a second later a horse galloped out from the redoubt towards the village, carrying, doubtless, a messenger to headquarters. The Turks are notoriously bad watchmen; a line of batteries had been built under their nose, and nearly ninety thousand men had gathered in front of them during the night without their pickets firing a shot; and apparently their first intimation of what had transpired was derived from this 90-pounder messenger of iron which had dropped in upon them. But they were not long in answering. Hardly a dozen shots had been fired from the various Russian batteries before a puff of smoke curled up from the Krishin parapet, and we saw the shell explode a long way in front of us. The second or third, however, fell squarely on the parapet, throwing the dirt in the faces of the Russian gunners, and one not long afterwards dropped in the bushes near our group, and caused us to move back to a more advantageous point of observation. The guns answered one another from every point of the two lines, and the ball was fairly opened.

It continued throughout the whole of this and the three succeeding days and nights, and grew monotonous. There were tentative infantry skirmishes here and there, developing almost into a battle at one point, but the characteristic feature of these four days was the cannonade. We watched it for hours with the glasses until our eyes grew dim; saw the dust of the exploding shells time after time in the very midst of the redoubts, and received the same in our own. The symmetry of the nicely-made Turkish works was sadly marred, and one gun after another seemed to be silenced; but the fire ever broke out in a new place, and still the stout piles of earth forming the parapets remained in place and warned the Russians that they could still give a murderous reception. The assaults had been originally intended for the 9th, but were postponed from day to day in the hope of their being made easier by the hammering of the artillery; but the dirt parapets were as uninviting as ever. The Grand Duke and his staff arrived and rode through all the batteries. Prince Charles, of Roumania, the nominal commander of the assembled troops, was daily on hand. The Emperor and his suite drove on to the field in barouches every morning, mounted their horses, and rode to one or another advantageous point of view; assembled at noon for a hearty lunch *al fresco*, and at dusk drove back to his headquarters at a village some ten miles in rear.

The thing began to drag. We rode from day to day from one end of the line to the other, we foreigners and newspaper correspondents (of which there were nearly twenty on the field) meeting at this point or that, and as we constantly discovered some new line of Turkish trench or battery which we had not previously seen, our bright enthusiasm of the first morning began to wane, and the dull, gloomy suspicion forced itself upon us that this was to be no holiday affair, deciding the war at a single blow, but a terrible battle, with the odds enormously against the chance of Russian success.

Finally, the assaults were fixed for September 11th, the Emperor's name-day. Four days' incessant bombardment had silenced nearly all the Turkish guns, which were far inferior in numbers and weight to those of the Russians; but it had also shown that the earthern parapets were practically but little injured, and that they would be in the same condition if bombarded for four weeks or months. Nevertheless, it was necessary to begin some time, and what better day than this? They have a sentimental fancy in Russia for anniversaries. For example, the negotiations for the treaty of San Stefano were allowed to drag on, through Turkish procrastination, for nearly five weeks, and were then brought to a conclusion in two or three days, in time to be signed on the 3d of March (February 19th, O. S.), the anniversary both of the Emperor's accession and of the signing of the ukase freeing the serfs. The 11th of September (August 30th, O. S.) is the feast-day of St. Alexander Nevsky, one of the most famous saints in the Russian calendar, and therefore the feast-day also of all who bear the name of Alexander. What more graceful compliment to the Emperor, who had come to encourage his men by sharing the hardships of the campaign, than to link his name with that of the great decisive battle of the war, and to give him a great victory as a name-day present?—as General Sherman offered the city of Savannah to Mr. Lincoln for a Christmas gift in 1864.

During the night of the 10th the rain fell in torrents; this was succeeded by a fog and mist so dense that it was hard to tell when day broke, and when our watches told us it must be broad daylight, nothing could be seen at the distance of a few hundred yards. Nearly all the regiments had left their knapsacks and shelter-tents at the villages where they had bivouacked a few days before, and had nothing with them but their muskets, cartridges, overcoats, and a small amount of rations. The men awoke cold, wet, and stiff; the ground was covered with a slimy paste of mud; the air was raw and damp. It was altogether a most dismal day.

The assaults had been fixed for three o'clock in the afternoon, and were to be preceded by an elaborate artillery programme, which, however, was altogether disconcerted by the fog. Early in the morning a sharp rattle was heard through the mist from Skobeleff's position, off on the left; and the troops in the center became involved in a very brisk affair, in which they lost over two thousand men without any advantage whatever. The Emperor arrived before noon, and, with the Grand Duke, Prince Charles, and their numerous suites, took up a very advantageous position (had there been no fog) on a hill near the right of the Russian lines, from which, on a clear day, the whole position could be very distinctly seen.

The fog lifted and settled again during the day; the artillery burst forth from time to time, occasionally mingled with the rattling from the picket lines; the men lay in the mud, behind the shelter of the various hills and ridges, chatting, joking, and making as merry as possible in their dismal surroundings. At three o'clock, on every part of the line the troops were formed and moved forward, grouped in three principal columns for assault on three specified points. In company with some German newspaper correspondents, I selected a good point of observation, a few yards from the batteries on the left of the Radishevo ridge, and nearly at the center of the whole line, and we watched the assault at that point. The hill on which we stood was fully one hundred and fifty feet higher than the Turkish redoubt known as No. 10 on the Russian maps, and about two thousand five hundred yards from it. The hill sloped gently from us, and completely overlooked the whole basin—filled with redoubts and batteries—to the commanding ridge of Krishin, opposite to us, and about three miles distant. While the guns redoubled their activity, firing with the utmost rapidity and a deafening racket, the infantry slowly filed past us in column of platoons, the men looking serious, but not sad, and crossing themselves and muttering their prayers incessantly as they passed the brow of the hill and moved down the slope. When they arrived at the base of it they were under the shelter of a little ravine, and the redoubt (No. 10) lay on their left, and about fifteen hundred yards from them, the greater part of this distance being nearly level, or sloping gently up to the redoubt, part of it covered with standing corn, and part of it (the greater part) entirely open, the corn having been cut.

The troops composing this particular column numbered six battalions, or about five thousand men; when they reached the little ravine just mentioned, they halted and lay down for a few minutes of rest; then they turned by the left flank, and, leaving one battalion in reserve, moved forward in line, the center battalion being in company column. They were not long in coming on the brow of the slope leading to the redoubt, and in full view of it. They moved forward, preserving a fair alignment, steadily, slowly, grandly. Nothing can be finer as a mere spectacle than the sight of a line of troops moving forward with blind, unthinking obedience and faith into battle.

They were fully twelve hundred yards from the Turkish redoubt when the smoke began to curl up along the line of its parapet, and the pop, pop, of its muskets gradually increased in sound till it resembled the drummers' long roll. The fog had partly lifted, and the redoubt, as well as other parts of the field, could be fairly well seen; the Russians answered back at the Turks and still kept advancing. The columns on either side of us were by this time also fully engaged, the din was very considerable, and the smoke was beginning to collect in low dense clouds, gradually drifting across the landscape, before the wind.

The Russian line gradually moved on; to us above them, and some distance on one side, the rate of progress seemed terribly slow, but it never halted. Individual men could be seen running forward, firing and falling; a few others in the rear moving back, throwing up their arms and falling, but the main line—a black, irregular, waving band, of which the individuals could only be distinguished by the glass—still stretched across the stubble-field, and still moved on. Finally they had passed half the space from the little ravine to the redoubt, and then they stopped and lay down, and the firing increased in rapidity. A few minutes later they got up again, the center battalion now deployed in line, and again moved forward. They were soon so near the redoubt that the batteries near us ceased firing for fear of injuring their own men; the gunners leaned on their pieces watching their comrades below, and the silence in our neighborhood was oppressive, although the more distant noise became ever louder and more boisterous. Finally the line of Russians seemed to be within only one hundred or two hundred yards of the redoubt; the line could be seen to break into a run, and then all was lost in a confused mass of smoke, through which the fire from the muzzles leaped back and forth from end to end of the parapet, like flashes of lightning, and out of which was heard the sharp, continuous rattle of the muskets, but no individual sound. It was the critical moment; nothing was in sight but the cloud of smoke, and we held our breath in suspense awaiting the result. My God! they are coming back! Black dots began to emerge from the smoke, increasing in numbers, until it was seen to be the whole line, confused and irregular, but still intact, gradually moving back to the rear. The sound of shouts came through the smoke, and now the fire of the Turks seemed to increase with the fury of hell itself. As the smoke partly blew away, the parapet seemed made of sheets of flame; and outside of the redoubt there was a regiment or more of Turks fighting in the open, and still others behind them climbing the slope from the direction of Plevna. And now a mass of black objects were seen streaming over the parapet at one corner, jumping and running forward toward the retreating Russians. The Turks were following up their victory. But this lasted but a few minutes. The Russian line stopped, turned, lay down, and sent back a greeting of death as warm as that which they were receiving. It was but a second before the Turks were swarming back into their redoubt as rapidly as they had come out. Then the Russians got up and continued their retreat—a few running, but the great mass steadily walking in a confused line, stopping now and then to return the fire. As they retreated, the battalion which had been left in reserve came hurrying forward at a run, but it was a bagatelle in strength, and merely joined their comrades and returned with them. The whole lot were soon back under the shelter of the ravine again. It was a little over thirty minutes since they had left it to advance; and fifteen hundred of their number now lay in the furrows among the corn-stalks. The Turkish hurrahs came echoing over the field; their men stood defiantly on the parapet; the Russians sat exhausted and bewildered under the shelter of their little ravine; the firing simmered down to a few scattered shots; soon it ceased altogether, and was succeeded by the stillness of death, in painful contrast to the noise of a few minutes before. The stubble-field was covered here and there with black objects. Three of these were noticed to rise, and two began to run; then the firing recommenced; thousands of bullets came chasing after these three lone objects; first one threw up his hands and plunged headlong on his face, then the other; the third went on at a walk, defiantly, with head erect, swinging his arms; then, either losing his nerve, or stung with a bullet, he began to run, but before he had gone ten steps he too fell headlong. Everything was quiet again, and over the whole field not an object moved.

Meanwhile, the distant firing continued uninterruptedly on both sides of us, but we could make nothing of it through the fog and smoke, and our hearts were too sick with what we had just seen to feel much interest in it. If nothing could be finer than their advance half an hour ago, certainly nothing could be sadder than the sight before us now. Brave men had done their best, one in four giving up his life in the effort, but they could not accomplish the impossible. They came slowly up the hill again to where we stood, their faces sad but not panic-stricken, filed down the reverse slope, stacked arms, and lay down to sleep, overcome with fatigue and bewilderment.

As they passed by us, another disjointed attack was going on against the same redoubt by other troops off to our left. The assaults were not simultaneous, and the Turks had only to turn to the other side of their work to drive back this more easily than they did the first, for it was not pushed so far. The line was withdrawn, the fire slackened, and darkness, smoke, and fog gradually settled over the whole field. The sun, which never shone, had set on the Emperor's name-day, and his name-day gift was only a roll of five thousand killed and ten thousand wounded of his own subjects, without counting the losses of his gallant young allies, the Roumanians, who had borne the principal part in the assault on our right against the Krishin redoubt.

I turned my horse down the hill and met a party of English correspondents and the English military attaché, who had witnessed the same struggle as myself from a point a few hundred yards to the left; leaving them, I rode rapidly over to the Emperor's point of observation. On my way I met the younger Grand Duke Nicholas, who eagerly questioned me for information, and then galloped on to relate it to his father. When I came up the elder Grand Duke was standing at the steps of the Emperor's carriage. As the Emperor returned my salute, I got a good look at his face; his expression was sad and very thoughtful, but still dignified. It seemed simply as if he had an unusual load of care in addition to that which his face habitually gave signs of. The two brothers kissed on the cheek after the Russian fashion, and the Emperor drove off, followed by the carriages and cavaliers of his suite, and the half-wild, grotesquely-dressed Cossacks of his escort. What must have been his thoughts during this ten miles' drive in the drizzling rain and darkness! Fortunately, being but a man, he could not realize it all. Could he feel the measure of his misfortune in the same proportion that a captain of a company in that death's hollow near him felt his, the weight of it would grind him to powder.

I dismounted as the Emperor drove off, and the Grand Duke beckoned to me, took my arm, and walked a few steps to one side, saying in English, "Come, tell me what is this?" It seemed that I was the first officer to arrive from that part of the field which I had witnessed. I told him, in short, what I had seen—that the assault had been most gallant, but had totally failed; that the losses could not be less than twenty-five per cent.; that the failure was due to a lack of *ensemble* in the attacks; and that everything was now quiet, the Turks making no signs of taking the offensive. He listened intently, asking a few questions, and then, noticing that his staff had gathered around us, terminated the conversation by remarking, "Beautiful evening, is it not?" (the rain had just begun falling rapidly) and moved off.

Near by were a dozen carriages belonging to the Grand Duke and some of his staff. The rest of the officers and the headquarter escort had nothing but their overcoats. Some Cossacks were sent off to the stacks of grain piled on the sides of the hill, and bringing it in, they made a bonfire, and we gathered around it. At that time the news from the Krishin redoubt was that three desperate assaults had been made by the Roumanians, assisted by a Russian brigade, and that all three had been repulsed with great loss. From the center, the news was what we have seen. From Skobeleff, away off on the extreme left, the latest information was several hours old; it was to the effect that he had carried one of the redoubts near the town on the Lovtcha road, but the fighting was still going on unabated, and the result could not be predicted. On all sides there was nearly the same sad story of defeat. It was a gloomy evening; the air was cold, and full of a sharp, fine rain. We were most of us wet through, and, more depressing than all, in those cornfields and vineyards between us and the town lay the fifty thousand or more men who had passed through the fiery furnace of to-day's battle, and who had done their duty in it so loyally, though with so little success—many of them lay dead, others in agony longing for death, and the rest in their troubled sleep thanking God that this day was over and they still lived, but wondering whether they would be able to say as much twenty-four hours hence.

As we sat chattering around the fire, the sound of a horse on a hard gallop through the mud was heard, and in a minute there jumped into the group Genghis Khan, a major-general in the Emperor's suite, and descendant of the famous conqueror of the thirteenth century—a great, burly, good-natured creature, with high cheek-bones and black hair and beard, almost a perfect type of the Tartar as depicted in the child's geography. He had been sent to learn something of the course of events near the center of the line, and in returning past the village of Krishin he had nearly galloped over a man in the road, who told him he was carrying a message to a brigade commander for more troops to garrison the Krishin redoubt; that the redoubt was actually taken, and he had himself been in it! This tale was listened to with wide-open mouths and eyes and ears. Two officers were immediately sent off to verify the report; they went splashing away through the mud and darkness, and were soon out of hearing.

Then the Grand Duke stepped over to Prince Charles's carriage, woke him up, told him the news, and suggested certain orders for the Roumanian troops, insisting that this or that should be attended to in order that the redoubt might be held when day broke and the Turks tried to regain it.

Before the Roumanian officers rushing off with these orders were out of sound, up dashed another major-general named Stroukoff, a handsome young fellow of thirty-two, with long blonde mustaches. He had been sent to the Krishin troops for news before dark, and had entered the great redoubt with them. He had been riding post-haste to bring the news, but had lost his way in the darkness, and so Genghis, with his second-hand account, had arrived first. Stroukoff corroborated all that Genghis had told, and gave the details of the final capture of the redoubt just after dark; the Turks had fought to the last with curses of defiance, refusing to surrender, and the last remnant of the little garrison had perished by the bayonet.

The fate of the Krishin redoubt being settled, at least till morning, the Grand Duke prepared to go to sleep—it was between ten and eleven o'clock—leaving word that the first messenger from Skobeleff should come to him immediately upon his arrival. There were about a dozen carriages here, belonging to the Grand Duke and the more important members of his staff; the horses were unharnessed and hitched to the poles, the curtains and boots were unrolled and fastened together, making very passable places for a nap. Others lay on the ground under the carriages, and the rest found what shelter they could. For myself, I picked out a place not far from the fire, where a small bush formed a partial protection against the piercing cold wind and mist. I had no cover with me but a ten-ounce mackintosh overcoat, and I wrapped this round my shoulders, though with no particular object, for they were thoroughly wet. I soon found I had made a bad selection, being directly in the line between the embers of the fire and the carriages. After three or four men, with their big boots and spurs and sabers, had fallen over me, I concluded to change, and found a more quiet place, although it was openly exposed to the cutting wind.

In this dismal situation we struggled for a few winks of sleep throughout the long hours of the cold night. Toward morning it cleared, with a high wind, and the stars came out, and just at daybreak several wagons drove up with food from the Grand Duke's commissariat. There was bread, cold mutton, a few eggs, and a great brass "samovar" five feet high and holding sixty gallons. We were soon drinking tea by the quart and devouring cold mutton by the pound, few of us having had anything to eat in nearly twenty-four hours. Our stiff joints and rheumatic backs began to loosen and lubricate, and our spirits rose accordingly. The sun soon rose bright and clear, disclosing the whole field and drying our clothes. Smoke could be seen rising from the woods of Skobeleff's position on the extreme left, about six miles from us in a straight line over the heads of the Turks; there was also some firing going on around the Krishin redoubt. Word had been received during the night from Skobeleff explaining his precarious position, and answer was sent back to him at seven A. M. to retreat slowly, for no reinforcements could be sent to him.

About eight o'clock the Emperor and his suite drove up, and we all rode forward about half a mile to the point of the hill, and there strained our eyes through the glasses trying to make out what was going on with Skobeleff, away off on the other side of Plevna. We could plainly see two dark lines of troops hotly engaged and moving backward and forward, but, being ignorant of the details of the topography of that vicinity, and almost equally ignorant of the actual course of events. in Skobeleff's command, we could not make out anything definite as to what was going on, or even which side was Russian and which Turkish troops. I stepped over to General Levitzky, the assistant chief of staff, and discussed with him the probabilities as to which was which. He knew no more about it than I did. We could only see that a very hot fight was going on. We watched it for two or three hours, and then the Emperor mounted and rode back to the site of our bivouac of the night before. About noon a lunch was served of cold meats and preserves, bread, biscuits, and an abundance of claret and champagne. An improvised table was set up for the Emperor, his brother, his nephew, the Duke of Leuchtenberg, Prince Charles of Roumania, old Prince Suwaroff, and the Minister of War. The rest of us, numbering nearly a hundred in all, squatted about on the ground,—but the lunch was very good. After it was over the improvised table was used for a council of war, in which the Emperor, the Grand

Duke, the Prince of Roumania, the Minister of War, the chief of staff, his assistant, and the chief of staff of Prince Charles, all took part. It lasted during the greater part of the afternoon. The air was warm and sunny, and we sat about in groups chatting and enjoying the balmy air as at a picnic in early spring. Meanwhile, the smoke was still curling up from the woods over where Skobeleff's troops were, and we could just distinguish the noise of their musketry fire. We did not know it, but just then his terrible two-days' fight, in which he lost eight thousand men out of eighteen thousand, was culminating, and he was beginning to withdraw as best he could the remnants of his troops. The council finally broke up late in the afternoon, and the Emperor drove off. It was told to us, in general terms, that it had been determined to make no more assaults on this position which had already cost the Russians thirty thousand men, but to remain in *statu quo*, fortify their own positions against any counter-attack, and await the arrival of the re-enforcements which were already *en route* from Russia. Upon their arrival the place would be regularly invested and besieged, if the Turks did not meantime evacuate it.

So ended this memorable assault,—at least the acute part of it. Its effects,—the long lines of creaking little carts, which could be seen any day for a week afterward carrying men groaning with wounds to the Danube,—the unburied dead which lay in plain sight in front of the Turkish redoubts for the next three weeks, until the terrible stench compelled the Turks, in self-defense, to throw a few spadefuls of earth over them; these and other horrors, necessary and unnecessary, I have no desire to dilate upon.

On the 10th of December Plevna fell. On that day Osman Pasha found his provisions reduced to but a few days' supply, and saw that the place which he had so gallantly and stubbornly, though perhaps unadvisedly, defended for nearly five long months, was at last doomed to fall through starvation. But he would make no tame surrender, like Bazaine and Pemberton, of mere hungry mouths; if perish it must, his army should perish in the hot blood of battle. Massing all his troops during the night, he broke forth at daylight, striving to pierce the Russian lines on the west side and escape to the Balkans. It was one of the maddest, fiercest, least hopeful onslaughts ever made; it swept over the first two Russian lines like a whirlwind, and was barely checked at the third and last. But once checked, the Russians closed in on every side, and by noon Osman was wounded and his army was a mass of angry, stupefied human beings, without cohesion and without leaders. A few hours later it marched back with sullen faces within its own lines, laid down its arms in the ditches along the road, and became a mere herd of ill-fed, ill-clothed prisoners of war.

I was not at Plevna on the 10th. Sharing the feeling then current that the siege might last for several months, and weary of walking through the muddy trenches and conning for the thousandth time with field-glasses the outlines of the Turkish redoubts, I had joined General Gourko, who was leading a detachment of about forty thousand men into the Balkans, near Sophia, to prevent any re-enforcements or supplies from coming to Plevna. Hearing of the surrender by the field telegraph, I rode back as rapidly as possible, and reached Plevna about noon on the 13th. The burying-parties were still busy on various parts of the field. At the first one I met, an officer of the grenadiers was seated on the ground eating a few bits of hard bread and sausage for lunch. A dozen yards from him was a trench sixty feet long and twelve feet wide about half full of bodies. The men of his detachment were moving over the field, picking up the dead Russians, straightening them out, and rolling them up in their overcoats; they were then brought to the trench and dropped in it with some uniformity, heads and feet alternating, like sardines in a box. When about two hundred had been put in the trench, it was filled over with earth, a short service read by the chaplain, and a good many signs of the cross made by the men; a rude wooden cross, with two cross-pieces, after the fashion of the Greek Church, was then placed over it, and the burial was over. So fared the dead Russians. For the Turks the process was somewhat abridged: the little batteries and trenches which covered the field, and whose parapets bore the footprints of many a fierce hand-to-hand fight three days before, were now utilized for graves; the Turkish bodies were first stripped of their clothing for immediate use, it being in many instances superior to what the Russians had themselves, and they were then dragged to the nearest battery and tumbled headlong into the ditch. There the naked bodies lay, their arms and legs tangled in inextricable confusion, reminding one of Doré's illustrations of "The Inferno." When the ditch was nearly full the loose earth was shoveled down from the parapet to cover the bodies, and the ceremony was complete.

I had been riding over the field among these scenes, gleaning as much as possible from the survivors of the events of the battle, and had grown somewhat hardened to the sickening sight, when suddenly, on passing near a ditch full of naked bodies, my horse plunged violently and stood quivering and snorting with fear. Among the corpses was a living man; his head and one arm only were visible among the tangled mass of bodies and legs; his face was purple, and he was already so far gone as to be speechless; with his hand he beckoned very faintly to me to come near, and in his face and eyes there was the most ghastly death-agony I have ever witnessed. I called a passing soldier to bring some water; he replied he had seen none since early morning; there was none on the field nearer than the river, two versts off; my own brandy-flask and cigarette-case I had emptied a few minutes before among a group of wounded. There was nothing to be done for this poor fellow, and I moved on; he was probably dead before many minutes. For all the volumes that have been written in all the ages of the horrors of the battle-field after the battle, how little do they or can they portray its reality!

War is at best brutal and brutifying; in the midst of it men are too busy with the object to be attained to have any time for human sentiment, and they think of their fellow-men as mere units, like horses, guns, muskets, and wagons. Afterward, when the brain is less heated, its daily events group themselves together in the memory like a confused and unreal nightmare, of which some more than usually vivid scenes are the only tangible features.

The next day the Emperor came over to the field

to review the troops, thank them for their victory, and take leave of them prior to his departure for St. Petersburg. From the Grand Duke's head-quarters, at Bogot, to the battle-field, near Dolni-Etropol, the distance was fully fifteen miles. It was a cold, drizzling day, and I gladly accepted the invitation of one of my colleagues to take a seat in his barouche and send my horse on ahead by an orderly.

The scene in the town of Plevna just after the surrender defies all description. The lack of ready wit of the Russian Tchinovniks, the total want of transport and medical service of the Turks, the vast numbers of sick which had accumulated during the bad weather of the last few weeks of the siege, the vile, filthy streets of the dirty little Turkish town, all combined to make up a scene whose like I doubt has been witnessed since the plagues of the middle ages. You could barely open a door on any street without the chance of stumbling over two or three corpses in the hall,—men who had crept in there to die of their fevers. The yards of the houses presented nearly the same spectacle; no sanitary precautions seemed to have been taken, and the yards and streets were one foul mass of filth and mud, which combined with the stench of dead bodies to make the place a vast pest-house. Many of the houses had been destroyed by the bombardment; all those belonging to Turks had been deserted by their owners. The streets were filled as in a mass-meeting, — Bulgarians, Russian soldiers, creaking carts full of wounded, supply-wagons, artillery-wagons, horsemen, all blocking one another's way without order or direction. It seemed as if Pandemonium had settled down in the mud of this filthy village. On this day two long rows of gendarmes lined the streets, shunting every vehicle or being into the nearest by-way or yard, and keeping a single, continuous passage open for the carriages of the Emperor and his suite. As we emerged from the farther end of the village we came upon another striking scene; it was a collection of not less than twelve hundred carts, each with a pair of uncouth buffaloes tied to the end of the pole, and all crowded into a space so small that it was barely possible for a person to thread his way on foot between them. In this caravan were all the camp-followers of Osman's army and the Mohammedan inhabitants of the town. They had been brought together by Osman, with orders to follow his troops the moment he should break the Russian lines. Here they had been for four days. Standing like a fringe along the front were the men, dressed in every variety of gayly-colored and picturesque Oriental costume, staring in silence at us as we passed, with stolid indifference or sullen defiance on their faces; behind them, peering from under the covers of the carts or playing about the wheels, were the women, dressed in blue or yellow gowns, the "yashmak" tightly drawn over their faces, and the children laughing or gaping with wonder as they toddled about in their striped baggy trousers.

Across the river, on the wide plain where the battle had been fought, were the prisoners, herded together like cattle, in three great herds, about ten thousand in each, and a line of Russian sentries around the outer edge. The Russians had not tents or blankets enough for themselves, the Turks had none whatever, and the miserable town afforded no facilities for shelter; there seemed to be no way to guard them but the way that we saw. We had arrived an hour or more before the time fixed for the Emperor, and I passed the interval wandering through the midst of the herds of prisoners. More than half of them were hearty, stout-looking fellows, with deep, broad chests, and well-knit muscular frames; among the others were many whose emaciated and sallow faces told of the bad food and suffering in the trenches. Not a few were crouched on the ground, shivering with the cold wind and the still colder hand of death which was beginning to rest upon them. For clothing, every man wore the Turkish fez, and a majority had a rather shoddy overcoat with a capote; further than that there was no uniformity, the dress being of every variety from the rudest of homespun to a handsome suit of stout blue cloth, cut *à la Zouave*, and adorned with red or yellow trimmings. They were badly shod, great numbers of them having no other protection for the feet and ankles but raw hide tied with strings. The expression of these men was, as a rule, frank and gentle; but there were many scowling, defiant, and savage faces. I found a few who could speak some words of French, enough to tell me that they had not tasted food since the morning of the battle, four days before; they had been all this time herded in the open as now, their position being moved once in twenty-four hours to avoid the accumulated filth, and to give an opportunity to bury those who had died meantime.

The Emperor arrived about one o'clock. The troops formed for review consisted of the corps of grenadiers, three brigades of Roumanians, a division of cavalry, and one hundred and eighty guns—about fifty thousand men in all. They were drawn up, about half a mile from the herds of prisoners, in the usual Russian fashion—the cavalry on the flanks, the infantry in a line of battalion masses (double column of platoons on the center), and the artillery in rear of the infantry. Even in this compact formation the troops of the three arms covered a space over a mile long and half a mile deep. The review was conducted in the customary form. The commanding general—in this case the Grand Duke Nicholas—took his position on the right of the line, with his staff immediately in rear of him. As the Emperor and his suite approached, the Grand Duke galloped out alone to meet him, saluted, and handed him the consolidated report of the troops present. The Emperor then rode along the front of the line, the Grand Duke's staff joining in the suite, swelling its numbers to nearly three hundred. As he approached each regiment the men presented arms and the officers saluted, all turning their heads toward him and watching him with the most intense interest. He then wished the men good-morning in the usual manner, and they returned his salutation as the regimental band struck up the national hymn—an air whose grand harmony is long remembered by those who have heard it. The men kept up an uninterrupted series of hurrahs so long as the Emperor remained in their front. Now and then the Emperor stopped to call out some soldier wearing the St. George's Cross, and ask him to relate the circumstances under which he had gained it. The answers were usually brief and modest, and the Emperor would compliment him at the end with "Tee molodetz!"—"Thou art a fine fellow!" and the man would grasp his hand, his sleeve, his skirts, and cover them with kisses, often dropping his musket in the confusion of a moment which he would remember to the last day of his life, and which he considered ample reward for any sacrifice or risk of life. Opposite the regiments of Siberia and Little Russia, which had borne the fiercest part of the Turkish assault, the Emperor stopped and called the officers about him to make a short speech of a few appropriate words, telling them their regiment had earned its place in Russian history, and would henceforth carry the colors of St. George entwined on its standards. It was more than an hour before the Emperor had finished riding down the line of infantry, and thence back to the other flank and down the lines of batteries, each of which was saluted in turn by name. Then the Emperor took position in front, and the troops filed past him, consuming something more than another hour. The infantry went past in company fronts (two hundred men each), and to those who preserved a good alignment the Emperor shouted, "Koroshoh!" "Very well!" to which the men yelled back, "Otchen radom, Vass Imperatorsky Veleetchestvo!" "We're glad to serve your Majesty!" Each regiment, after filing past, returned directly to its own quarters, and then the Emperor and suite rode back to their carriages and returned in them, giving their saddle-horses to their orderlies.

One often sees reviews,—the hopeful, bright recruits setting out for the war, the saddened veterans returning with thinned ranks,—reviews at great ceremonies, reviews for mere inspection or drill. They do not vary greatly in different countries; the men are usually dressed in their best, their arms are bright, the ground is well selected, the movements are precise, the scene is brilliant. But it is rare that they have an air of reality about them; the most they tell of actual war is occasionally some reference to their fallen comrades, such as leaving gaps in the ranks where they had stood. But this review was none of these. It was a review of the survivors of a battle fought but four days before, and it was held on the very ground where they had fought, and in full sight of the men they had conquered. It seemed to me to be most intensely dramatic, and full of a vivid savagery, which had nothing in common with the grand march of Grant's and Sherman's armies along Pennsylvania Avenue in April, 1865, but rather to recall the stories of the old Roman triumphs, where the conquered were dragged through the streets chained to the chariot wheels. It represented all that there is in the pomp and circumstance of glorious war— and all its emptiness. Here were fifty thousand men, victors in a great battle, shivering, with their gaping boots in the mud, but shouting themselves hoarse at the sight of their beloved Emperor, who typified to them all they had fought for; over yonder, listening to their shouts, were herds of disorganized men, the remnants of soldiers who had but a few hours before met them in fierce fight, but who now had no shouting to do, no commendation to receive, no future, but a dull blank in their minds; no feelings but suppressed rage, alternating with the gnawings of hunger; and between the two groups lay the carcasses of horses, pieces of clothing, parts of belts and cartridge-boxes, broken ammunition and wheels, and all the numerous odds and ends which lie strewn on every battle-field, including here and there a dead man who had escaped the notice of the burying-parties. Yet the two enemies, the victors and the vanquished, have an almost equal claim to every soldier's admiration; without stopping to inquire into the justice of the causes for which they respectively fought, or into the errors which their commanders had made, but thinking merely of the great mass of the soldiers on either side, one can only recall that in the historical drama of Plevna which this day's review closed, both sides had shown qualities of endurance and devotion, of daring spirit and dogged courage, of faithful obedience and cheerful sacrifice, of all those soldierly qualities which in all the ages have commanded the admiration of men. But one quality had they lacked—that of mercy to their fallen foes —and in a war of religious fanaticism perhaps this could hardly be expected.

CHAPTER V.

THE WINTER CAMPAIGN.

WITH the fall of Plevna and the capture of Osman's army it was thought that the backbone of the Turkish resistance was broken, but it was only a few days before every one knew that there was to be no rest in the campaign. Orders were immediately issued sending the troops who had blockaded Plevna to one or the other of the advanced guards in the Balkans, and at the end of a week they were all in motion. Every one obeyed cheerfully, nobody knowing what would come of it, but nine out of ten believing it could only result in terrible disaster, to be brought about by lack of food and extreme suffering from cold. These views were only confirmed by a change in the weather, which hitherto had been raw and wet, with occasional snows, but now suddenly changed to a temperature of about zero Fahrenheit, accompanied by a raging snow-storm of three days' duration. Everything was frozen solid, the roads became beds of ice, the animals staggered and fell dead with cold, and the men huddled together in silence, shivering in their ragged clothing which had not been renewed since summer.

I left Plevna and the Grand Duke's head-quarters on the 20th of December, two days after the departure of the ninth corps, which had been detailed to General Gourko at the Orkhanie Pass. I intended to overtake these troops on the road, and follow the campaign with General Gourko's army. At the close of a long day's ride the storm increased in severity, and I was preparing to leave the road and seek shelter for the night in a village bivouac, whose smoke I could see not far off, when a weird picture attracted my attention just in front of me. Alone in the road, without a human being in sight, stood a company wagon heavily loaded with the men's rations; the ground was frozen hard beneath it and covered with snow on all sides; the snow was driving furiously through the air, and the eye could penetrate its mass but a short distance; against this white background stood the black silhouette of the middle horse of the "troika"; the other two lay dead and stiff at his feet on either side, and he alone was still standing, gaunt and feeble, swaying backward and forward in sad and terrible silence before the blasts of the storm, and waiting, half insensible, his turn to fall.

I found refuge for the night with a captain of a "park" of reserve artillery ammunition which was bivouacked in the village. He occupied one room of a little hut, the other being filled with a family of some ten or twelve Bulgarians, of both sexes and various ages. His reception was in unison with that which I invariably received from every one of his class, and the open-hearted warmth of which I was often puzzled to account for. He spoke but a few words of French and German, barely more than the few phrases of Russian which I had by that time acquired, but it was enough for him to understand that I was an American. Everything was immediately placed at my disposal: my horses had the best stalls in the wretched little stable, and plenty of forage to eat; the *samovar* was immediately set boiling for tea; whatever meat he had was at once put to cooking; his little flask of brandy was half drained to warm my chilled stomach; his chest was opened to take out the one or two delicacies which he possessed in the way of food; his one knife and fork were cleaned for my use; his servant was called a fool and a blockhead for not being quicker with the supper; his few St. Petersburg cigarettes were forced upon me; and when it was time to go to bed he insisted long and urgently, though I would not yield, that I should sleep on his camp-bed while he took the mud floor.

In the morning, he was equally urgent that I should take the greater part of the half-dozen cans of potted meats which he possessed, on the ground that I would need them out in the storm, while he might remain where he was for ten days or more. In a word, everything that was possible was done to make us change places for the night,—he to become the ill-provided traveler, and I the comparatively comfortable lodger in a house, such as it was. I never saw this man before nor after the one night I passed with him, yet, had I been his foster-brother and playmate from childhood, now rejoining him after a long absence, he could not have done more for me. The same thing happened to me on dozens of occasions, and as I found that more than once, when I was mistaken for an English officer or correspondent, my reception was very cold, I at last became convinced that all this kindness was due to my nationality. It is a fact, strange as it may appear to some people, that there exists throughout the length and breadth of Russia a sentimental attachment for Americans, of the depth of which we have very little conception at home. The policy of the rulers of Russia, from the time of Catherine to the present, has been one of uniform and unbroken friendship for the United States; this is a well-known fact in politics, and people account for it on the ground of self-interest, or of genuine admiration, according to their political opinions. But what is not generally known is the fact that this friendly feeling permeates all classes of society, and is far more firmly rooted in those portions of the community which never see St. Petersburg than it is in the more cosmopolitan court circles of that capital. It is of no use to argue that the feeling is superficial, that it has no substantial foundation, that the political customs and the habits of the people of the two countries are diametrically opposed, and that they have no interests in common. The feeling does exist, and it is a very strong one. Certain reasons may be given for it, which, although at first sight they may appear insufficient and superficial, have nevertheless a great deal of force. Remoteness and the lack of clashing interests are, no doubt, among the prime causes, coupled with the fact that Russian interests do clash so constantly with those of other European nations; in addition to this, there are elements of sympathy in the fact of mere geographical bigness, Russia and the United States standing first among civilized nations in point of continuous territory and number of inhabitants of one race; each of us is sensitive to foreign criticism, and each, while conscious of its own strength, has felt the sneers of other countries; but, above all, Russia has come to look upon itself as the inveterate and eternal enemy of England, and it rightly judges us to be the natural rival of England in all those elements of commercial success which have made her present greatness. Russia looks to see England decline as we advance, and this decline she considers her greatest advantage. A wide-spread illusion also exists, which I never succeeded in dispelling with any one with whom I conversed, that the minute England becomes involved in war we will destroy her commerce by precisely those means which certain Englishmen employed in our hour of trouble to destroy ours. Our feelings and probable action in the event of England being involved in a Continental war are more correctly appreciated at St. Petersburg, but in the country at large—as represented by the army officers—the opinion is universal that we would at once send out cruisers to depredate on English commerce the moment England's fleet was occupied elsewhere. Both being enemies, the Russians argue, of the same power, we must naturally be friends of each other.

One other incident, which is almost forgotten at home, made a deep and lasting impression in Russia; this was the mission of Mr. Fox in 1867. The sending of a fleet of vessels, partly composed of monitors, which had proved their merit in action at home, but had never before been seen in European waters, to convey an embassador bearing a special message from the whole American people, as represented in Congress, of good-will to the Russian people and hearty congratulations on the escape of their emperor from assassination—all this had a flavor of generous sentiment in it peculiarly acceptable to the people of Moscow and "old Russians" generally. The fame of this mission penetrated to the ends of the empire, and consolidated a friendship which has been growing for years, and the very inertness of the Russians, which prevents them from receiving a new idea every day, makes them hold very fast to those they do receive and accept.

I left my generous host early the next morning, and making my way through the storm, arrived two days afterward at General Gourko's head-quarters, on the northern slope of the Balkans, near Orkhanie. The troops destined to re-enforce his army arrived the same day, and on the next the orders were issued for the advance. The following day, Christmas morning, in intense cold and in the midst of a dense, impenetrable fog of particles of ice, the Russians set out to cross the Balkans. The troops found almost insuperable obstacles in dragging their guns up the steep, icy slopes of the narrow road which had been made over the mountain to enable them to turn the position of the Turks in their front. The guns had to be taken apart and dragged piecemeal by ropes up the mountain, and late that evening, at the time when it was intended that more than half of the troops should have been at the southern outlets of the mountain passes, not a gun had reached the summit. The position was a precarious one; the troops were spread out over an immense length, and there was the greatest danger that the movement would be revealed to the Turks and might be wholly aborted by flank attacks as the isolated detachments should reach the southern valleys. At nightfall, General Gourko reached the summit and lay down in the snow for a little rest, thoroughly harassed by the anxieties of the moment. It was one of those critical periods when success or failure hang in the balance, and the general's impatience knew no bounds, as successive reports came to him of the difficulties and delays which the different columns met with. After admiring the magnificent view which was disclosed from the top of the mountain, at the base of which lay the broad plain of Sophia, clad in snow, but dotted here and there with the numerous dark clusters of huts and curling smoke of the villages, I declined an invitation to pass the night on the mountain, and determined to push forward to a regiment which held the outposts in the valley below. Several hours after nightfall, when I was beginning to fear I had wholly lost my road and was wandering into the Turkish lines, as I once did at Plevna, I stumbled upon the village where the Russians were bivouacked; applying at once at the first hut, I was received with the usual cordiality by the half-dozen officers quartered in it, and was immediately offered more than my share of whatever creature comforts they possessed.

While the troops were slowly dragging themselves and their guns over the mountain range, I took advantage of the delay to pass a day or two with the brigade of Caucasian Cossacks, who were employed in scouting and skirmishing with the Turks in the valley of Sophia. These men are of an entirely different type from the Russians proper. They come from the mountains and valleys of the Caucasus, not very far from that portion of the earth which is spoken of as the cradle of the human race, and they are of a remarkably pure Caucasian type—ruddy complexion, dark hair and eyes, short black beards, and compact, well-knit frames; their wild, picturesque costume consists of a black, woolly, sheepskin hat, one or two long tunics coming to their heels, the inner one of red or black silk and the outer of brown woolen cloth, a pair of trowsers, and low boots outside of them. The tunic is gathered in at the waist by a very narrow belt of leather, ornamented with silver worked in enamel; the scimitar-like sword is hung by a similar piece of leather passing over one shoulder, and over the other hangs the carbine, in a sheath of sheep-skin; on each breast are half a dozen cases for cartridges. Their horses are the counterpart of themselves—short, thick-set, extremely hardy, and very intelligent. The men are wonderfully bold riders, though their seat and appearance—with short stirrups and high saddles—have little in common with what we are accustomed to call good horsemanship.

These people differ as much from the Russians in their character as in their appearance. Though among the most faithful of the Tsar's subjects, they are all Mohammedans, understand but very little of the Russian language, are very quick-sighted and self-reliant, never at a loss to take care of themselves, and render the best service when left to their own resources. They are a species of amiable barbarians, devoted to their friends and absolutely relentless to their foes; they talk but little among themselves, have a serious expression of countenance, rarely smile, and do not sing except when they give themselves up to a dance around a campfire, which bears a strong resemblance to the sun dances of our Indians, although the motions are more varied and graceful. They have little of the regular discipline of European troops, though they are by no means disorderly, and they love nothing so much as danger and wild adventure for its own sake.

The brigade was bivouacked in one of the little villages of the Sophia plain when I joined it, just at daylight, a day or two after Christmas. The village was wrapped in snow, and showed no sign whatever of the thousand men who were hid in it, except that a good many horses were in the yards of the huts. I found the hut of the commandant, who was just rolling out of his blankets, and refreshed myself with a few glasses of the customary hot tea. Half an hour afterward the men were in motion, and moved out through the deep snow toward the town of Sophia, to reconnoiter the strength of the Turks at that place. As they passed from one to another of the villages, where no Russians had previously been seen, the Bulgarians met them in large numbers at the entrance of each, usually preceded by their priests bearing a cross and the elders of the village bringing salt and bread. At their approach they bowed their heads to the ground and cried "Welcome, welcome," and then rushed up to kiss their hands or clothes. Whatever knowledge they had concerning the Turks was cheerfully given (though their reports were often unintelligible and contradictory), and their ample provisions of grain, bread, geese, and poultry were freely placed at the disposal of the Russians. But as they saw that the latter did not remain, their enthusiasm cooled most decidedly, as they remembered that to-morrow might bring a body of Turks back upon them.

As the Cossacks approached one village, they were received with a few shots coming from behind the hedges. The column was halted and some skirmishers thrown out, who reported a body of Turkish infantry in the village, engaged in crossing a deep little stream which was covered with a thin coating of ice, not strong enough to bear a horse. Those of the Turks who had already passed were drawn up in line on the opposite bank, and as the Cossacks could only approach the ford through a narrow street they were at a considerable disadvantage, considering that their object was merely a reconnaissance, and nothing was to be gained by losing forty or fifty men. So they only skirmished with the Turks for half an hour, when all the latter being across the stream, they broke into a double-quick on the road to Sophia. The Cossacks put after them, but the ford was very narrow, and it was some time before they were over; the Turks got a start of a good half-mile, and as soon as the Cossacks came near them they stopped long enough to give them a warm fire and then ran on. The Cossacks could easily have caught them on the road, which was firm and hard, but would have lost thirty or forty men in doing so, and there was no object in it, as it was only a small force of five hundred or six hundred men retreating from an outpost in the mountains. Then the Cossacks tried to go around and get ahead of them, but the deep soft snow in the fields made their progress slower than that of the Turks. So they merely kept up the chase for three or four miles, until they came to the main high-road at a point where it crossed a considerable stream about three miles in front of Sophia. The Turks got safely across the bridge, and then the Cossacks were saluted by a fine, rattling fusilade extending over a length of about a quarter of a mile of the opposite bank of the stream, and they saw a regiment or more of Tcherkesses* deploy on the opposite bank. Here they were in full sight of the town, and the officers had a good opportunity to sketch the position of its fortifications, so the Cossacks fell back to about 1200 yards and, spreading out over a long line, kept up a good skirmish fire. A curious and very interesting incident now occurred. The Cossacks sat there exchanging shots for nearly an hour, and while with my glasses I could plainly see many a Turk knocked out of his saddle by the Russian Berdans, not a man on the Russian side was hit, and not a bullet was heard to whistle. The Tcherkesses were armed with the Winchester repeating carbine, which only carried about 800 to 900 yards, and the Cossacks were wholly out of·range! A week later another skirmish took place at the same locality. This time it was the main body of Gourko's troops forcing their way to Sophia; they met with resistance at this same bridge, and a smart skirmish took place, last-

---

* Caucasian cavalry in the Turkish service.

ing about an hour, and costing the Russians fifty or sixty men. On this occasion I was with General Gourko's staff, and we stood watching the fight on a tumulus about three hundred yards in rear of the place where I had been before; this time the bullets flew fast and thick, and a few horses in our group were wounded; but now it was Turkish infantry opposed to us, armed with the Peabody-Martini rifle, a splendid weapon which carries with deadly effect to 2,000 yards.

As the sun began to go down the Cossacks gradually withdrew, having gained as much information as was possible with their force. Along the road were the evidences of an affair in which these same troops had been engaged a few days before, and which was more to their taste than to-day's gentle skirmishing. Pieces of broken wagons, dead horses, immense stains of blood in the snow, men with their heads severed in two pieces—these were the marks of an attack on a transport train guarded by a company of infantry, every man of which had been cut down. And yet—so strange are the anomalies of semi-civilized nature—at the end of that affair, an infant, not over six months old, who had been discovered deserted among the *débris*, was picked up, wrapped in a big cloak, tenderly cared for during the night, and the next day carried back on horseback, thirty miles over the mountains, to the nearest hospital, and there delivered to the Sisters of Charity of the Red Cross, by whom it was taken in charge and sent to Russia for adoption. The picture of the rough Cossack carrying this child, laughing in his face, on the pommel of his saddle through the snow, was a most attractive one; and yet the same man, without a moment's hesitation, would pull out his sword and hack off the head of its wounded father, lying on the ground and begging for mercy; and, while enjoying the zest of it at the moment, would forget all about it the next day.

While this reconnaissance had been going on, the main body of the troops were still tugging painfully at their guns on the mountain range. It was six days before they had pulled them up one side, slid them down the other, and then put them together again, mounted them on their wheels, and turned them over to the horses for draught. Finally the troops were all assembled in the valleys on the southern side; and an attack was made at Taskossen, on the last day of the year, on the position which the Turks had taken up by throwing back their left flank to oppose the Russian advance against their rear. Their troops were commanded by the well-known Valentine Baker, who made a short but good defense, keeping it up until a dense fog settled just before sunset, and prevented Gourko's getting in the rear of the main Turkish army and bagging it entire, as the Turkish army was bagged at Shipka.

It was a pretty fight to look at. The Turks had a good position along a pass in a spur of the mountain through which the road passed. They were on high ground, and the Russians had to advance through an open valley. In front of them, directly opposite to the Turkish position and about two miles from it, was a high spur on which we were situated, and from which every movement of the battle could be seen with perfect clearness.

The Turks gave way about three o'clock in the afternoon, but it was impossible to follow them for any distance at that late hour of the short winter day, as the weather was inclement and the men were exhausted. The next morning, New Year's day, the troops were put in motion, the general and staff preceding them with a small escort. As they rode through the pass they came into a small valley not over four miles in width, in rear of the main range of the Balkans, which bounded it on the north, while natural spurs encircled it on the other sides. The principal body of the Turks had been on the Balkans, and the general looked eagerly to see whether they still remained there; nothing could be discerned. But off on the right he noticed a few black dots moving toward the south over a snow-covered slope. With our glasses we thought that a large body of troops could be seen massed in and near the village at the foot of the slope, about three miles off. The leading Russian battalions and batteries were immediately hurried in that direction, and, in a few minutes afterward, an enormous black mass, like a swarm of busy ants, was seen slowly ascending the mountain. Evidently a portion of the Turks were in retreat, but the Russians knew nothing of what had transpired at their principal position, and scanned eagerly the sides of the main range in search of further developments, while a few officers were sent forward to reconnoiter. Soon afterward, a long winding column made its appearance, descending the southern slope of the main range. Was it the rest of the Turks, or was it a portion of the Russians? Officers were sent off post-haste to learn. In less than half an hour one of them came galloping back to say that it was their own men, and that the whole position on the Balkans had been abandoned during the night. The troops we saw off on our right were, therefore, a large rear-guard of the Turkish army. The general took out of his pocket a piece of chocolate,—the only delicacy he had with him,—and divided it with his staff in congratulation of their success; for, in fact, the supposed impassable line of the main Balkan range had been passed in the depth of winter, and the Turks were in full retreat. Short dispatches were at once written and sent to the end of the field-telegraph on the other side of the mountains, and others, more at length, were written later in the day and given to an officer, to take with the utmost speed and deliver into the Emperor's own hands at St. Petersburg. It was a New Year's congratulation worth offering.

Five days later the Russian troops entered the town of Sophia, which the Turks had evacuated during the preceding night. At the entrance of the town they were met by a procession of two or three thousand people, headed by a large number of priests of the orthodox church, attired in the robes of their office. Some of them bore crucifixes of silver, which were presented to the Russian commander, who devoutly uncovered his head, crossed himself three times, and kissed them. Others carried a silver platter containing a loaf of bread and some salt—the ancient emblems of hospitality. Behind them was a choir of several hundred voices, that immediately began singing an anthem. The rest of the crowd was made up of Bulgarians, who broke forth into loud cheers and shouts of welcome as the Russians rode along past them.

This town, which was founded by the Byzantine Emperor Constantine in the sixth century, captured by the Bulgarians and made their capital in the ninth century, conquered by the Turks in 1382, and now reconquered by Christians in 1878, presented strange scenes—scenes which have little in common with the nineteenth century as we understand it, and are possible now in no other civilized land but Turkey.

Nearly all the shops had been owned by Turks or a few Greeks. The Turkish population had either fled with the Turkish troops or had hidden out of sight, and for about eight hours—from two o'clock in the night, when the Turks left, until ten o'clock in the morning, when the Russians entered—the Bulgarians had been engaged in indiscriminate and ruthless pillage. Every shop in the town had been broken open, and its contents carried off or scattered about the streets. The Russians very quickly brought order out of this confusion. Their Cossack whips were freely used on the backs of the Bulgarians, and any person found with goods in the street or suspicious-looking property in his house was required to bring it into one of the open squares of the town, where it was heaped up in great piles and guarded by sentries until its ownership could be clearly proven.

The only solitary instance of pillage by the troops —a Cossack who was found guilty of stealing a watch from a man in the street—was summarily punished by hanging within an hour from the time of the robbery.

This instance of pillage by the Bulgarians was, unfortunately, not the exception—it was the common rule on similar occasions; and as the war went on and instances of it multiplied, it sadly dampened the ardent enthusiasm with which the Russians had begun the war for the relief of their suffering co-religionists. Misgovernment extending over centuries cannot be righted without the hatred which it has engendered finding vent in horrible excesses, and this war will stand out pre-eminent among those of modern times for the suffering which it inflicted upon the non-combatant population. Whenever the Russian armies approached a village, the Turkish population abandoned everything and fled before them; when the Russians were obliged to fall back and the Turks followed in pursuit, the Bulgarians fled before them; when, finally, the Russian advance surged forward during the winter without interruption to the gates of Constantinople, a large portion of the entire Mohammedan population left their homes and villages, and packing a few possessions and still less food in one or two bullock wagons, they formed the nucleus of caravans of refugees—one of which, receiving fresh additions at every village, finally stretched out over a length of twenty miles and contained two hundred thousand souls!

This great train became mingled with the retreating Turkish troops, and was caught between two fractions of the advancing Russians—General Gourko from Sophia and General Skobeleff from Shipka. Its escort of a few battalions foolishly made a defense against the troops of the latter general, and being beaten it took refuge in flight toward the Rhodope Mountains, followed by all the ablebodied portion of the community, who left the old, the sick, and the babes to perish in the snow. The train was at once plundered of all its possessions by the Bulgarians of the neighboring villages, who mercilessly put to death all those who had not yet perished of cold. For three successive days we marched through the remnants of this caravan, scattered over a length of seventy miles,—broken wagons, scattered contents, dead animals; here a man and his wife, who had stretched a blanket in the snow and lain down to die side by side; there a stately old Turk, with flowing white beard, green turban, and brightly figured robe, lying by the ditch with his throat cut from ear to ear; and again a naked little infant frozen stiff in the snow, with its eyes upturned to heaven. Our blood curdled as we saw a Bulgarian clot, grinning and staring at us from the road-side, who answered as we asked him who murdered those two Turks lying a few feet from us:

"Nashe bratte!" (Our brothers, we did it.)

In the villages which the Turks had left, their houses, land, and effects were all promptly seized and used by the Bulgarians. On the other hand, in the wagons of the caravan were found silver altar-pieces which the Mohammedans had stolen from the Christian churches before beginning their flight.

Meanwhile, the refugees of this particular caravan eked out a precarious existence in the Rhodope Mountains until spring, when, aided and led by one or two English adventurers, they began an insurrection against the Russian troops who had been left to guard the line of communications. When this had been subdued, some months later, the tale of their sufferings reached Constantinople, and a commission of foreign consuls was sent to investigate the matter. They reported that more than a hundred and fifty thousand homeless and starving refugees were scattered about in the villages of this inhospitable region, with no resources of food or clothing for the coming winter. Subscriptions were opened in England for their relief, and measures were taken, the war being now over, to return them to their homes. Arriving there, they found all their property appropriated by others, and they met with a bleak reception from the Bulgarians, who imagined they had seen the last of their long-time enemies and oppressors; and it is questionable whether it would not have been more humane in the end, as several Russians suggested, to make them continue their flight to Asia.

The caravan of which I have spoken was the largest, but it was only one of many. The migration of the others continued all the way to Constantinople, where, on the arrival of the Russians, there were reported to be three hundred thousand refugees. The mosque of St. Sophia alone contained nearly three thousand of them when I first saw it. They were herded about in mosques and in open squares until the typhus fever broke out among them, when the Turkish authorities displayed unwonted energy and in a few days dispersed the whole mass, sending about half of them over into Asia and the other half back toward Bulgaria.

It is probably within the limit of fact to say that seven hundred thousand Mohammedans abandoned their homes and possessions during the war, and set forth on a long journey the aim and end of which they knew not, and that not one-half of them have ever returned, and a large proportion have perished. In addition to this, about three hundred thousand Bulgarians abandoned their homes at the time of Gourko's retreat in July. A million of people were thus wandering about during the course of the war, with only such possessions as two or three families could pack into one bullock-wagon. The sufferings which they endured can never be told, much less appreciated. Even now, more than two years after the events of which I am writing, we constantly read in the papers of a new commission being formed to make arrangements for returning the Turkish refugees to their homes.

The Russians stayed at Sophia just a week, recuperating the men and getting together the supplies for a further advance. Their way then lay on the ancient Roman road to Adrianople. They had to cross a second range of mountains, where the same difficulties were encountered with the guns as before, only lessened to the extent that smooth roads are less difficult than mountain paths, although both be covered with frozen, icy snow. Emerging from the mountains at last in the wide and beautiful plain of the Maritza, they came nearly up with the retreating Turks, and then for three days, marching from daylight to dark, and always in sight of each other, they kept up the exciting chase, hardly stopping long enough to extinguish the blazing fires in every village which marked the line of Turkish march.

On the afternoon of the third day, the advance guard, under Count Shouvaloff, with whom I was marching, were met by some cavalry which were scouting on their right, who reported that a column of Turks were moving directly toward a village just abreast of them, with the intention of crossing the Maritza River and gaining the high-road on which they were. Count Shouvaloff immediately turned his men to the right, and they plunged into the stream—a river more than a hundred yards wide and four feet deep, filled with cakes of floating ice which struck against the men's breasts as they forded it. Arrived on the other side, their clothing was soon stiff with ice; but the men pressed on through the village and formed on the opposite side. But the Turks had already seen their movements, and had turned back to the railroad along which they were marching, and continued their retreat in that direction. The rear of the column, on a good run, was over half a mile from us; the sun was just setting, and Shouvaloff had only about 5,000 men at hand. He rightly argued: If they have a large force, I am too weak for them to-day; if a small force, I would rather they escape than that my men should freeze to death with their icy clothes in these fields to-night. So, sending a small force of cavalry to reconnoiter their strength, he turned his men back to the village and bade them crowd twenty or thirty into each hut, and dry their clothes around blazing fires. The general picked out one of the squalid little huts for himself, and invited the two foreign officers who were present, Major von Liegnitz and myself, as well as his chief of staff and two aids-de-camp, one of whom was his son, to share it with him. We got some black bread of the peasants, and each one contributed a little tea or potted meats—whatever he had in his saddle, the wagons being all behind—to make a meal. Afterward we discussed the probabilities of the next day. There was plainly visible from our hut a long line of fires stretching across the country, about three miles from us. Liegnitz had, as the sequel proved, the best military instinct, and argued that this was a line of bivouac fires of a large body of Turkish troops, who had selected that position to give battle; the others inclined to the opinion that the fires were caused by burning the tops of the rice stalks which projected above the snow. In any event, the necessary orders were given by the general for the disposition of the troops for the morrow—for an attack if the Turks stood firm, or for a pursuit if they should retreat. Then we sandwiched ourselves about on the floor, and slept during the night. Two thoughts kept running through my mind: one was the contrast between the present squalid surroundings of Count Shouvaloff and his large estates and beautiful home in St. Petersburg, and his patriotism in leaving all this and asking to come to the army in an inferior position after having been passed over in the first assignment of generals; and the other was about my own position—going again into a battle in which I might lose my life as easily as any one else, but in which I had no more direct concern than that of an observer watching the development of an interesting problem, in which if I got hit I would neither receive nor be entitled to any sympathy, and to the result of which I was incapable of contributing in any way whatever. There is a peculiar sense of foolishness in the feeling of being hit as a bystander in a row. But our thoughts are mastered by physical needs, and one sleeps easily after bodily exhaustion, no matter in what surroundings.

We were up before daylight the next morning, and just as the sun arose—a bright morning of intensely bitter cold—the troops which had come up during the night, and slept in the fields on the other side of the river, began crossing the stream. As they had to fight all day in the snow it was very important that their clothing should not be wet, and they were therefore ordered to strip naked, roll their clothes in a bundle and carry them on their heads. As they came out of the icy river they were as red as boiled lobsters, but made merry as they squatted about in the snow to put on their clothes. They then formed and marched through the village, where the general saluted them as usual.

"Good-morning, my men."

"Good-morning, your Highness."

"Did you burn your feet coming over?"

"No, indeed, your Highness!" they answered in a shout, as a broad grin stole over their good-natured faces.

The troops were soon deployed in the fields outside the village, and, looking in the direction of the fires we had noticed the night before, we saw a ridge of slight elevation rising out of the rice-fields, and at intervals along it were several batteries, and we knew very well that plenty of infantry lay either between or behind them. The advance was gradually made toward this position, and when the line of skirmishers came within about two thousand yards of it, the artillery opened fire, accompanied by some straggling infantry shots. The men were ordered to advance slowly, or to lie down in the furrows of the field, as it was not intended to attack seriously from this side.

The Turkish artillery kept up a good racket, and one battery in particular singled out the general's staff and followed us closely, as we moved over the field, with its shells and shrapnel; for the former we cared little, as they buried themselves in the ground, spattering the mud and snow over us, but the shrapnel breaking in the air just over your head, and its pieces and bullets screaming past you, has an ugly and disagreeable sound. In about an hour the men had got up in good range, and the battle was in full play. It was not an exciting spectacle. The whole plan of the fight, which lasted this day (January 15th) and the two following days, was to hold the Turks, with whose rear the Russians had caught up, in place, while other portions of the Russian troops should pass around their right and rear, and either capture the whole force or cut them off from their line of retreat along the high-road, and drive them into the Rhodope Mountains. The part assigned to Count Shouvaloff's troops was therefore to simply engage the Turks with sufficient energy to keep them in position. This sort of affair was entirely deficient in the dramatic grandeur of the magnificent advances in line at Plevna. The two lines now lay down, firing away at each other with right good will, and the artillery on each side increasing the din. But on either side there was no movement visible, except of couriers or generals moving along their men, or occasionally a battery shifting its position. We sat on our horses, a few hundred yards behind the line of skirmishers, nearly an hour, watching the monotonous progress of the fight. We were a group of perhaps twenty horsemen in all, counting the orderlies, and we were under a large branching tree, hoping that this would make us less prominent. But the singing of the bullets gradually increased in such a degree as to let us know that we were becoming a special target. Finally the well-known " s-s-s-s-st*up* " of a bullet that has struck, as distinct from the "whiss-*s-s-s*" of one that has gone by, made us all turn, and we saw a young orderly officer in the rear of the group bending over his saddle, with his hand at his head. He fell from his horse into the arms of a couple of Cossacks who had dismounted to help him, and was laid down in the snow, while the nearest passing stretcher was called to carry him off. The bullet had passed through his forehead, and he was dead when he reached the nearest temporary hospital. In taking off his overcoat, it was then noticed that he had another bullet directly through his heart.

Strange fate, that out of twenty men standing quietly under fire for an hour, but one, and he the youngest, should be hit, and with two bullets simultaneously, either one of which was certainly fatal!

This incident warned us to move away from this place, and we rode slowly across to a part of the ground where a small brook, with banks about four feet high, meandered through the field. The general peremptorily ordered his staff to dismount and sit down under the shelter of the bank, and to have their horses led behind a neighboring clump of bushes. He, Major Liegnitz, and myself then walked up and down for a while, looking at the Turkish line, and talking of the probable result of the day. Presently two or three of the horses were hit, and the general then politely requested Liegnitz and myself to also shelter ourselves under the bank. He was then left alone on the bank, and I shall long remember the picture of him, in his long overcoat, pacing up and down in the snow, the noise, but inertness of the battle, and the incessant whizzing of the bullets over our heads. Many of them, plunging just over us, traced little furrows in the snow, barely beyond our feet; and we commented on the infinite variety which could be made in the simple sound of " whiss-s-s-s."

Two or three hours later, as no new developments were taking place here, I determined to set out to find General Gourko, the commanding general, and learn the news of the battle on the other flank. I rode back with my orderly over the field, past the reserves and back into the village. Here were some temporary hospitals in the huts, and here also were the skulkers, who are always found in the rear of every battle-field. Little groups of five or six men, who had probably got there by bringing back the wounded, were crouched against the hedges of the gardens here and there, laughing, chatting, eating, amusing themselves in any way, in as utter disregard of the battle which was roaring in their ears, and in which the lives of their comrades were at stake, as if they had been at home in Russia.

Crossing the river again, I saw considerable

masses of troops in reserve lying down in the fields, and was warned by an officer that the direct road to the left of the Russian position was commanded by a very heavy fire, and that I would do well to circle around behind the troops. The river was bordered with quite a considerable growth of small trees, which shut out the Turks from direct view, but the bullets which came whistling from that direction gave very plain indication of their whereabouts.

The plain was dotted here and there with ancient tumuli, about eight to ten feet high, and I rode from one to another of these in search of General Gourko. I finally saw in the distance a considerable number of horses and dismounted men behind one of these, and riding up found it was the general and his staff. He and his chief of staff were stretched flat on the top of the mound, peering over the top with their glasses, and the rest of the group were crowded together at its base. As I came up he turned around and slid down the mound for a short distance, and asked me to sit down and tell him how things were going in Count Shouvaloff's front, and also asked if I had seen anything on my way of a certain brigade whose arrival he was awaiting with the utmost impatience, as they were to move around the flank of the enemy and block his retreat.

How very prosaic a modern battle can be with its long-range muskets, and especially in the middle of January, with the thermometer away below freezing! There was a deafening roar, two curving lines of black dots could just be distinguished in the snow, and the bullets were singing over our heads as we squatted behind a mound—and that was all of the picture. Yet it would have been the merest masquerading for the general and his staff to go parading up and down the field to draw the fire of sharp-shooters. He was in the most central part of the field and on the greatest eminence—insignificant as it was—that the field afforded. Nevertheless, at the time I could not help thinking how tame it all was, as a mere spectacle—how little action there was in it. Yet this is the characteristic of nearly all battles now up to the last moment of the final advance, which is decisive of victory or defeat, but which seldom lasts half an hour. The range of the infantry aim is so great (a mile and a quarter) that the action may become fierce, and many thousands of men can be hit without either side clearly seeing its opponents, and one must be well inside the line of infantry fire to follow the movements clearly, even with a glass. Cavalry charges cannot stand under the withering fire of rapid breech-loaders, and the final advance of infantry will only be made after hours of preliminary but possibly deadly maneuvering have been passed. The dramatic features of battle have become very short-lived and infrequent.

This day's fight brought no permanent result. The brigade that was to get in rear of the Turks came too late, and the latter slipped through the gap and took up another position a few miles in rear. As night came on the firing simmered down, and the general and staff sought the nearest village for shelter.

In the morning, the battle was renewed on the same principle as before, of trying to hold the Turks on one side and get around them on the other. While it was going on, the general and staff rode along the road toward the left of his position, near the large town of Philippopolis, about four miles off. This town is peculiarly situated. It was founded in the days of the conquests of Philip of Macedon, when war was made at short range, and the party who was the highest had a great advantage; and when a town situated on an eminence, from which an advancing enemy could be seen in time, was sure of a good defense. For these reasons, the town was perched on the sides of three abrupt rocky eminences which rise in solitary grandeur from the midst of a plain, which is hardly broken for twenty miles in one direction and sixty in another. Its appearance is at once unique and striking. It stood boldly out against the sky as we rode toward it, and our thoughts naturally drifted back through the long series of strange scenes it has witnessed during these last three and twenty centuries. There is no bloodier cock-pit in all Europe than these plains of ancient Thrace, the fertile and beautiful valley of the Maritza or Hebrus. Here the Macedonians, under Philip and Alexander, first subdued the Thracian tribes; here the Romans, under Trajan and Adrian, passed on their conquests of the lands beyond the Danube; here they built roads and other public works during their administration, which still exist to-day. Here the Bulgarians fought for the foundation of their kingdom out of the tottering ruins of the Roman Empire in the East; through this same valley the contending hosts of Christians and Turks have surged back and forward for the past five centuries; and here, finally, under the shadow of the three rocky peaks on which Philip of Macedon founded the town of his own name in the fourth century before Christ, was now being fought the last great battle of the latest war in the long series of those which have been fought on the questions of whether the Turks shall live and govern in Europe. The mind is staggered by the long retrospect of history which the associations of this place call forth, and we felt that we were now assisting at one of the not least important steps of that development of historical sequence. The advance of this Christian army and the retreat of the Mohammedan, and the still more important migration of the immense numbers of refugees in front of us, marked one of the final periods—not the last, but very near it—of that retrocession of the Turkish wave of conquest, which came into Europe only to blight every land where it penetrated, and which has now been surely receding for two centuries, and early in the next century, at the latest, will be gone forever.

The battle of Philippopolis lasted throughout the 15th, 16th, and 17th of January. On the afternoon of the last day, the Russians had gained positions on three sides of the Turks, and cut them off from their line of retreat toward Adrianople. The latter fought with their backs to the mountains, and fought hard and well, as the Turkish rank and file always do. But, on a final advance of the Russians, they were obliged to abandon all their artillery and train, and disperse in small bands over the Rhodope Mountains to the Ægean. Pursuit was impossible, and these scattered detachments pursued their way unmolested until, two weeks later, they reached the shores of the sea, and were picked up by ships of the Turkish navy and transported to Constantinople.

The Shipka army having been captured in bulk,

and Suleiman's Sophia army having been routed and dispersed, no armed force of any magnitude lay between the Russians and Constantinople. They entered Philippopolis and remained there four days to refit, then pressed on to Adrianople, where we found General Skobeleff's detachment, which had arrived two days before us. From there the advance again pushed forward and came in front of the lines of Tchekmedje, the defenses of Constantinople, on the 31st of January, just fifty-two days after the fall of Plevna. On the same day the armistice was signed which put an end to active operations.

In these fifty-two days, the column which I had the honor to accompany had marched six hundred miles and had crossed two high ranges of mountains. The combined Russian forces had captured one army of 40,000 men, dispersed another of 50,000 men, had taken 213 pieces of artillery, over 10,000,000 rounds of cartridges, 12,000,000 rations, and enormous numbers of tents, baggage, pontoons, and military supplies of every description. They had, in short, for the moment annihilated the military power of Turkey, and were only deterred from entering Constantinople by questions of political expediency. The manner in which the men lived, and the sufferings which they endured in the snow and ice of these fifty-two days of midwinter, I have endeavored to explain elsewhere;* their self-abnegation and cheerfulness under great physical suffering, to which their brilliant success was pre-eminently due, are excelled by nothing of which we have any record in history, and they entitle every man of those trans-Balkan columns to the lasting gratitude of their own countrymen and the friends of Christian government everywhere, no less than to the admiration of the entire world, which still appreciates the value of military heroism.

---

* "The Russian Army and its Campaigns in Turkey in 1877–78." Pages 369–374.

CHAPTER VI.

RUSSIAN GENERALS.

THE advance-guard on the march from Adrianople to Constantinople was commanded by Lieutenant-General Skobeleff, and while with it my previous acquaintance first began to ripen into great intimacy with two men—General Skobeleff and Mr. J. A. MacGahan—who stand, as I believe, at the head of their respective professions; professions widely apart—one of them as old as the history of man, and the other the product of the last thirty years; professions which can hardly be said to be equal in responsibility and importance, yet between which the gulf is not so great; for the world is governed not so much by battles as by politics; politics, even in the most despotic of countries, are now directed by public opinion, and public opinion is largely formed by the newspapers, and by their correspondence rather than their editorials. These are well-established facts of the times we live in, and the vast influence of the daily press, disgraced though it may often be by license and abuse, should cause it to receive that consideration to which its importance entitles it, from military men as well as from other functionaries of government.

Newspaper correspondents will hereafter form a most important element in every war, every great diplomatic conference, every other great event of any character; and the way to treat them is not to foolishly banish well-trained professional men, as the English tried to do in Afghanistan, and take in place of their reports the crude, biased, and incorrect statements of tyros in the form of subaltern officers, but to treat the real correspondents with dignity, increase their sense of responsibility, and give them every facility for acquiring correct information of facts that have already transpired and are concluded; in short, to make the position one that will be sought by men of brains, energy, and a high sense of honor, and thus to see that the world, which will have news of some sort, shall have truthful news

But of the generals first, as being the senior profession.

Mikhail Dimitrievitch Skobeleff was born in October, 1845; his grandfather rose from the ranks to be a famous general in the Caucasian wars of the first Alexander; his father was an officer of the guards, and his mother came of a noble and wealthy family intimately connected by marriage with the persons in the court most nearly attached to the Emperor's person. At the age of eighteen he became concerned in some disturbance while at the University, and was dismissed. His father, who then commanded the Emperor's body-guard, immediately entered him in one of the regiments of the guard, and he was sent to Poland, where he saw some active service during the insurrection of 1863. After this war he returned to St. Petersburg, but soon tired of the inactive garrison life, alternating in barrack duty and the endless round of social gayety. As he himself expressed it, the fine gentlemen of the guards drove him out. He entered the Staff College, and at the conclusion of his two years' service of instruction was made a captain and sent to the Caucasus about 1869 or 1870. After two or three years of the ordinary guerilla service against the mountain tribes of that region, he was transferred to Turkestan, and took part in the Khivan campaign of 1873 as lieutenant-colonel of a regiment of Cossacks. At the close of this campaign he made a wonderful and famous journey through the desert, accompanied by only two or three Kirghiz, under orders to discover what was actually the nature of the country along which the Krasnovodsk column was to have advanced from the Caspian, but which had turned back when half its men had perished of thirst. He was made colonel at the close of this war and attached to the staff of General Kaufmann, whom he accompanied two years later in the first expedition against Khokand. For his services in this campaign he was made a major-general, and in the following spring, at the age of thirty-one, he was placed in command of an independent force of about 4,000 men, with the aid of which he completed the conquest of Khokand, and annexed to the Russian empire a fertile province of nearly 30,000 square miles and a million of inhabitants. The province received the name of Ferghana, and Skobeleff was made governor of it. For his services in the Khivan campaign he received the fourth class of the order of St. George, and for the conquest of Khokand the third class of the same order—the latter being a reward whose value may be estimated from the fact that in the whole war in Turkey only thirty-seven of them were bestowed.

Skobeleff remained as Governor of Ferghana until a few months before the breaking out of the war, thus completing a tour of nearly seven years' consecutive and active service in the Caucasus and Central Asia. In this school he learned his trade as a soldier, and I have often discussed with him the value of it, advancing the well-known theory, "*la petite guerre gâte les militaires*," and asserting that great generals were not formed in small wars against semi-barbaric, nomadic people, and he, on the other hand, always maintaining that the first essential to a general or any other officer is the habit of being accustomed to danger and the responsibility of command under fire, and that these habits are acquired in the wars of Central Asia, of Algeria, or on our own plains. Having once acquired them, a man can pass readily to the command of large bodies of troops if he has the necessary talents; and, on the other hand, his talents will never be the worse for his previous experience in small wars. Without discussing this question, it may be said that Skobeleff affords no argument on one side or the other, for he is a man who is altogether exceptional—one of those few who have the power of rising superior to their own surroundings, and make their fate rather than follow it. He is a voracious reader, and his wealth puts all books at his command, no matter in what part of the world he may be. In the intervals of his campaigns he must have devoured books, for I never met a man so thoroughly posted in all the salient facts of military history, of the principles of modern warfare, and of the questions of Central Asiatic and Indian government. And he read, too, not as one reads at home or in a university, but in the midst of events, with a realizing sense of responsibility, seeing actualities and not mere pictures in what he read. For instance, in his garden at Bokhara he read (in English) the story of the destruction of Elphinstone's column between Cabul and Djelallabad in 1842. Every word of that terrible tale sunk deep into his memory, for he stood in precisely the same position —had just conquered a race of Asiatics of the same type—and while he read he half expected that any minute, as he sat in his garden, he might hear of an insurrection of the Khokandians, as the English at their newly-formed clubs in Cabul heard of the rising of the Afghans. He once gave me a summary of this tale of disaster, and I listened to him in eager silence for several hours, as I have listened to General Sherman narrate some story of our civil war. He is, indeed, the rival of Sherman as a fluent and graphic speaker.

Skobeleff came to Russia in the winter preceding the war, under a cloud of suspicion none the less heavy because of its entire injustice. In the period of inaction after the Khokandian campaign, his combative nature had determined to wage war on the rascals of the Supply Department. They, in turn, waged war on him, and, being no less skillful than unscrupulous and corrupt, they succeeded in sending charges to St. Petersburg of the gravest character against Skobeleff. One of the Emperor's aids-de-camp was sent out especially to investigate the matter, and, as he was courted by the people of the Supply Department and but little heeded by Skobeleff, he went back and made his report that

Skobeleff was a million of roubles short in his accounts! As soon as Skobeleff heard of this he got leave by telegraph from Kaufmann, and, without delaying longer than to pack up his vouchers, he started for St. Petersburg. There he appeared before the officials of the Treasury Department and submitted his papers. A thorough investigation was made, and Skobeleff was entirely acquitted, and received the official statement of the Treasury Department that his accounts were clear and correct in every particular. But a man of his pronounced and aggressive nature never lacks for enemies, and he is, moreover, one of those very, very rare instances of a man in Russia who dares to make his own career without asking the aid of court influence and "protection." The result was that, although officially vindicated, the cloud still rested on him; and the jealousy of a man only thirty-two, who had the rank of major-general and two crosses of St. George, was so great that he could obtain no command. The most that he could get was a nominal position on the Grand Duke's staff, *en disponibilité, i.e.*, having no particular duty, but to be disposed of when something turned up. It was not long before something did turn up for a man of his character. At the passage of the Danube he asked permission to accompany the commander of the leading division of troops—a major-general only slightly superior in date to himself—in the quality of a mere aid-de-camp or orderly officer, a position usually filled by lieutenants and captains. To show the stuff he was made of, he was not content to cross in the boats, but rode his horse into the river and swam the entire width of it—a stream as large as the Missouri near its mouth. The general whom he accompanied had never before been in battle, and Skobeleff's assistance and advice to him at the critical moments were of the utmost value—a fact to which the latter bore willing and generous testimony in his official report.

A few days later, in the organization of the detachments for the advance, Skobeleff received a command—the same brigade of Caucasian Cossacks of which I have given some account in the previous chapter. With these he was engaged in reconnaissance duty for the next four weeks, until they came into pitched battle at the second affair at Plevna, on July 30th. Here he handled this mere handful of men with such consummate skill as to save the left flank of the army from annihilation, and to prevent what was in fact a very serious defeat from becoming a hopeless rout.

He was then sent to reconnoiter the position of the Turks at Lovtcha, which he did in a most thorough manner; and, some infantry being placed under his command, he prepared all the details of the subsequent attack on that place so effectually that when the main body of troops came to make the attack, their commander had only to confirm his dispositions. In the attack he commanded the left wing of the Russian force, and to such purpose that the Grand Duke's brief telegram announcing the affair to Russia concluded with the words, "General Skobeleff, Jr., was the hero of the day."

From Lovtcha he came to Plevna, and receiving the command of the 18,000 men who formed the left flank of the Russian army, he made that heroic but unsuccessful assault on the redoubts just south of the town which, on a larger scale, has already taken in the Russian annals a place similar to that of the charge of the Light Brigade at Balaklava, in the English, or the final assault of Sheridan at Winchester, in our own. He lost 8,000 men out of his 18,000, and was driven out on the next day by overwhelming numbers. The attack was faulty in principle, and with the force which he had, was doomed to failure from the beginning—but this was no fault of his; he simply obeyed his orders, and did his utmost to accomplish the impossible. And although nearly fifty per cent. of his command perished under him, yet from that day his name was spoken of among the soldiers of the entire army in words of fables, as a man whose bravery could not be described. I have heard them speak of him as a general under whom they would rather fight and die, than fight and live under another; for with him they knew they could never come to disgrace, but were sure they would achieve the fame of military heroes whether they gained or lost the day. whether they lived or were killed.

On the following day Skobeleff was made lieutenant-general, being then not quite thirty-three years old, and was appointed to the command of the Sixteenth Division, which command he retained, in addition, at times, to the command of other divisions, till the close of the war. He then set to work to make that the most famous division in the army, and he succeeded. It is commonly spoken of to-day as "the famous Sixteenth Division." He won the unalterable affection of the men by his ceaseless care for their wants. They were the best-clothed and the best-fed troops in the army; they were never short of ammunition; they were never needlessly moved or exposed. If he was without public funds he never hesitated to advance, or give outright, whatever private funds he had, if it could in any way contribute to their comfort. At Constantinople, for instance, when there was considerable delay in transporting the sick to Russia, Skobeleff advanced over 15,000 roubles out of his own pocket, and succeeded in chartering an English steamer then in port, and obtained permission to ship the sick of his own division in it to Odessa. They thus reached home several weeks in advance of their regular turn. When his friends expressed their admiration at his generosity, he replied, "I owe everything in the world to these men, and the least I can do is spend a few thousand roubles to help them in their sickness." He passed his whole time in the midst of his men, tasting their food, inspecting their arms, learning their every want with his own eyes, and supplying it with orders based on his own knowledge. He was always with them in their most exposed positions, and when he was slightly wounded he refused to go to the rear, but had a cot brought up and placed in the trenches, and remained on it there until he was able to mount his horse again. At the instant of going into a fight he called as many officers as possible about him, to explain the exact purpose and object of it, and the manner in which this object was to be gained; and then he always made a short speech to his men, telling them what he expected them to do, and that he felt sure they would do it. In a word, he made himself and his division one—he representing the brains and they the body, and the heart being in common. He succeeded so thoroughly in accomplishing this union, that his men responded to his thoughts as readily as the muscles obey the will. I have listened in wonder at the enthusiastic admiration with which they spoke of him, and the no less enthusiastic way in which they obeyed him; and I doubt if a more thoroughly ideal relation between a general and his men has existed since the days of Cromwell.

In return for his care of his men he demanded of them, first of all, unhesitating, unflinching, unquestioning obedience to his orders. If he ordered a man to do anything, where immediate death was as certain as the sun in heaven, he expected to be instantly obeyed, without so much as even a look of question or surprise. Himself a man of wide reading, speaking many languages, and having traveled in many lands, he gathered about him, in his personal staff, as rough and uncultured a lot of men as I ever saw in officers' uniform; but they answered his purpose to carry orders, and, as he said, if he ordered one of them to ride his horse against the muzzle of a discharging cannon, he would do it instantly. One morning that I was with him on a reconnaissance, we came to a small brook; an officer of his staff, with whom he had had some cause of dissatisfaction just before, rode forward to try its depth; while he was cautiously feeling the bank, another officer—a Cossack—rode toward it, and, as his horse drew back, plied both spurs and the whip with all his force; the horse sprang forward into the middle of the little stream, and as it was very deep, though very narrow, both horse and rider disappeared under the water.

"There," cried Skobeleff to the other, "that's the way I want my officers to do things."

The first officer, greatly nettled, then put spurs to his horse, and, though Skobeleff, seeing his purpose, yelled at him to stop, in an instant he and his horse disappeared under the water. Both men were then dragged out, dripping from their cold bath. Every one laughed, and Skobeleff was in the best of humor.

"Now go home and dry your clothes. You're both fine fellows (Vwee Molodetzee). But," turning to the first one, " after this *never hesitate* in what you have to do."

On another occasion Skobeleff heard one of his colonels, just as he was going into action, trying to make a speech to his men, but hesitating, and stammering, and breaking down in it. He relieved him instantly. "If at such a moment," he said, "a man can't find a few simple words to tell his men what he expects them to do, then he don't know it himself. At that moment a man can't lie; his heart will speak if he have a heart for fight, and if he can't find words it is either because he is a coward, or because he has no notion in his head of what he is going to do."

Again, he punished his men without mercy for

the slightest depredation on unarmed inhabitants or their property. "Not that I care anything for these miserable people—their sufferings are nothing to those of my men—but because they had no orders to do it. If it served my purpose, I would give them a village to plunder and burn without a moment's thought. But they must do it only on my order. I want them to feel that they are merely my creatures—that they exist simply by my will."

These little episodes read queerly; they seem to be almost the doings and talk of a madman; but it was madness with a direct method—the insanity which is merely another name for intense concentration of thought and energy on a single purpose.

Of his officers he required that they should know their own business; not that they should be cultured, should present a fine appearance, should be gentlemanly in their speech. He demanded none of these things, but only that they should combine unflinching bravery and obedience with a thorough knowledge of the way to handle the number of men each commanded, so as to obtain the greatest results with them. If they answered these requirements there was nothing he would not do for them: he continually praised them; he secured them rewards and promotions; he shared with them whatever he had. If they failed in these qualities he pursued them relentlessly, abused them in unmeasured terms, and sought the first opportunity to get them out of his division.

His personal bravery was not only of the most reckless character, but at times it seemed to partake of the merest bravado, in which only extraordinary luck prevented him from reaping in death the well-earned reward of his foolishness. He always wore a white coat, a white hat, and rode a white horse in battle, simply because other generals usually avoided these target-marks. He was perpetually riding at breakneck speed over some fence or ditch, leaving half his staff and orderlies sprawling in it. He never lost an opportunity of *displaying* courage. He went into battle in his cleanest uniform and fresh underclothing, covered with perfume, and wearing a diamond-hilted sword, in order, as he said, that he might die with his best clothes on. For a long time he wore, with evident affectation, a coat in which he had been wounded, and which had a conspicuous patch on the shoulder.

Yet all this was not mere bravado and nonsense, but was the result of thought and almost cold-blooded calculation. It was intended to impress his men, and it did so. They firmly believed he could not be hit, and whenever they saw a white horse, coat, and cap among them, they knew that was Skobeleff, and so long as he was there they felt sure that everything was going well. At the beginning of the war he made up his mind firmly that he would never come out of it alive. (After reading me the telegram announcing the armistice, one of the first things he said was, "Well, perhaps I won't get killed after all.") With this idea firmly fixed in his mind, that his death was only a question of a few weeks or months, his one thought was how to best use his life so as to make an impression on his men, and gain such a control over them that they would follow him anywhere. In everything that he did he tried to eliminate the idea of danger from their minds, and to make the most dangerous exploit appear as an ordinary every-day affair. His bandsmen were kept up to their full strength, and their musical instruments as carefully inspected as the men's arms; when they went into battle it was with colors flying and the bands in their parade positions, with orders to play till they had not a gasp of breath in their bodies. At the battle of Shenova he moved over the snowy ground in this order, and got over thirty per cent. of his musicians killed and wounded. But this device of giving to a bloody assault the air of a customary afternoon parade, helped not a little to encourage the men to do their usual part in it.

All these little affectations were mere superficialty, calculated and employed for their effect on his men; but behind and below all this, forming the solid structure on which these airy trifles rested, was his stupendous military genius. I use the words advisedly, and firmly believe that should he live twenty years more he will be commander-in-chief in the next war about the Eastern question, and history will then speak of him as one of the five great soldiers of this century, side by side with Napoleon, Wellington, Grant, and Moltke.

Napoleon defined the requisite qualities for a great general to be, first, greatness of character, or moral courage, which produces resolution; second, coolness, or physical courage, which masters danger; third, a well-grounded knowledge of the guiding principles of his profession; and fourth, and above all, the capacity to see things as they are, and not to make pictures in his mind.

Although all these men have differed widely in their personal character and in the bent of their minds, yet they have all possessed these qualities in an eminent degree. And Skobeleff possesses them all, no less eminently. But without trying to penetrate what the future has in store for him, he already belongs to history. Though he has lived but thirty-five years, he has commanded twenty thousand men in battle; he has received the surrender of an entire army of nearly forty thousand; he has led more assaults than any living man but Grant, and in no one of them has he failed to carry the line he assaulted, though in one case he was subsequently overwhelmed with numbers and driven out. His name is forever linked with the battles of Lovtcha, Plevna, and Shipka, and with the Russio-Turkish War of 1877-'78.

The two other generals whom this war brought to the front were Radetzky and Gourko, both of whom have made good records, but who will never rise into the first rank of great commanders.

Radetzky was born in 1820, and was therefore fifty-seven years old during the war. He had seen service in the Hungarian campaign of 1849, and at various periods in the Caucasus, but he had not been in the Crimean war. He commanded the Eighth Army Corps from the beginning to the end of the war in Bulgaria. It was this corps which forced the passage of the Danube, and which held on to the Shipka Pass with such heroic tenacity from its first capture, in July, till the final capture of the Turkish army opposing it, in the following January. He is not a man of brilliant abilities, but is greatly endowed with those stubborn qualities of determination and perseverance which have made the name of George H. Thomas memorable in our own history; and, like him, he was unwearying in his devotion to his men, and his kindly, fatherly solicitude for their welfare.

Gourko is eight years the junior of Radetzky, and was not quite fifty during the war; he has been all his life a cavalry officer of the guards, and had seen service as a subaltern in the Crimea and as a colonel in the Polish insurrection of 1863. At the beginning of the war he commanded the Second Cavalry Division of the Guard, but before this was mobilized he came to the field as a volunteer, and was selected by the Grand Duke Nicholas to command the advance-guard which pushed forward over the Balkans immediately after the passage of the Danube. The success which he attained in this expedition is known to all the world, and it was a success due entirely to his own energy and skill. On the conclusion of this expedition he resumed command of his own division, which was then on the way to the field, but a few weeks later he was selected to replace an incompetent general in command of all the cavalry assembled in rear of Plevna. Not long afterward the guard and grenadiers arrived as re-enforcements, and Gourko submitted to Todleben his plan of capturing the redoubts which guarded Osman's line of communications, and converting the paper blockade of Plevna into a real one. Gourko received command of all the troops destined to accomplish this, and for the first time in his life he had a large body of infantry (forty-four battalions) under his command. He attacked these redoubts, carried them, and completed a tight investment—but at a terrible sacrifice. In the principal redoubt, Gorni-Dubnik, the Turks had but 4,000 men in all; Gourko brought nearly 16,000 against it, and in the assault lost 116 officers and over 3,000 men! The blow was a heavy one, for the troops were all picked regiments of the guards, and their officers nearly all belonged to the nobility; it brought the sufferings of war home to the higher classes in a way they had previously had no idea of. The fault was not so much Gourko's, but rather that of the men themselves and their subordinate officers; yet it was a generous fault, for they had rushed forward impetuously in advance of their orders, filled with the pride of their birth and position. But the breech-loader is no respecter of persons, and there was a wail of lamentation throughout St. Petersburg and Moscow.

The sanguinary result of this affair, and the maledictions which fell on Gourko's head from the widows and orphans, seem to have made a great impression on him. After that he was as untiring as ever in his own restless activity; he gave his men no respite of long marches, and bold, quick movements; but he never again led them to a vigorous assault. He commanded a semi-independent army of 80,000 men during the winter, and was the first to cross the Balkans, by turning the enemy's position near Sophia; after this he followed them energetically, and in the three days' battle of Philippopolis he completely routed and dispersed them. The whole of his campaign was a series of admirably executed turning movements, but the losses in battle were less than from freezing. Had he thrown his whole force impetuously upon Valentine Baker's position at Taskossen, and, though he lost 5,000 men or even more in the assault, carried this position by ten o'clock in the morning instead of late in the afternoon, he would have come squarely across the one line of retreat of the main Turkish army, and in all probability would have captured the army in bulk just as the Shipka army was captured. But he nursed his men, losing only about 500 in all, and the Turks escaped. Though he routed and dispersed them two weeks later, yet they still lived, and not as prisoners of war; five months afterward they stood facing him with arms in their hands in the growing fortifications of Constantinople, and they formed the veteran nucleus of the army which at that time rendered Constantinople safe against a *coup de main*.

Gourko is the least popular of the Russian generals: his manner is brusque, he is very harsh with his men, and never pays personal attention to their wants. The men worshiped Skobeleff as a legendary hero, they loved Radetzky as a kind-hearted father, but they never developed any personal affection for Gourko. He is a man of restless, untiring energy, a high order of abilities, and he has rendered services of the greatest value; but he never made himself one with his men. He has the brains of a leader, but lacks those qualities which gain men's affections.

It would, of course, be idle, in speaking of the Russian generals, to pass by General Todleben, who is the first military engineer of his age. But to be the first engineer is not to be the first general. His great and lasting fame was made in those days when, as a colonel of engineers and a major-general at thirty-seven, he was the guiding genius of the defense of Sevastopol. In the last war he was called to the army only to direct the siege of Plevna. All the details of the latter part of the siege are due to him, and the credit of the final success is largely his. But he was present at only one battle —that in which the Turks finally tried to break out —and he was, so to speak, out of sympathy with all the aggressive features of the war. His counsel was always on the side of prudence; he had a large "factor of safety" in all his plans, and he advised against that bold and successful winter campaign which alone brought the war above the dead level of mediocrity and placed it in the list of brilliant campaigns. He was not quite sixty years old at the time Plevna fell. He has grown stout with advancing years, but he is still full of activity, both physical and mental. In personal appearance he bears a strong resemblance to Bismarck, and is a man who at once impresses you by his agreeable manners, polished address, and dignified bearing. After the treaty of San Stefano, when the Grand Duke Nicholas gave up the command of the army, Todleben came to Constantinople to succeed him; but his ability as commander-in-chief was never put to the test, for hostilities were not resumed.

I have previously spoken of the men who by their abilities alone forced themselves to the front; but in the three great military empires, and most of all in Russia, every prince of the reigning family is carefully educated as a soldier; when he attains maturity he becomes, *ex-officio*, a great general, just as he is lord lieutenant or governor-general of a province, or councilor of state. On the outbreak of a war the great commands are usually given to princes. It is foreign to my purpose to argue the advantages and disadvantages of such a system; under the existing conditions of such governments there are far more advantages in it than we Americans would suppose; it is, in fact, almost a necessity of the system. In such cases the commander-in-chief directs his army as the Emperor rules his country: *i.e.*, by his own will, if he be a strong man—by the advice of his counselors, if he be weak.

Under this system twelve members of the Imperial family came to the army, occupying positions from commander-in-chief to aid-de-camp with the rank of captain. One of them, the Grand Duke Serge of Leuchtenberg, nephew of the Emperor, was killed in a reconnaissance.

The most important were the Emperor's brother Nicholas, who was commander-in-chief of the troops in Bulgaria, and his three eldest sons—the Cesarevitch Alexander, who commanded the left wing of the army; Vladimir, who commanded a corps under him; and Alexis, who, as rear admiral, commanded all the naval operations on the Danube.

The Grand Duke Nicholas was forty-six years old at the beginning of the war; he is a man of remarkably frank and genial nature, and the exact opposite of his brother the Emperor in the apparent ease with which he carried his responsibilities. He has a soldierly bearing and a soldier's nature, and, had he not been a grand duke, would probably have made a dashing leader of a cavalry division. While no one ever claimed that his military talents alone would have made him a commander-in-chief, yet, under the system which I have referred to, it is doubtful if any general could have been selected who would have been more acceptable to the army, or who would have better fulfilled his difficult task. It is impossible to be jealous of the Emperor's brother. Unfortunately, he selected for the chief of his staff and his assistant two men of very mediocre abilities. The first was never more than a chief clerk, and the second was reduced to being one after having committed two or three crass blunders early in the campaign. Yet these two men, whose incompetency nobody disputed, were, for reasons never fully understood, retained in their places to the end of the campaign. As a result, the Grand Duke was practically without any staff at all. While the campaign waited for the fall of Plevna, Todleben supplied the place of chief of staff; after that there virtually was none.

At the close of the war the Grand Duke returned to St. Petersburg, almost the most unpopular man in Russia. The cause of his unpopularity lay in the growing discontent of the Russians, who feared that the results of the war were being lost by diplomacy. They blamed him in unmeasured terms for not having occupied Constantinople—an act which would certainly have embroiled Russia in war with England and Austria, and to no purpose—and sought to trace the responsibility of all the early delays of the war directly to him; whereas, in fact, they were due to the insufficiency of the force with which the war was begun against the Grand Duke's remonstrances. No people are more given to criticism for its own sake than the Russians, and particularly when their wounded vanity is in question; but it passes over in due time. The day will soon come when the Russians will realize that their war would have been a dead failure but for the winter campaign, and they will acknowledge their just debt of gratitude to the Grand Duke Nicholas, who undertook that campaign against the advice of those most entitled by their position and experience to give it.

The Cesarevitch, at the age of thirty-four, commanded from first to last the two corps to whom was intrusted the task of masking the Turkish fortresses on the left flank of the Russian advance. Assisted by an able chief of staff, about fifteen years older than himself—from whom, however, there is no reason to suppose that he received any more assistance than a commanding general always derives from a good chief of staff—he fulfilled this most important duty in a thoroughly satisfactory manner; and although the many battles in which his troops were engaged have been forced into the back-ground by the bloodier deeds around Plevna and Shipka, yet his military achievements are well known in Russia, and have greatly increased the popularity, as well as the respect, with which he is regarded by the army and the Russian people generally.

CHAPTER VII.

WAR CORRESPONDENTS.

THE position of a newspaper correspondent, representing one of the great journals, and writing daily history for an audience of hundreds of thousands of people, by whom he is believed much more readily than those even who are making the history, is, as I have said, one of great responsibility. The class of men who hold these positions is every day growing in responsibility, in their qualifications for their work, in the value which is set upon their services, and in the consideration and dignity with which they are treated. Their duties require ability of a high order, a keen judgment of men and events, readiness and skill in literary composition, energy, courage, and indifference to hardship. The more consideration is shown to them, the more facilities are given to them for writing of events where publicity is possible, so much the more will men of a high order enter their ranks, and so much the better will they do their work, to the benefit of the whole world.

I believe that no one was more fitted for this

work, or has yet done it better, than J. A. MacGahan. He was born in Ohio, where his parents still reside, about thirty-eight years ago. Of his early life I know nothing. He first turned up in Europe, at the time of the Paris Exposition of 1867, as a correspondent of the New York *Herald*. Three years later he followed the Franco-Prussian war in the same capacity. In 1873 he succeeded, after the greatest difficulties, in getting permission at St. Petersburg to accompany the expedition to Khiva. He traveled, in company with Mr. Eugene Schuyler, as far as Fort Perovsky, on the Syr Daria, where they parted; Schuyler going on to Tashkend, and MacGahan setting out to make his way across the desert and overtake Kaufmann's column, which was supposed to be on the Oxus. With two or three Kirghiz, and twice as many horses, he started to cross the sandy, trackless desert, known as the Kyzil Kum, with the intention of reaching the Oxus, the nearest point of which was over four hundred miles distant! He hoped, on reaching this river, to fall in with the Russian column, but the chances were equal that he fell in with the Khivans or some band of Turkomen.

After he had ridden three hundred and fifty miles he finally came upon the trail of Kaufmann's column, at a small post called Kala-ata, which Kaufmann had left behind him. Here he was arrested by the commandant, and held in confinement until instructions should be received as to what should be done with him. But he knew that, long before these instructions could arrive, the Russians would be in Khiva, and he determined not to have the object of his long journey defeated at the critical moment by the assumed authority of a subordinate. He managed to escape from the little post during the night, and, although Cossacks were sent out in pursuit of him, he eluded their search; and at last, after a journey of thirty days in which two of his horses had perished of thirst, he came in sight of the Oxus —but only to hear the noise of a battle between Kaufmann's men and the Turkomen who were hovering about them. He rode on as cautiously as possible, and had the good luck to fall into the hands of some Kirghiz allies of the Russians, instead of the hostile Turkomen. He thus reached Kaufmann's head-quarters in safety, and was received with hospitality and admiration.

The story of this wonderful ride has been told with equal modesty and skill by MacGahan himself, in his interesting book, "Campaigning on the Oxus," but we must look to others to know how it was appreciated in the Russian camp. The fame of it spread throughout Central Asia, and it became one of the most celebrated exploits of the whole campaign. It would never have been credited—

so impossible did it seem for a man to make such a journey alone—but for the two incontrovertible facts that he disappeared suddenly from the little post on the Syr Daria, and reappeared as if from the heavens four weeks later among Kaufmann's men on the Oxus.

Schuyler says of it, "His ride across the desert was spoken of everywhere in Central Asia as by far the most wonderful thing that had ever been done there, as he went through a country which was supposed to be hostile, knowing nothing of the roads or of the language. Even the officer whose scouts had failed to catch MacGahan, from whom long afterward, on coming from Khokand, I first heard of my companion's safe arrival at Khiva, was delighted at his pluck, and used the significant Russian expression, *Molodetz*—a brave young fellow—the greatest possible praise under such circumstances."*

After the conclusion of the Khivan campaign, MacGahan returned to Europe and wrote the "Campaigning on the Oxus." He was then transferred to Spain during the Carlist war, and had an amusing experience in being arrested and imprisoned on suspicion as a spy, which came very near, however, to having a sudden and tragic termination.

After he left Spain he joined a yachting party which went to Iceland in the yacht "Pandora" dur-

---

* Schuyler's Turkestan, vol. i., p. 66.

ing the summer of 1875. Of this he has given us a very readable account in his "Under the Northern Lights," one of the most charming books of its kind in the English language.

We find him then, at the end of ten years' travel from one end to the other of Europe and beyond its borders, familiar with men and affairs, a ready and accomplished writer, speaking French and German fluently, and having no small knowledge of the Russian language, and an intimate knowledge of the Russian character. He was well prepared for the work in which he now engaged, and in which he lost his life.

In the meantime affairs had been growing more and more critical in Turkey, and it was evident that another acute period of the "Eastern Question" was approaching. MacGahan took service in the London *Daily News* and went to Constantinople, where, immediately on his arrival, he heard those stories of massacres in Bulgaria which were then floating about Constantinople, and a portion of which had been telegraphed to England, though with some doubts as to their accuracy. He immediately determined to proceed to the locality and investigate the matter on the spot. He persuaded Mr. Schuyler, then consul-general in Turkey, to accompany him; they proceeded to Philippopolis, and from there, either in common or separately, they visited every portion of the insurrectionary district. From here MacGahan wrote those celebrated accounts, the substantial accuracy of which has never been successfully impeached, of the "Bulgarian massacres," which astonished and horrified the civilized world, and which were far more potent than any other cause in bringing about the recent war, and the liberation of the greater part of Bulgaria from Turkish rule.

But for MacGahan, or some other correspondent who would have done what he did, the tale of these barbarities would have been hushed up by the Turks, a truce with Servia might have been patched up, and the Eastern question allowed to slumber again for another twenty years without any progress being made toward its final solution. No more marked instance could be cited of the influence, of which I have spoken, of correspondents upon public opinion, and public opinion upon the course of events. The manner in which the policy of the British cabinet was deranged by the storm of indignation against the Turks which these outrages raised in England is a matter of common notoriety.

MacGahan remained in Constantinople, and at the close of the year (1876) the conference met to deliberate on the affairs of Turkey. During the whole of this he was received on terms of unusual consideration by all the plenipotentiaries, particularly General Ignatieff and Lord Salisbury. When this conference broke up in failure MacGahan repaired to St. Petersburg, knowing that war was inevitable, and made his way to Kishineff, where the Russian troops were assembled.

On the outbreak of the war he moved forward with the army, and remained with it uninterruptedly until his death in Constantinople, in June, 1878. He was with Gourko in his first passage of the Balkans, at Shipka in August, at the great battles of Plevna in July and September, at Osman's sortie in August and at the surrender in December, and at the first battles in Gourko's second expedition toward the Balkans in November. During the whole campaign he suffered greatly from a severe injury to his leg, caused by the falling of his horse in the Balkans in July; and after the fall of Plevna he was delayed so long at Bucharest by the aggravating nature of this injury, which had resulted in stiffening the knee-joint, that he was unable to overtake the rapidly advancing columns before they reached Adrianople. He arrived at Constantinople with the advance-guard in February.

I first met him in a way that was characteristic of his quiet, unobtrusive character. In company with several other foreign officers, I was traveling on the 31st of August from the head-quarters at Gorni Studen toward Plevna, where the great battle was expected. About midnight we had stopped at the bank of a little stream and lain down for a few hours' sleep. At daylight, just as we were waking up, a rough, shaggy pony, carrying a man wrapped in a large ulster and wearing the correspondent's badge on his arm, came ambling along the road and stopped to speak to us. It was MacGahan, who had passed the previous day in watching the battle in which Osman attacked the Russians at Zgalevitza, on the east of Plevna, had written his dispatches during the early part of the night, taken a few hours of sleep, and started off at two o'clock in the morning to carry the dispatches forty-five miles to the Danube, where he had a courier waiting to carry them to Bucharest, the first point where they could reach a wire open to ordinary business. He gave us a short but clear account of the fight, and, mounting his pony, ambled off again. The next morning his account of the battle was read by every one in London and New York.

MacGahan was universally esteemed by the whole Russian army, throughout the length and breadth of which his name was as familiar as a household word by reason of his exploits in Central Asia. The secret of this popularity lay in the simple fact that he applied the plain rules of ordinary morals and common honesty to his calling as a correspondent. No one has criticised more freely than he the mistakes of the campaigns or the faults of individual men, but he never did so with malice, he never used his paper to ventilate personal revenge; his criticisms were the result of long and intense thought, and were an honest judgment founded on the best information he could obtain. Not one of them ever gave offense, and I have heard the justice of some of the most severe of them freely acknowledged by the Russians themselves. Considering the haste with which that large portion of the two volumes of the "War Correspondence of the *Daily News*" which came from his pen was necessarily written, there is remarkably little in it which even at this day needs correction. He applied this same rule of honest, manly dealing in utterly rejecting that theory of certain journalists who disgrace their profession by maintaining in practice the principle that news, being the commodity of their business, and priority in publishing it being the first essential of their success, is to be obtained in any manner whatever, not even omitting means which would be considered utterly dishonorable in any other business or profession. According to the practice of these men, whatever they overhear by chance, whatever they learn at a dinner or at other times when men are off their guard, whatever is told to them under the trust of secrecy, is to be used as freely as their notions of its value may seem to require. Otherwise, they reason, some one else will in some way get an inkling of it, and then they have lost a piece of property; for fresh news is the article they deal in, and stale news has no market value.

All such ideas as these MacGahan condemned, not so much in words as in his acts, for he never once employed any of them. In the intimacy which he enjoyed with more than one Russian officer of high rank, he became possessed of unusual information, not only of what had already transpired, but also of what was planned for the future. Not once did he betray a confidence, and never did he commit an indiscretion in using the abundant material which came into his hands.

Facts which it was indiscreet to publish at the moment, and which a few weeks later, in the rush of events, had lost their value as news, he was content to store away for some future time, when they might be used in a continuous history of the war which he proposed writing.

MacGahan was a man of a wonderfully sweet and gentle nature, almost womanly in tenderness, though he never lacked for a man's strength in all he wrote and did. Often, in the midst of his correspondence, he turns aside at the end of some long discussion of politics, or narrative of battle, to describe some touching little incident. He had an equable temper, never fretted, never worried over his hardships, never nursed his anger against any man. He met every one frankly—not failing in the respect due to high rank or position, but not overawed by the mere greatness of the person with whom he was talking. He had an acute penctration, which enabled him to detect quite readily the dust which some persons attempted to throw in his eyes, under the guise of unusual confidence.

His death was sudden, although mainly due to overwork during a long period. He came in from camp to Constantinople to nurse me when I was ill of the typhoid fever. Two days later he fell ill himself, the disease taking the form of the typhus with spots; it attacked his brain, which was the most vulnerable part of him by reason of long-protacted mental strain, and he died in convulsions at the end of a week. On the 11th of June, 1878, he was buried in the little Greek cemetery on the hill behind Pera, his funeral being attended by the United States minister and other members of the legation, by the officers of the U. S. S. *Dispatch*, then in the harbor, and by a large number of Russian officers, prominent among whom was General Skobeleff. Masses were said for the repose of his soul in St. Petersburg and at other points in Russia.

No man of his age has in recent years done more to bring honor on the name of American, throughout the length and breadth of Europe, and far into

Asia; no man has more faithfully served the English-speaking races, by telling them the truth about great events in an attractive form in their daily papers. His letters may be studied as models by those who propose to adopt his profession, and his sterling character, his pluck, and his energy, by every man who aims at honest success in any walk of life.

At the beginning of the war, the Russian military authorities received the press in a way that it has probably never been received before. Regulations were drawn up, which permitted any regularly accredited correspondent of a responsible journal to accompany the army, provided he agreed in writing to a few simple rules. The principal of these were that he should always carry on his person his photograph, on the back of which was written his authority to accompany the army, as a sort of passport by which he might at any time be identified; that he should wear a band around his arm bearing the word "Correspondent" in Russian letters, and his number, and that he should give his word of honor not to report the numbers of troops, the intended movements of the army, or any other information which might compromise its success. As it only required about forty-eight hours for news from the Russian head-quarters to reach the Turkish camps, *via* London and Constantinople, the propriety of such a pledge could not be questioned. The object of the badge and the photograph was to give the correspondent a known status in the army, which would protect him from accidents, as well as let every one know with whom they were conversing. It is probable that some more efficient means might be devised for this purpose, such as compelling them to wear an entire uniform of a distinctive character; and considering the good or harm which may result from their letters, and the impossibility of supervising them before they are sent, it would not be asking too much to require them to sign their names to whatever they write. The position and responsibility of every man about an army should be sharply defined.

Something over eighty correspondents joined the army under these conditions, about one-third of whom were Russians. The London *Times* sent in succession three officers of the army—Colonel C. B. Brackenbury, R.A.; Colonel Sir Henry Havelock, M.P., and Captain Herbert—as special military correspondents, in addition to its regular correspondent, Mr. E. M. Grant, an ex-officer of U. S. Volunteers, who followed the whole campaign, and who had been in the East for the two previous years, and had accompanied the Servian troops in the field, and to several others who acted under his orders.

War Correspondents.

The London *Daily News* sent Mr. MacGahan, Mr. Archibald Forbes—who had previously followed the German armies in 1870, and subsequently was with the English troops in Afghanistan and Zululand—and Mr. F. D. Millet, an American artist residing in Paris, who desired to see the war for the studies it might afford him in his own profession, but who was also specially fitted for his position by his literary skill.

The *Telegraph* and *Standard*, *Illustrated News* and *Graphic*, various other papers in England and Scotland, several papers in America, in France, and in Germany were also represented, some of the latter by officers of the army.

All the great papers had a special office or "bureau" in Bucharest, the nearest large town, through which their telegrams were received from the field, and their other business transacted, including supplying their correspondents with the necessary money for their expenses, which were sometimes enormous. Several of these papers had a regularly organized line of couriers to carry their telegrams from the field to Bucharest.

When it is remembered that some of the correspondents received $10,000 a year, besides, all their personal expenses; that they had a wagon, tent, and complete camp outfit, three or four saddle-horses and equipments, one or two servants, four or five couriers—all at the expense of the paper—and that they often sent telegrams of two and three thousand words for a distance of as many miles, some idea may be gained of the expense which a "leading daily" can afford, in order to give the world its news before breakfast.

Of all the correspondents, none achieved so large a reputation as Mr. Forbes. Every one remembers those graphic accounts which he sent from the battle-field itself, so clear in every detail that whoever read them felt as if he had the original scene before his eyes. In power of picturesque description of this sort with the pen, it is doubtful if he has an equal in the world. No small measure of his success is also due to the fact that he arrived in England while the war was still at its height; as people listened to his lectures or read his articles at the same time that fresh news was coming in from the same fields, they felt that the actual reality of the war was brought closer before them. He left the army, however, on the morrow of the great repulse at Plevna, and the conclusions which he formed about the Russians and about the course of the campaign were founded on somewhat incomplete data.

Of these eighty correspondents about half were at the front throughout the summer, and the greater part of them exposed themselves with the utmost fearlessness in battle, and endured the greatest hardships without flinching. One of them, Mr. Millet, received a decoration for extraordinary bravery in aiding the wounded under a very hot fire. For the other half, the comforts of Bucharest possessed the greater attraction. They came to the army occasionally, visited the camps and hospitals, studied the Russian character, and went back to Bucharest to digest their studies. But when the winter came on, the ardor of nearly all was benumbed, and their interest began to flag. Some went back to Paris and London, others remained in Bucharest. But only four of them, MacGahan, Grant, Millet, and Villiers—the latter representing the *Illustrated News*—trudged through the snow in the Balkans and arrived at Constantinople with the troops. Of these four, the first three were Americans.

CHAPTER VIII.

CONSTANTINOPLE.

I FIRST entered Constantinople under such amusing circumstances that, although the story is entirely personal, I venture to relate it.

After the armistice was signed on the 31st of January, I remained with the advanced guard under Gen. Skobeleff, whose head-quarters were at the little village of Tchataldja, about thirty-five miles from Constantinople. Ten days later, I had passed through the Turkish camps in company with a mixed commission of Russian and Turkish officers, who fixed the lines to be occupied by the outposts, and the "neutral zone" between them; had ridden my horse into the waters of the Black Sea one day and of the Marmora the next, and had caught a glimpse in the distance of the glittering domes and minarets of the ancient city. There was nothing in particular to do, and I began to weary of inaction and to long ardently to see the city itself. After sounding General Skobeleff on the subject, and learning that he had no personal objection to my making my way thither, though of course it must be done entirely at my own risk and on my own responsibility, I made up my mind to quietly ride in through the Turkish lines.

Early the next morning I packed my one remaining suit of presentable clothes on the horse of my Russian servant, strapped a Cossack cloak (boohrka) on my own, and in my ordinary uniform started out. I knew enough Russian by this time, and was sufficiently well known to Skobeleff's men, to pass the Russian outposts, and I felt sure that the Turks were quite tired enough of war to be slow in firing on any one approaching them during an armistice. The respective outposts then stood at two bridges, about five miles apart, on the ancient road along the shore of the Sea of Marmora. The Russian sentry saluted me as usual, but did not accost me. As I approached the Turks half an hour later, my uneasiness as to what they would do was relieved by seeing them turn out the whole guard! I rode up slowly, the twenty men of the guard presented arms, I returned their salute gravely, and passed on. The village near this bridge was filled with soldiers lounging in the streets, a brigade or more of troops being quartered there. Most of them stopped to salute me, but the others paid no attention to me beyond a short stare of wonder. Once out of the village, I made a circuit through the fields in order to avoid a large camp, and then regained the high-road.

It was a superb, cloudless day of such weather as we have in the Middle States in the latter part of April; fresh from the snows of the Balkans and the filthy huts in which I had passed my nights for the past three months, the change was almost as great and as sudden as is experienced in descending in a few hours on the overland train from the snows of the Sierra Nevada to the flowers of the Sacramento plain. The road was crowded with endless lines of creaking *arabas* filled with refugees, or bordered with parties of them stopping to rest on the wayside; dead animals, dead men, and broken wagons, the remnants of previous caravans, also lined the road, but the suffering which these sights suggested had no effect on my spirits, thoroughly intoxicated with the balmy air and the beautiful, warm, blue sky.

Suddenly, during the afternoon, on reaching the summit of a hill, Constantinople stood before me in full view, not five miles off. In front, beyond a succession of rolling hills and deep valleys, stretched the long, gray line of the ancient walls—the most superb ruin in existence—parts of it here and there hidden from view by masses of tall, dark cypresses; beyond the walls lay the white domes and tall, slender minarets of the mosques, and the masses of bright-colored houses. The dwellings are all covered with plaster, painted in some warm tint, usually a light pale pink or yellow, though shades of blue are not uncommon; the setting sun behind my back wrought these into the most gorgeous but harmonious patches of color. Off on the right, this side of the Asiatic shores, lay the placid Sea of Marmora, which rivaled the sky in the intensity of its rich aquamarine blue; out of it in the distance rose the bold, abrupt shores of the Princes' Islands, some of them covered with red ochreous clay, and others with immense dark groves of olive-trees; still beyond them lay the range of mountains which culminates in the broad, snow-clad peak of the Asian Mt. Olympus. The variety of features of the landscape, and particularly the intense, rich warmth of the coloring, combined with the softness of the air to make one of the loveliest pictures I have ever beheld.

Continuing my ride in keen enjoyment of the scene, I passed through the broad belt of cemeteries which extends for several miles along the walls on the western side of the city. Nothing gives such an impression of the antiquity of the cities in the East, as the great number of cemeteries, in which every foot of ground is occupied, and whose silent occupants exceed so many times in numbers the living population of the adjoining cities. The Turkish graveyard, however, has none of that cold, gray solemnity so repulsive in our own, whose monuments are of cold marble or granite. The gravestones are usually small, are made of sandstone, and brightly decorated with colors in paint or with long inscriptions in golden characters on a black background. Those marking a man's grave are surmounted by a *fac-simile* of his head-dress — the ancient ones with a turban, the more modern with a fez, cut in the stone; the headstones of women are plain slabs with a wreath of flowers at the top. The brilliancy of the colors contrasts well with the tall, dark cypresses, which are almost invariably planted around them.

As I came nearer to the walls the beauty of their ruins impressed itself still more strongly upon me. It was originally, when built by Justinian in the sixth century, a triple wall, the highest being thirty feet, each line crenelated on top and flanked at intervals by high towers; in front was a broad, deep moat with dams at intervals to hold the water when flooded. Now there are long gaps where the masonry has crumbled and fallen, the ditch is used in places for a vegetable garden, and the wall itself is overgrown here and there with ivy. Twenty-three times have these same walls been besieged, and four times have they been captured. Here, where the ivy trails so gracefully along the gray masonry lit up by the setting sun, in the final siege and capture, the Emperor Constantine, the last of his name and his dynasty, fell in the fierce struggle which put an end to the Eastern Empire of Rome, and firmly consolidated the Turkish power in Europe.

But my mind was diverted from these thoughts by curiosity as to how the Turkish soldier, pacing under the archway of the gate, would receive me.

I rode across the bridge quietly, as if engaged upon most important and legitimate business. That seemed to be his idea also, for he stopped and presented arms with every sign of respect. I returned his salute and passed through the gate into the town.

I was, of course, entirely unfamiliar with the streets, though, from a careful study of the map, I knew they were very crooked, and I was prepared to find them narrow, as is common in Eastern cities. The sun was still half an hour high, and I hoped to pilot myself by its shadows so as to keep an easterly course, and, traversing Stamboul and the Golden Horn, come into the semi-European suburb of Pera, where I trusted to luck to find the house of Mr. Schuyler, who was then our Consul-General for Turkey.

I soon found, however, that the streets were so very narrow that for long distances I got no glimpse of the sun or its shadows; and as they curved in various directions, and were met by others at every variety of angle, I could only trust wholly to chance to keep the proper course. I had made up my mind that it would be very injudicious to ask any questions (my servant knew a few words of Turkish), and thus excite suspicions as to my character or business. I was still, however, in a comparatively unfrequented part of the town, and the few people on the streets paid no attention to me beyond a slight stare.

Presently, on reaching an intersecting street, considerably less narrow than the others, I noticed that there was a horse-car track in the middle. The thought at once flashed across my mind that in all probability this railroad would lead either to Pera or to the Golden Horn; so I determined to follow it, though it was apparently considerably off my course. This street proved to be the great main thoroughfare of the city, and before long I was in its most crowded part. There are only a few streets in Constantinople that have any sidewalks at all, and those which do exist are only three or four feet wide, and utterly inadequate to the crowd of foot-passengers. The result is that people ordinarily walk in the street, and in the principal thoroughfares the number of pedestrians is so great that great persons, like ambassadors and ministers, have a mounted man, who precedes their carriage to open the way; and even the horse cars find that a loud bell, incessantly ringing, is insufficient to clear the track, and at certain hours of the day every car is preceded by an athletic runner with a stout stick, who trots a short distance in front of the horses, blowing a loud horn, and freely applying his stick to all those who do not heed its notes.

Through this motley throng I slowly threaded my way without molestation of any kind; people turned their heads toward me, some stopped to stare, others muttered " Moscov" or " Giaour," but no one accosted me in any manner whatever. It was only when I saw this large crowd, and realized their calm forbearance, that I reflected what a risky business I was engaged in, and how foolish an ending it might easily have. But the Turkish character, as I afterward learned, is a peculiar mixture of contemptuous tolerance and fanatic frenzy; they are patient and even polite for an indefinitely long period, until suddenly their religious fanaticism is excited, perhaps by some incident of a trifling character, and then their mad excesses, as in the murder of the consuls at Salonica, know no bounds.

They merely passed me by now in careless scorn, as not worth thinking about; but had some urchin thrown a stone at me, or some hot-headed fanatic yelled " Down with the Giaour," as an Anglo-Saxon in similar circumstances might easily say " Hit the damned foreigner," the crowd would have jumped upon me and torn me limb from limb.

It must be remembered that this was three days after the British fleet had passed the Dardanelles; it was at the time when the English ambassador was telegraphing home that the Russian army was advancing on Constantinople "in spite of the armistice;" when the city was full of the wildest rumors, and when no Russian had yet been seen in the streets. My uniform differed in general appearance from that of the Russians only in the cap, which it would have required an expert to detect. My horse had Russian equipments, and the well-known Russian cloak was on my saddle; I was, moreover, covered with the mud of a long day's ride, and evidently came from the army. Every one took me to be a Russian officer, as was evident from their remarks of "Moscov."

Two officers had, a few days before, come down by train from Adrianople bearing diplomatic dispatches; they had been met at the railway station and driven at once in close carriages to the palace where they were lodged. With this exception, I was the first man to enter Constantinople from the Russian army, and, as I said, I was the first one to appear on the streets. What would have been the fate of a German officer entering Paris alone during an armistice in the siege?

I watched the crowd carefully, but rode on as if I was in the habit of riding there daily. There were many novel sights to attract my attention which I longed to stop and examine: the curious costumes, the bright little shops, now and then a gorgeous little fountain of marble and gold, or a magnificent mosque; but all these could only be noticed with a glance, for I knew it would be imprudent to stop. The journey seemed to me a very long one, it being, in fact, over five miles through the town as I rode; the sun had now disappeared, and though I had passed over one or two hills, the streets were so narrow and so thickly built up that I had never been able to get a bird's-eye view of the town and the Bosphorus, and thus orient myself by the map which was photographed in my mind. I began to fear that I was not going toward Pera at all, but that nightfall would find me still wandering around in a circle through the crooked streets. Finally I reached the mosque of St. Sophia, though I did not then know it from the other mosques; here the street suddenly turns almost completely on itself, following along the walls of the old Seraglio. This was very discouraging, and the streets being here less crowded, I ventured to ride up to a drug-shop bearing the sign, "*Hier ist Deutsch gesprochen*," and inquire the way to Pera. But I was answered by a Greek—the partner, I suppose, of the one who spoke

German; I got no intelligence from him, and a crowd quickly collected, so I determined to push on at once. My suspense was soon relieved by coming abruptly on the Pera Bridge over the Golden Horn. I rode on to it with such an air of assurance that the man collecting toll stepped back and bowed to me, instead of stopping me for money, as he invariably did afterward.

This bridge is one of the world-famous sights, and is familiar to every one who has read anything of modern Constantinople. It is a rickety old wooden structure, nearly half a mile long, resting on boats; its two sides are lined continuously with beggars, and between them, from sunrise to dark, surges an incessant throng whose numbers are counted by hundreds of thousands at the close of the day. In its blending of Europeans and Asiatics it is the type of Constantinople itself. Here may be seen, at any hour of the day, the Turkish Minister in his coach or on his horse, the western merchant in the dress of London or Paris, the Turkish priest in long robe and green turban, the hermaphrodite Greek merchant in Parisian coat and Turkish fez, the Jewish money-lender and the gayly dressed Circassian, the merchants from Arabia and far in Central Asia, and the Turkish women with the *yashmak* drawn tightly over their faces, their curious bundle of skirts lifted high above their ankles, disclosing ugly feet cased in cheap French shoes, a parasol over their heads, and a small satchel in their hands.

Every variety of the Semitic and Indo-European races here jostles each other in the course of the day, producing a moving and highly-colored panorama of kaleidoscopic variety.

The diversity of shipping alongside the bridge is no less extraordinary. Here are the high-pooped little Greek junks, of the same form as that in which Paul set sail from Troas, side by side with the Mediterranean steamers of the Austrian and French lines, the Turkish ironclad of latest English pattern, and the screeching little pack-boats of the Bosphorus, built on the model of those that ply from Dover to Calais. In and out through them all, dart hundreds of the graceful little *caïques*, with their no less graceful oarsmen in turban, white shirt, and baggy white trowsers. It is a scene of endless, bustling activity, full of life and color.

Threading my way slowly through the crowd, I finally reached the streets of Pera. Immediately I was surrounded by an eager, curious crowd, composed principally of Armenian boatmen and *hamals*.* I at once asked if any one spoke English or French. A burly Armenian pushed his way through the crowd and said, "Me Inglis." I told him I was an American, and wanted to find the

---
* Baggage porters.

American Consulate. He answered promptly, "I know," and forthwith began hustling the crowd, opening a passage, and beckoning me to follow him. He led me along a street close to the Bosphorus, in the lower part of Galata, which I afterward discovered was largely occupied by sailors' boarding-houses. At the end of half a mile he stopped before a large house, and pointing to it with an air of satisfaction, kept repeating, "American, American." The surroundings of the place seemed to me rather strange for a consulate, but I dismounted, and, leaving my servant with the two horses, went up the steps, entered an open door, and, finding no one, ascended a pair of stairs, and saw a large hall with several seats in it, and a sort of primitive stage at one end.

There was no one in the hall, but presently a man, dressed in European clothes, but having the appearance of a Greek, came out of a neighboring door. He answered me in bad French, and I told him I had been brought here in search of the American Consulate. He replied that it was not in that building, and he did not know where it was; that this was the *Café chantant Américain*, or American concert and dance-house, of which he was proprietor!

Retracing my steps down the stairs, I found my servant holding the horses with a terrified air, surrounded by a crowd intent on examining and feeling the horses and their equipments, and plying him with an infinite number of questions in various languages. The guide was holding forth in Armenian, with a self-satisfied manner, explaining at great length who I was, and all about me. The crowd extended for two hundred feet or more in each direction, completely blocking the street; two horse-cars were ringing their bells, and their runners were blowing their horns and fighting with the crowd, but it refused to yield.

I sharply accosted my guide, telling him, in phrases which must have increased his knowledge of the English language, that he was a fool, that he had brought me to a concert house, and that I wanted him to show me at once the way to the American Consul's. He asked me to repeat the word, and then his face fell; his temporary importance vanished, for he had never heard of the place. But from the crowd of eager listeners, another Armenian came forward with smiling face and an air of confidence, not unlike that of a Chinaman in San Francisco under similar circumstances, and said, "I know him." I repeated the word "consul" several times and asked him if he was sure, but he only answered, "I know him," and immediately set to work to open a way through the crowd. I got on my horse and followed after him, as he led the way through a filthy little street not over twelve feet wide, and so steep that there was a high step in the pavement at every few yards. It was already quite dark, my horse slipped and tumbled over the wretched pavement, the various families of dogs who occupied this street in fee simple set up a tremendous howling, and behind me followed a motley crowd of not less than five hundred people. I had no confidence that this fellow who was leading me knew anything more about the consulate than the other one, and I began to have serious misgivings as to the termination of my adventure. My anxiety was unfounded, however. When we had nearly climbed the steep hill, the guide turned down a narrow lane, and presently stopped before a house over the door of which I could just discern in the twilight a blue board bearing the spread eagle in gilt, and the welcome words, "Consulate of the United States of America." Looking back, I saw that the crowd extended up the whole length of the lane. I gave the guide a small gold piece, about equal in value to what he would earn in a month, and he went off with radiant face, gesticulating to the crowd, who followed him with a Babel of questions.

Half an hour afterward I had washed, and donned my fresh suit of uniform, which only brought out in stronger contrast my unkempt hair and beard, and was dining at Mr. Schuyler's table. It was but a few weeks since I had been shivering in the snows of the

Balkans, and that same morning I had left a squalid hut like those in which I had been sleeping during the whole winter. The contrast between the thoughts which run through a man's mind in the midst of war and such surroundings as those I have mentioned, on the one hand, and a refined home and a gentleman's dinner-table on the other, was sudden and bewildering.

Constantinople was at this time the center of observation of the entire world. The Russian army, which but a few weeks before had been in the trenches before Plevna, had suddenly appeared almost at the gates of the city; the English fleet lay in the Bay of Ismidt, three hours' steam from the Golden Horn; the Russians and Turks had made an armistice in order to arrange a treaty on terms the basis of which had already been accepted by the Turks. The latter, for the moment, lay completely at the mercy of their enemy. Would he enter Constantinople? Would England declare war? Would the Sultan be deposed? Was the Eastern question to be at last finally settled? Was the war to spread and involve all Europe? Nobody knew what a day would bring forth. Diplomats and newspaper correspondents were in the keenest state of excitement; but not the least trace of it could be discerned on the surface of what one could see in the streets. The latter were thronged as usual during the day; they were silent and deserted during the night as the watchman made his rounds, striking the pavement with his iron-shod stick. One looked at any moment to see some one appear on the streets with news or rumors of news, to see crowds gather and discuss it, and give vent to their fanatical hatred of the first hostile army which had penetrated to Constantinople during the four centuries that the Turks had held possession of it. But nothing of this kind transpired. On the streets, in the great bazar, in the baths and cafés, people led their accustomed life, and from what one saw it would never have been imagined that a war was even in contemplation, much less that a great war was just terminating disastrously for them, and that the fate of their empire and the future of Europe were for the moment trembling in the balance.

I had made arrangements immediately on my arrival by which, in case the armistice was broken, I could be transported in a small steamer to some point on the coast within the Russian lines, and then I gave myself up quietly to sight-seeing. A week later we had news that the Grand Duke and a portion of the Russian troops had occupied the little village of San Stefano, on the Sea of Marmora, about eight miles outside the walls. I immediately proceeded thither, and found that, in consequence of the arrival of the English fleet, the Russians had made an agreement with the Turks by which they were to occupy a line very much nearer the city than that laid down in the original armistice. The Grand Duke and his staff had come down by train from Adrianople, and installed themselves in the village, and with them had come General Ignatieff, who had lately arrived from Russia as first plenipotentiary to negotiate the treaty of peace.

The village of San Stefano is beautifully situated on the shore of the Sea of Marmora, and consists principally of about twenty or thirty large houses owned by wealthy Greek merchants, who live in them during the summer. These houses were immediately occupied by the various members of the numerous head-quarter staff. I was fortunate in receiving a room in one of the largest houses facing the quay, which runs along the front of the village. Here we used to pass the afternoon enjoying the mild air, listening to the music of the various bands intermingled with the sound of the swell breaking against the wall, basking in the bright sunlight, and forgetting with marvelous rapidity the snow, the cold, the mud, the squalid huts, the sufferings, sickness, and death, which were our surroundings such a short time since.

Small numbers of officers were now allowed to go by train to Constantinople; no evil results followed, and the number was increased, and finally the privilege was extended to enlisted men. At last four or five hundred would go in every day, and the Russian uniform was as common a sight on the streets, and particularly in the bazar, as that of the Turks themselves. Both officers and men behaved themselves in such an exemplary manner as to call forth the highest commendation, even from their greatest detractors among the English. There were no street brawls, no instances of rowdyism of any kind whatever. One day two officers were reported to have been seen intoxicated on the streets, though not giving offense to any one. The Grand Duke immediately rescinded the permission to visit the city. But when it was learned that these men had done no harm, further than to expose themselves and their uniform to the criticism of indecorum, the permission was gradually extended again under certain stringent rules. I believe that no second case of drunkenness was ever heard of.

The officers spent their money lavishly in every direction; the hotels and restaurants were so crowded that there was great difficulty in getting a meal; the *cafés chantants* (the meretricious substitute which Pera offers for theaters) were crowded nightly, and the Jews and Armenians of the bazar found such customers as they had only known in their dreams—people who actually paid without an hour's bargaining the first price they demanded for their goods, which usually exceeded by four to six times the market value which they expected to receive. The Russian five-rouble piece became far more common than the piece of twenty francs or the Turkish lira; and merchants who had means of forming a fair estimate told me three months later that not less than six millions of roubles in gold (about $4,600,000) had been paid into the various shops.

On the 3d of March (Feb. 19th, O. S.), the anniversary of the Russian Emperor's accession to the throne, the long haggling over the terms of the treaty came to an abrupt termination. The treaty had been all agreed to the previous night, and was to have been signed at one o'clock in the afternoon, the troops were drawn up for parade at that hour, and the horses of the Grand Duke and staff stood saddled in front of his house. But at the last minute the Turkish plenipotentiaries raised fresh objections and refused to sign; couriers rushed back and forward between the Grand Duke's house and that in which Ignatieff and Savfet Pasha were deliberating. The afternoon wore on, and it began to look as if the anniversary day would pass without the treaty being signed. At half-past four o'clock, the Grand Duke and his staff mounted and rode to the edge of the village, the former sending word to the plenipotentiaries that he would wait there till the paper was signed. Not long afterward, one of his aids came running forward, bearing in his hand the pen still wet with the ink with which the document had been signed, and which he begged to keep as a souvenir. Following him came General Ignatieff, who saluted the Grand Duke, saying, " Your Imperial Highness, I have the honor to announce that the treaty of peace is concluded." The Grand Duke pulled off his cap and shouted " Hurrah," which was taken up by his staff as he went galloping off toward the troops.

The latter were drawn up on an eminence just outside of the village, and facing Constantinople, which was in full view a few miles off.

The usual form of review was held, and then the Grand Duke rode out in front, and calling the whole body of six hundred or eight hundred officers about him, he announced to them the signature of the treaty of peace, and the end of the war. A grand shout of joy broke forth, which quickly passed to the men, who understood what it meant, and sent up deafening cheers; looking back, the whole air seemed black with the caps which the men were throwing up, and I doubt if any man got his own cap again in the course of a week.

A moment afterward, the Grand Duke wanted to say a few words more to the officers, and they began signaling to the men with their swords to keep silence, but the latter paid no attention; a lot of aids were then sent to stop them, but it was found impossible. Like a fire checked in one place, the cheering broke out in another in a dense roar, drowning every other sound, so that few people heard what the Grand Duke had to say. It was only a few simple but well-chosen words, thanking the officers and men for their bravery and endurance, and telling them they had their reward in the great results which they had achieved.

Then, after waiting a few minutes for the men to stop cheering from sheer exhaustion of their lungs the Grand Duke stepped forward to the place where the priests had arranged a sort of altar on the ground, and stood ready in their green and gold robes to hold service. All uncovered their heads, and the ordinary form of mass was chanted in monotonous tones. My next neighbor in the crowd, an admiral in the navy, nudged my arm, and said in English, "Solemn moment." I replied, "Very solemn!" But in reality it was a solemn moment: the climax of the most momentous events which have taken place in the East since the Turks crossed the Hellespont, nearly five centuries ago—events involving the welfare and habitation of two whole races of people—liberating one race, overthrowing the power of the other, and preparing the way for their speedy exit from Europe.

The greatest religious ceremony of these later days will be the mass to be held in St. Sophia, when finally it is restored to the hands of Christians; but this not being possible now, twenty-five thousand Russians knelt at prayer with arms in their hands, on a spot where no Christian army had ever trod since the Turks conquered Constantinople, and looking in the dusk of twilight at that dome of St. Sophia which has occupied so prominent a place in the imagination of all their countrymen since the days of Catherine! Well might the Grand Duke say to them, "You have reason to be proud of having been the instruments to accomplish such grand results."

To my own mind, looking on as a foreigner sympathizing in their cause, but without any of the realizing sense of sympathy springing from personal interest or attachment, the affair failed of its impressiveness—first, because I had been impressed to my full capacity by a similar scene, which I have already described,* at Plevna some months before, and one cannot have the same emotions twice; and secondly, because, although heartily glad to be out of the dangers and horrors of the war, and rejoicing also in the success of the Russian cause, which I believed to be the cause of right, yet I could not overcome a strange feeling, not exactly of regret, but of

---

* Page 11.

emptiness and languor, because the future seemed so tame and devoid of occupation.

When one's mind has been concentrated for several months on one set of ideas, wondering each day what the next will bring forth, leading a life of the utmost excitement, novelty, and danger, and involving from hour to hour such fundamental questions of fact as life and death; when one has had during a considerable period a diet of such strong nervous food, and then suddenly sees it come to an end, and has to contemplate the return to a quiet and comparatively inactive life—after the first sigh of "Thank God" at the escape from danger, there comes an indefinable feeling of horrible dread of *ennui*. It lasts but a few days or hours before one returns most contentedly to his accustomed life, but it is none the less strong for the moment.

Already, while the review was going on, the following message from the Grand Duke to the Emperor was traveling over the wires. It represented fairly the feelings of the army, though its phraseology sounds queerly to western ears:

"SAN STEFANO, Sunday, Feb. 19 (Mar. 3), 5 P. M.

" I have the good fortune to congratulate Your Imperial Majesty on the occasion of the signing of the peace. God has granted to us, Sire, to accomplish the great, the holy mission that you had assumed. It is on this anniversary day of the emancipation of the Russian peasants that Your Majesty has liberated the Christians from the Mussulman yoke. NICHOLAS."

Immediately after the conclusion of peace the Grand Vizier and other high Turkish officials, both civil and military, came out to San Stefano to pay their respects to the Grand Duke, and negotiations were at once begun to arrange a visit of the Grand Duke to the Sultan. But questions of etiquette and other details delayed it for more than three weeks. Finally it was arranged that the Grand Duke and staff should proceed to Constantinople by water and be received by the Sultan at his palaces on the Bosphorus, after which they would land and be driven to the Russian Embassy, and pass the night there.

On a beautiful bright morning the Grand Duke and about seventy-five members of his staff embarked on board the Emperor's yacht "Livadia," and another vessel which had meanwhile arrived from the Black Sea, and we steamed around Seraglio Point into the Bosphorus. The harbor presented a gay scene, the Turkish men-of-war and all the foreign *stationnaires* displaying their bunting and manning the yards. Opposite the palace of Dolma-Batche, about three miles above Pera, the ships stopped and the Grand Duke went ashore in a state *caïque*, being received at the landing by the Sultan. The ships then continued their way a few miles up the Bosphorus to the palace of Beyler-bey, on the Asiatic shore. Here we all went ashore, and a half hour later were joined by the Grand Duke, at whose disposal this palace had been placed in order to allow the Sultan to make a return visit. This palace, although small, containing not more than thirty rooms, is one of the most exquisite of all those which line the shores of the Bosphorus. It was built comparatively recently, and was completely renovated in 1867 for the Empress Eugenie, who occupied it during her visit to Constantinople. A sea-wall runs along the Bosphorus in front of it, at each end of which is a little *kiosk*, or "summer house," whose sides are almost wholly of glass, the interior furnished with a broad divan in blue and straw-colored satin, on which one could easily be content to pass hours in simply watching the beautiful stream. Behind the wall is a series of gardens surrounding the palace, filled with flowers and fountains, and rising in tiers above one another on the abrupt hill. At the top of this are cages of wild animals of various kinds, one of which contained at that time a far-famed tiger of great beauty and wonderful size. The palace stands in the midst of the lower terrace of the garden, not over two hundred feet from the edge of the stream; it is three stories high, built of pure white marble in the ornate style of the renaissance, which is well fitted to a building of its small size. Ascending the steps, we passed through a broad vestibule into the grand central hall, which was about fifty by sixty feet, and extended up to a highly decorated skylight in the roof. The galleries of the floors above were upheld by marble columns, and the walls, floor, and ceiling were also of marble. In the center was a grand fountain, the basin of which was about twenty-five feet in diameter, and which had innumerable small jets playing from the side and from a group of figures in the center, producing that moisture in the air and that gentle sound of rippling water which are so agreeable and soothing to the senses in hot weather.

The various rooms opened off of this main central hall, and into one of them we were shown, where we were served with coffee, and every variety of sweets and wine, several of the large dishes being of solid gold.

After partaking of these, we were asked to walk about the palace, pending the arrival of the Sultan. The rooms were all in keeping with the hall which I have described. One of them in particular attracted my attention; it was in the second story, in the corner looking toward Constantinople; the ceilings, walls, and floors were all of wood mosaics, principally different varieties of olive wood polished to the highest degree, and of a beauty of design in figures which I have never seen rivaled. In the center of the room stood one of those queer—and very unhealthy—articles of furniture, resembling an ancient brazier, which is found in nearly every Turkish house, and which, when filled with live coals, answers the purpose of a stove. They are usually constructed of brass, and many of them are of handsome design. But this one—which was not less than three feet high—was of a single piece of carved crystal! On the inside were a few metal projections on which the pan of coals would rest when used, and whose brilliancy of reflection in the surrounding crystal can be easily imagined.

It was a queer sight to watch the Russian officers, dressed in full uniform, but not free from the rough appearance of men just from a campaign, striding over these exquisite floors of wood and marble, in long boots and spurs and clanking metal sabers.

While we were still examining the building, word was brought of the approach of the Sultan. In former times he used always to travel over the Bosphorus in a *caïque* of twenty-four oars, seated on a dais, and the rudder held by the Minister of the Navy. Now he usually travels in a little steam yacht of exquisite proportions and beautiful furniture. He arrived in this, and the Grand Duke met him at the water's edge, and they two led the way into the palace. Nothing could be in greater contrast than these two men. The Grand Duke is a man of about six feet three inches in height, with full chest and broad shoulders; he was dressed in a general's full uniform, and wore high boots and a clanking sword. The Sultan wore a plain fez, and that peculiar single-breasted, high-buttoned black coat which the Turks in late years have invented to agree with western ideas, and adopted as their full dress; it resembles most closely the conventional coat of a Methodist parson. The Sultan is a small man, and the top of his fez barely reached the Grand Duke's shoulder; he looked haggard and frightened, and his eyes darted rapidly but stealthily from side to side, as if he feared injury from some one in the crowd. These two men walking side by side suggested the relative position at that moment of the two nations they represented—big, burly, noisy, victorious Russia; and weak, timid, humbled Turkey.

The members of the staff were presented to the Sultan in the upper hall, and then the two, accompanied by an interpreter, went into the room I have mentioned to take a cup of coffee and exchange compliments in a few minutes' conversation.

The visit being over, the Sultan was escorted back to his yacht, and most of the staff seated themselves in the various imperial *caïques* which were in waiting. The one in which, in company with three other officers, I took passage, was about twenty-five feet long, made of some wood resembling the Spanish cedar in color, and highly polished and oiled. It had ten oarsmen, sitting in pairs, dressed entirely in white except the red fez, and their necks and breasts exposed to the air. In the stern-sheets were soft cushions of blue satin, so low (on account of the crankiness of the craft) that it was necessary to recline rather than sit on them. The Sultan's *caïques* certainly surpass any row-boats in the world in their gorgeous splendor, and they are the equal of any in grace and beauty of outline. The pleasure of riding in them on the Bosphorus is equaled only by that of moving about in a gondola at Venice, or in an Indian canoe on our western lakes.

On arriving at the outskirts of Pera, on the European shore, we were met by carriages which conveyed us into the city. The Grand Duke and a few others entered the Russian Embassy, whose black eagles over the gate had just been uncovered for the first time since the declaration of war, eleven months before.

The war being now over, every one thought only of returning to Russia, and began counting the days to their departure. The mails came quickly direct from Odessa, naval and supply vessels came from time to time to anchor in front of San Stefano, news was brought that a large fleet of transports was being collected at Odessa to take the troops home, and every one hastened to the bazar to buy some souvenir to take home from Turkey, or hurried up his sight-seeing. It was announced that the first troops would embark on the 20th of March from Buyukdere.

This is a little village on the Bosphorus, about half way between the Sea of Marmora and the Black Sea, and it was selected on account of its good harbor, San Stefano being perfectly open and without docks or piers where large ships could land. But, as the above date approached, the troops received no orders to move, and then it was learned that the English Ambassador had protested to the Turks against allowing the troops to march around Constantinople, on the ground that in so doing they would become possessed of certain positions commanding the city. The Turks thereupon declined to allow the Russians to embark from this place.

It being impossible to embark any number of men and horses from San Stefano, the contract for the transport fleet was revoked. A few days later, on April 1st, appeared Lord Salisbury's famous circular, criticising the San Stefano treaty, and plainly intimating that England would not accept its terms. The project of embarkation was then indefinitely postponed.

And now followed a curious instance, reflecting the highest credit upon Russian discipline, of a victorious army being held completely and absolutely subservient to political necessities. Having for the time being completely destroyed the military power of their enemy, the Russian army had arrived in front of the capital of the defeated nation—a capital too, on which their eyes had been fixed for many long generations—and quietly remained there without entering it.

Their only desire was to return to their homes and families, receive congratulations for their glorious deeds, and resume their ordinary avocations. But the defeated nation, at the instance of a neutral power, interposed insurmountable obstacles to their departure. Still they remained outside, while as yet the capital lay entirely at their mercy, and could have been possessed the moment the order was given. Nor was this all; for while longing only for home, and anxiously awaiting the development of diplomatic events, the remnants of the Turkish army were reorganized and recruited, and under their very eyes the Russians saw springing up, and growing day by day, a long line of defensive works, which six weeks later rendered Constantinople safe against a *coup-de-main*, and were soon afterward so strong that some persons deemed them invulnerable, and all acknowledged that they could not be carried in open assault without the loss of fully fifteen thousand men.

No wonder that the spirits of the men began to languish. Their position was one to command the sympathy of every soldier; they had been in the field for fully a year, had fought a war marked with checkered successes and failures in the beginning, but concluded with a brilliant success, due almost wholly to their patient endurance of hardship; part of them had marched six hundred miles without seeing their knapsacks and without changing their clothes; their boots were dropping to pieces, and they had no tents; everything was, in fact, worn out except the guns in their hands, the cartridges in their pouches, and their own splendid devotion; they were herded about in small villages, the little huts of which afforded a miserable shelter to only about half, leaving the rest out in the open.

Their mental condition was quite as trying as their bodily discomfort. During the campaign, the intense excitement of rapid marching, sharp fighting, and success, had buoyed up their spirits and enabled them to endure what seem incredible hardships; now they were idle, longing to go home to receive their reward, but kept here in perfect inaction, and in necessary ignorance of the object or result of it.

The effect upon health of a sudden change from a life of intense mental and physical activity to one of dull inaction is well known to all physicians; in addition, these men had been marching for several weeks in intense cold, with but the one shirt which was on their backs; and, finally, in their bivouacs the plainest principles of sanitary hygiene were utterly disregarded. Dead animals lay a few feet off, rotting in the spring sun for weeks before they were buried; there were few latrines, and what there were were insufficient; different regiments bivouacked along the same stream, the filth of those near its source being washed down into the drinking water of those below them. This subject was one of universal remark among foreigners, and there is but one word to apply to their bivouacs—they were simply filthy.

All these causes combined, and produced their natural result. Toward the last of April every variety of camp fever broke forth, from the mild forms of malarial ague. through the typhoids to the typhus, and finally the typhus with spots, which is not greatly different from the plague. They spread so rapidly that throughout the months of May and June fully one-half of the whole Russian force near Constantinople lay on their backs; so many doctors and nurses died that it was not unusual for one surgeon to have over a thousand patients dependent solely on him—so large a number that, for sheer lack of time, the lighter cases could not be visited more than once in three or four days.

Toward the latter part of June, the sickness

seemed to diminish, and a month later it had nearly disappeared. During these three months over thirty thousand sick had been transported to Odessa by the Red Cross Society, and those who remained had been provided with fresh clothing and tents, and had moved their camps to higher ground. Of the mortality of those who were dispersed through the hospitals of Russia, I am unable to speak; but of those who were treated on the spot, it was singularly small, not amounting to over five per cent. of the total number of those taken sick.

Some of the Cossacks who returned to the Caucasus carried the seeds of the disease with them, and, inflamed by local causes, it broke forth with great malignity the next spring as the plague, whose ravages in southeastern Russia during the summer of 1879 are well known.

In Count von Moltke's history of the campaign of 1828-29, there is given a very full account of the sickness which broke out in Diebitch's army after he had reached Adrianople, and which increased to such an extent that one-third of his force was helplessly ill, and the rest took turns of doing military duty one day, and shaking with intermittent fevers the next. In this case, however, the mortality was exceptionally great, nearly forty per cent.

The same sickness on a still greater scale was repeated at the close of the Crimean War. As neither the Crimea nor Roumelia are naturally unhealthy countries, the main cause of it must be found in the traditionally bad sanitary arrangements of the Russian camps.

There is something peculiarly sad and cruel in the fate of a brave soldier who survives the perils of many a bloody field only to fall a victim to an insidious disease a few months later. This was the fate of only too many of the Russians. A terrible gloom spread over the army, and was reflected at once throughout Russia. The pitiable condition of these gallant men, waiting helplessly on diplomacy in front of Constantinople, watching the enemy's fortifications grow under their very eyes, and falling sick daily by thousands, called forth the bitterest feelings throughout Russia. Without due reflection, people at home visited their discontent upon the Grand Duke Nicholas, as has been already narrated. Ostensibly on account of his health (which in reality was not good, for he was suffering from a return of a complaint of the liver, which had troubled him more or less throughout the whole campaign), and at his own request, the Grand Duke was relieved from command on the 24th of April, the anniversary of the declaration of war, being promoted to the rank of field marshal on the same day. He returned to Russia, the object of such unpopularity that it was difficult to secure him the respect due to his position, much less to his great and eminent services. He was succeeded in the command of the army by General Todleben, but no active operations were afterward resumed, for the treaty of Berlin was signed a few weeks later. The troops began gradually returning to Russia in the following month of August.

CHAPTER IX.

ST. PETERSBURG.

THERE is but little in the general appearance of St. Petersburg which is distinctively Russian, the only great city of the pure Russian type being Moscow. In St. Petersburg there is here and there a gilded dome, or one covered with stars on a blue field, but the city is essentially of the cosmopolitan modern type, resembling Berlin more than any other, but not differing greatly from the more recent additions to Paris and Vienna. The streets are broad and straight, usually paved with stone, and the buildings are long rows of stuccoed structures of a barrack-like character, singularly devoid of architectural variety.

The whole appearance of the place is essentially military and bureaucratic, and a large proportion of the people one meets on the street are in uniform. Those who wear spurs and trail a sword clanking at their heels are officers of the army, and those who wear a black uniform with white buttons and ornaments are civil servants; the total number of these two classes in the whole city amounts to a good many thousands. The policemen are old soldiers, and wear a uniform closely resembling that of the army, and they also carry a sword. No small part of their time is taken up in keeping a lookout for officers, every one of whom, whether on foot, on horseback, or in a carriage, they are required to face and salute.* When a junior officer meets a general, he not only salutes him, but stands fast on the curb, facing the general and holding his hand at his cap, until he has passed. When a member of the imperial family, no matter how young, passes in his carriage, every officer, of the highest as well as the lowest grade, stops and faces him in the same way during his salute.

This great number of uniforms gives an air of brightness to the otherwise gloomy streets, overshadowed by the never-varying dull gray sky; and an additional element of life is given by the equipages, which are of an entirely unique character. The picture of the fashionable carriage of the West, with dignified Jeames seated high on the box, immovable, with his whip on his thigh, and a reduced edition of himself on a lower plane to his left in the form of Thomas, sitting equally immovable, with arms

---

* This has been changed by a recent order, dated March 20, 1880, of General Melikoff, Chief of the Supreme Executive Council, which limits the salutes to the Emperor and members of the imperial family, in order that the police may give their whole attention to the maintenance of public order.

folded, and before them a pair of clipped and banged three-quarter-breds, their eyes covered with blinders and their heads checked very high, throwing their feet well in the air but not advancing above six miles an hour—all this is as familiar in Vienna and Paris as in London and New York, but it is never seen in St. Petersburg except in the case of some young guardsman, who considers it a swell thing to have one of his turn-outs *à l'Anglaise*. The fashionable carriage of St. Petersburg is totally unlike this; it is a *calèche*, or victoria, built very heavy, and is drawn by two coal-black Orloff trotters, with curved necks, long manes, tails reaching nearly to the ground, and shaggy fetlocks; the collar and traces are strong, but there is no blinder, check-rein, saddle, or breeching, and the bridle is composed of such small pieces of leather that it is hardly visible; the reins are of blue cloth, and there is one for each side of the bit, making four for a pair of horses; there is no footman on the box, and the driver, who seems to be chosen for his large girth, is dressed in the costume which is worn by every coachman, whether driving a prince's carriage or a little *droschke* at ten cents an hour. It consists simply of a low-crowned stiff hat, and a long blue tunic, crossed over his breast and reaching quite to his feet. But what principally distinguishes the Russian equipage is its animation; they drive at ten miles an hour through the most crowded streets, yelling at people to get out of the way; the horses' eyes and nostrils are full of fire, and the coachman, whose short little whip hangs by a string from his wrist and is rarely used or seen, is no less animated, as he stretches both hands forward, watching his animals most intently, and looking as if he were driving in a race. They are the best drivers as a class that I have ever seen.

When the Russians drive more than two horses they hitch them up abreast instead of in pairs, and their favorite team is the *troika*, or three horses abreast, the middle one trotting and the outsiders galloping. The excitement of rapid driving in this style is very enjoyable, and one of the principal amusements of winter is to get a sleigh and *troika* and go out to some of the concert halls in the suburbs to hear the gipsies sing and watch them dance. Another swell equipage for a young bachelor is a handsomely-mounted little *droschke*, with two horses, —one jet-black, trotting in shafts, with head erect, and the other a light gray, galloping by the side, with his head kept out and down by a side line. The effect is very pretty, though the constrained position of the free horse uses him up after a couple of years at the most.

The furious gait at which they drive, and the rough stone pavements, tell very severely on their horses, and no one who pretends to keep a handsome turnout ever drives the same horses on successive days.

The streets are much less crowded than in other great cities. Peter laid out his town on both sides of the Neva, and he also applied the principles he had seen in Holland, by building radial and concentric canals through the main part of the city. These canals are faced with fine granite walls throughout their length, and in summer they afford the means of transporting heavy merchandise without recourse to wagons. No heavy hauling is permitted on any of the main streets in the fashionable quarter, except in certain hours.

In summer, all the "world" leaves town, not from any necessity, for it is never hot, but because it is the fashion. They go to their estates in the interior, or to the German and French watering places. Those who are obliged to remain amuse themselves in the evening by driving to Yelagin Island, or, as it is commonly called, "the Point." The various channels of the delta of the Neva form about a dozen islands of various sizes on the north of the main Neva, and four of these, of which Yelagin is one, lying next to each other, constitute a great park of over fifteen hundred acres. There are here and there some private country-seats in it, and a few public gardens with out-door theaters, but fully half is covered with forest-trees, from which the underbush has been cut away and replaced by lawns, and through which are numerous well-built roads.

In midsummer the sun does not set until about ten o'clock, and the twilight lasts for a full hour later; these four or five hours after dinner are occupied by everybody in a drive to "the Point," or a visit to one of the gardens. The sun shines more or less in summer, though rarely on two days in succession; the air is pleasant, barring a little dampness which renders a light overcoat necessary at sunset, and this great park, though but little cultivated by art, is a very agreeable place for recreation.

In winter the whole scene changes. Snow begins falling in October, and by the 1st of November the sleighing is firmly established; the Neva and all the canals are tightly frozen, the sun is not seen for weeks at a time, and the snow falls in fine flakes during a greater or less portion of nearly every day; it seldom comes in storms with high wind, but seems to be sifting down with occasional intermissions nearly all the time. The cold compels every one in the streets to wear such a mass of cloaks and wraps that it makes little difference whether it is snowing or not.

About four inches of snow is allowed to remain

on the streets for sleighing, and the rest is hauled away. There are no thaws, and but very few extremes of cold; the average temperature is about ten degrees above zero, Fahrenheit, all the time.

The "world" has now returned, the streets are full of handsome sleighs, the celebrated jewelry shops are lighted to their brighest, the operas and theaters are all in operation. People of the upper class get up in a twilight at ten in the morning, have a cup of coffee in their own apartments, and are occupied with their private affairs until noon, when they breakfast at home or in the *cafés*. After breakfast they attend to their public business, or go out to do shopping for a couple of hours. Returning home between two and three, it is already dark, and candles are lighted. Then begins the round of afternoon visits, which continues till dinner, which is usually at six. After dinner they go to the opera or theater, and when that is over, at eleven, they go to a ball or a heavy supper, which ends the day at about two in the morning.

Every one, except a few very rich princes, who have their own great palaces, lives in a "flat;" not such miniature affairs as we are familiar with in New York, but a series of fifteen to twenty large, well-proportioned apartments, with broad halls. In order to provide such a suite of apartments on one floor, the houses are built from two hundred to two hundred and fifty feet long, and looking along the street, instead of seeing a door to every three windows, you see only one to over twenty windows; in a word, a man's house is separated from that of his neighbor by horizontal rather than vertical walls.

The outside walls are very thick and heavily stuccoed with plaster; the windows are invariably double, and the space between them is packed at the bottom with sand to exclude the draught, and a little salt to absorb the moisture which would congeal on the glass. One pane of the eight in each window is set on hinges, and is occasionally opened to admit fresh air. It is a common mistake to suppose that the houses are kept very hot; this is not so; the air is sometimes a little stale, but it is maintained throughout the large halls, as well as the rooms, at a remarkably uniform temperature of about 70° Fahrenheit. This is accomplished by means of an enormous brick stove in the corner of each room, reaching from the floor to the ceiling, and covered over in handsome apartments by porcelain tiles; this is filled with wood every morning, and, after the fire is well lighted, the dampers are tightly closed, and the wood smolders for twenty-four hours. The outside of the stove is never hot enough to burn the hand, but its radiating surface is so large that the room is kept at a very agreeable temperature. In addition to the stove, people who can afford it have an open fire in every room, for purposes of ventilation and adornment only.

The street entrance is provided with three sets of doors, which are evidently necessary in order to maintain a temperature of 70° inside against one of zero or below outside; in the hall are always one or two porters ready to take the wraps, which are removed immediately on entering. A huge mass of furs hobbles through the doors on great *goloshes*, and, a moment later, leaves the hands of the porter a graceful young lady of slender figure, a dapper young officer in tight-fitting uniform, or possibly a plethoric old general; wrapped up in their furs, they are all equally shapeless and undistinguishable, and it is often an amusing exercise of curiosity to watch the disrobing, and see what form of human insect will emerge from the chrysalis.

The building of St. Petersburg was the most despotic act ever committed in this most autocratic of modern countries. Had not Peter been the strongest man of his cotemporaries, his people would have clapped him in the mad-house when he ordered them to build a city out in a morass, where even to-day no great structure can be erected without disturbing the foundations of its neighbors. The Isaac Cathedral rests on a forest of piles, and still the unequal settlement defaces the walls so constantly that there has never been a year when workmen were not busy repairing them. It is a Russian proverb that in St. Petersburg " hearts are always dry and the streets are always wet." St. Petersburg is so little a natural site for a great city that to-day, when it is a hundred and seventy years old, it is approached from any direction only by riding over a hundred miles of well-nigh uninhabited country. From the edge of the city you emerge at once into endless, uncultivated plains, across which you would travel for days in a carriage before reaching any thickly settled region. But for an imperial command, no city would ever have arisen on the site of the present capital of Russia.

We often read of certain events in history " which changed the whole course of empire ;" as a rule, the expression is exaggerated, for the events were usually only the more salient features of a long chain of development depending on the action of many minds. But the building of St. Petersburg is an exception ; it was the isolated act of one man's mind, and it has determined the nature of the whole course of modern Russian development, which would have been totally different had he decided differently.

It is well known that when Peter came back from his travels in Western Europe, he was strongly impressed with the commercial greatness of England

and Holland, and decided that the first step necessary to rouse Russia from her lethargy, and bring her into the family of civilized nations, was to provide an outlet to the sea, by which not only could she begin to build up a foreign commerce, but learn the ways of the rest of the world.

He had two courses open to him—to pitch his new capital near the Baltic or on the Black Sea. In favor of the former, he saw that he already possessed land on the arms of the Baltic, from which he could reach the ocean without hinderance from any one nation, though his route would be closed half the year by ice; it was also the shortest route to England and Holland. In favor of the latter, he had a mild climate, better harbors, and a highway open all the year; but he possessed only a small and insecure footing on the Black Sea, and the route from it to the ocean led through straits, both shores of which were in possession of a foreign power—Turkey—then one of the most powerful states in Europe. It was absolutely impossible for him to hope to conquer possession of the straits during his own short life-time. He therefore chose the northern route, and was forced to build his city in the most thoroughly uninviting and unpromising spot that ever a city was founded upon. In order to give it life, he removed his court and his seat of government to it. Though it has prospered and grown, probably to the full measure of his anticipations, yet it is doubtful if it could survive even now were the seat of government removed from it.

All this is utterly opposed to the laws of natural selection, which have ruled in the establishment and growth of cities as in other matters. The modern characteristics of Russians have been the result of this mere act of one man, undertaken, not in accordance with the spirit of his time, but directly in the face of it. The mind is absolutely lost in trying to contemplate what would have been the result had he pitched his capital on the Black Sea. The effect of a warm climate and an easy existence would probably have so modified the Russian character as to make it incapable of the great sacrifices which it has from time to time shown since Peter's day; the Eastern question would have been forced to a settlement one way or the other three generations ago; we might have seen the dreams of Catherine realized long before the day of the Panslavists by an amalgamation of the Slav and Greek races of Turkey with those of Russia, and the founding of a Christian empire with its seat on the Bosphorus; or we might have seen the northern Slavs degenerate like those of the south, and the whole fall a prey to the Turks on the south and the Germans on the north. There is nothing on which to form any sure estimate of what would have happened; we can only affirm that the national character would have been entirely different, and the course of Russian history would have been totally changed. It seems hard to realize that one man actually had it in his power to, and did, cast a die on which such far-reaching consequences depended.

I have already said that the military aspect predominates on the streets, and I might add that it permeates the whole life of the ruling classes. The career of every young man in the great families is begun in the Guards; he remains in the army, or subsequently passes into the diplomatic or civil branches of the government service, according to his taste and ability; it is incumbent on him to serve the government in some capacity, and he always begins by the military service. The subsequent changes sometimes appear to a foreigner as very amusing; the present Minister of Finance, for example, began life as a cornet of cavalry, was afterward in a diplomatic post, then passed into the navy where he attained the grade of admiral, was then a civil governor of a province, which he left to become Comptroller of the Empire, and is now Minister of Finance. He is still young, being but little over fifty, and people say of him laughingly, that it only remains for him to be bishop or metropolitan in the church in order to make his career complete.

Similarly, the Minister of Public Works is an admiral in the navy, and the late Minister of the Interior was a general of cavalry. The number of ambassadors who have been generals is well known, and more than half of the civil governors of provinces are chosen from the army. While there is now less of this interchanging between different branches of the service than there was in the last reign and the one before it, yet it is still true, as it has always been, that the army is the pathway to any career in the government service.

This being so, the whole tenor of official life is essentially military, and the Emperor, as the actual head of the army, devotes no small portion of his time to his duties as commander-in-chief; this sets the tone of the court, of society, and of the governing classes, and it would hardly be saying too much to affirm that the country is governed for the benefit of the army, rather than the army being maintained for the benefit of the country.

Along-side of the summer garden, two squares from the winter palace, and separated from the Neva only by the houses along the quay, is a vacant space, over twenty acres in extent, known as the *Champ de Mars*, and used exclusively as a parade ground. About forty thousand men can be assembled in it, and here the great reviews are held in the spring and autumn, and on the occasion of royal visits.

During the winter, the extreme cold makes outdoor reviews impossible, and the Emperor therefore holds a weekly inspection of one regiment at a time in the great riding school, a structure covering in itself over three acres of ground, and well heated by the usual immense brick stoves. This inspection, or *rasvod*, is held every Sunday after church, between twelve and one o'clock, and forms one of the principal events of the week. It is attended by the Emperor, all his brothers and sons, in their various capacities as commanding officers of different grades, by all the generals of the guard, and by the military attachés of the several embassies and legations. Every one is in full uniform, the men are dressed in their best, their arms are bright, the horses' shoes even are polished like mirrors; it is altogether a pretty sight. The Emperor, Minister of War, aid-de-camp on duty, and the foreign officers are mounted; all the others are on foot.

There are stationed constantly in permanent barracks in St. Petersburg eight infantry regiments of the guard, the two regiments of mounted bodyguard, two regiments of Cossacks, the Emperor's escort, and several batteries of artillery. In the neighboring villages along the Gulf of Finland are stationed eight more regiments of cavalry, as many batteries, and four regiments of the line. Altogether there are in and near the city about fifty thousand troops at all times. Each regiment takes its turn at one of these Sunday morning inspections. They are reviewed, inspected, and marched past by the Emperor; the cavalry regiments, and particularly the Cossacks, give specimens of their dexterity in riding, jumping, handling the saber and pistol, and then the Emperor walks or rides through the ranks chatting familiarly with the men.

In addition to these Sunday morning inspections, each regiment is reviewed at the riding school on the occasion of its annual *fête* day; one of these *fêtes* occurs every week, on an average, throughout the winter.

Of a similar nature are the honors paid to the distinguished dead of the army. When a celebrated general dies, the Emperor attends his funeral service; on the anniversary of the death, forty days, half-a-year, or, possibly, even a year afterward, the Emperor, Minister of War, chief of staff, and distinguished generals, all attend a mass in the chapel of the palace, for the repose of his soul. The same thing occurs on the anniversary of the late Emperor's birthday, of the death of the present Emperor's eldest son, and on other anniversaries of a similar character. Again, on St. Alexander's day, the Emperor, important personages, and the diplomatic corps, attend a long service at the church of St. Alexander Nevsky; on St. Isaac's day, a similar service at the Isaac Cathedral, and so on. These forms of religious ceremonial, which have a strong military flavor and are attended in full uniform with military exactness, form part of the daily life. They consume an amount of time which to us is almost incredible; the best part of the day, from 1 to 3 P.M., is given up to one or another of them on about four days of every week. The same habits permeate all classes; a man is repairing your house, making you a suit of clothes, or doing some other tradesman's or mechanic's work for you; it is promised on a certain day, and you are disappointed at its not being done in time; he has a ready answer for you, which, in his mind, is a perfect excuse—yesterday, or the day before, was a *praznik*, or holiday, perhaps the saint's day whose name he bears, and he could not work! One often wonders how any business is ever transacted with the delays due to these *prazniks* and ceremonies, but it is the custom of the country, and people govern themselves accordingly. Things seem to go on, after all, about as smoothly as in America, where "time is money,"—an expression, by the way, which always affords great amusement to Russians.

These ceremonies naturally culminate in celebrating the great events of life; viz., birth, marriage, and death. In December, 1878, I assisted at the christening of His Imperial Highness, the Grand

Duke Mikhail Alexandrovitch, youngest son of the heir to the throne. He was born during the night preceding a grand review, and at the review the next day a battery was halted in marching past, and informed by the Emperor that it had a new chief in the person of this Grand Duke, an announcement which was received with loud cheering. The little fellow was honorary colonel of a regiment of infantry, of another of cavalry, and of a battery of artillery, before he was a dozen hours old. Two weeks later he was christened in the chapel of the Winter Palace. A large crowd gathered in the street to see him go past on his way from his father's to his grandfather's palace. He rode in the arms of his godmother, in a gilded coach, drawn by six white horses, with postilions; behind him was a similar coach containing the Grand Chamberlain and his godfather. In front and behind the coaches rode a platoon of Cossacks. At the palace, besides the Emperor and other members of the imperial family, there were the diplomatic corps, "the chamberlains and ministers, the first and second charges of the court," various other personages, and finally, " all those having the right to appear at court." The detailed programme of the form of proceedings, issued by the grand master of ceremonies, covered five columns of the official newspaper. Every one was in full dress—the men in military or civil uniform, and the ladies in the Russian court dress. This costume is very peculiar and striking in effect; the front of the dress is of cloth of gold, the back and train of red or blue velvet, and on the head is worn a sort of diadem (*kokoshnik*) of the same color as the dress, and studded with precious stones.

In the chapel the male members of the imperial family stood next the chancel-rail on one side, and the female members on the other. Next to them came the members of the diplomatic corps and their wives, then the gentlemen of the body-guard and the principal dignitaries of the crown, and behind them, extending out into the adjoining grand hall, were the other persons present—about a thousand in all. The child was brought in on a handsome embroidered pillow, borne by Princess Kourakin, his godmother. On either side of her walked the godfathers, Prince Suwarof and Count Kotzebue. The service was chanted in the usual form, but by the almost unrivaled voices of the Emperor's choir; then the child was christened by immersion by the priest; he howled and struggled with fine spirit, and was then taken out, wrapped up in some rich cloths and handed to the Emperor, who walked three times round the altar with the child in his arms. The exact significance of this I did not learn, but it was a pretty family scene to see the little fellow still shouting and kicking, every one present laughing at it, and the Emperor smiling benignantly, after the manner of grandfathers on such occasions.

After this, the little Grand Duke was handed to his nurse, the various members of the imperial family kissed each other in congratulation, and then passed out, terminating the ceremony.

The anniversaries of great battles are celebrated by the troops attending divine service in the morning, and having a dinner and an extra allowance of grog in the afternoon. On the occasion of the first anniversary of the fall of Plevna, the Grand Duke Nicholas gave a dinner at his palace near the bridge named after his father. The Emperor and all the members of the imperial family then in town were present, as well as about two hundred officers who had been present at Plevna. This palace is remarkable for the beautiful broad marble stairway which rises in a straight line from the entrance to the third story, but there is nothing unusual in the large dining-room, nor in the table service. The dinner was a purely Russian one, made to suit the Russian palate, and certainly unacceptable to any other. As an instance of Russian taste, I give the *ménu*. First came the *zakuska*, or appetizers, at a side table: caviare, a dozen varieties of native and foreign whiskies, brandies and cordials, including one bottle marked "American Cocktails;" as many varieties of cheese, of little fishes like sardines, of *pâté de foie gras*, etc. After we were seated at table, the first dish was a soup of cabbage with a peculiar white sauce of sour cream which was mixed in it according to each person's taste. With this was served Château Yquem. Next came a filet of beef with mushrooms, served with red wine. *After* the filet came the fish, which was a work of art; it was a gigantic sturgeon, weighing over ninety pounds, and about five feet in length; this had been cut into small pieces and then carefully put together again, so that the lines of division were only visible when you came to help yourself; it was gayly decorated with flags, etc., and was brought in on a silver platter borne by six men. The sturgeon was followed by the *pièce de résistance* of the dinner, which was a sucking pig, stuffed with the *kahsha* or buckwheat gruel, to which I have frequently referred as the staple article of food of the peasants. With this was served your choice of champagne, or the Russian sour beer called *kvass*. Next came a Roman punch, and after this there was game, some ducks and grouse with cucumber salad, served with the red wine of the Crimea; then some sort of pudding, sweetmeats, coffee, and cigarettes.

The health of the Emperor was drunk, as usual, on the simple announcement, "*Za zdarova Gosurdara Imperatora, hourrah!*" (To the health of our lord the Emperor, hurrah!) the hurrah being taken up vociferously and long continued by all present, and every one standing. The health of the Cesarevitch and of the Grand Duke Nicholas were also drunk, but of no one else; and there was no speech-making, except by the Emperor, who said a few words as he proposed each of the latter toasts. At a previous dinner of the same kind, at which the Emperor was not present (being in the Crimea), there was a good deal of speech-making accompanying the toasts.

The dinner, which began at six, was over at eight o'clock, and nearly every one present then went to the opera or to the circus; the latter is admirably conducted in a large iron tent, and is very popular with the younger cavalry officers. After the circus I accepted an invitation to one of the regimental clubs.

The two regiments of the Emperor's body-guard, one of which is called the *Chevalier Garde* and the other the *Garde à cheval*, are the most aristocratic organizations of any kind in Russia. Appointments of cornets in them are made only with the consent of the regiment and with the personal knowledge and approval of the Emperor in each case. The officers are all "gentlemen of the guard," and are present at all court ceremonies. Each of these regiments is quartered in a very desirable part of the town, their barracks, stables, riding hall, etc., occupying an entire square about one thousand feet long and four hundred feet wide. Each numbers about forty officers and six hundred men, the men being all selected, and over six feet in height. They are cuirassier regiments, and their horses are chosen, with no little difficulty, to combine grace with the strength necessary to carry about three hundred pounds. One regiment has all black, the other all bay horses. Every officer has from three to six private saddle-horses—English thoroughbreds, Russian Arabs, Cossack cross-breds, and other varieties of blooded animals, ranging in value from one to three thousand dollars apiece. The cost to the crown of one of these regiments is enormous—about equal to that of a division of ten thousand men of the infantry of the line—yet they have been called into active service only twice in this century; viz., in the wars against Napoleon and in the Polish Insurrection of 1863. Every one of the officers, however, who could obtain leave saw service in the last war as an aid-de-camp, or a volunteer in some other regiment.

Their barracks contain handsome suites of apartments for about half the officers, that number being supposed to be married; the junior unmarried officers have also two or three rooms apiece, though not so large or handsome as the others. Each regiment has also a large and well-appointed club-house, adjoining the barracks, maintained by the officers. This contains the usual reading-rooms, a good library, billiard-rooms, card-rooms, and restaurant. A supper is spread each night at midnight, in readiness for the officers as they come home from the theater.

The regimental clubs are so numerous and well appointed that there are but two other clubs in town, the club of the nobility and the yacht club, neither of which is equal to the clubs of the crack regiments.

The nobility of Russia is hospitable and open-handed to the last degree, but it is equally extravagant. A young man, as they say themselves, is considered enormously rich if he merely lives within his income, and keeps out of debt. While there is no more card-playing at the clubs than is common in other capitals, yet the play is for enormous stakes, frequently out of all comparison to the resources of the players. They are usually in the habit of leaving the entire management of their estates to their *intendants*, or stewards, and visiting them only for short periods once a year. The stewards are none too honest, as their masters well know, but the latter are averse to bothering themselves with the details of management, and let the steward steal a fair percentage so long as he remits regular installments of the income. This carelessness, combined with extravagant living, has its natural result in the financial crash of several families every year. The young men then sell out their household valuables and go off to the Caucasus and Central Asia, to win distinction in active service, and promotion to a grade whose pay is enough for their support. There is in a certain portion of St. Petersburg an immense bazar of the pure oriental type, known as the *Shtukin Dvor*, where, as in the other bazars, you can buy everything that is sold in commerce, but where also there are over a dozen large and well-known shops devoted exclusively to the purchase and sale of the *débris* of the establishments of the bankrupt nobility. Here you will find the rarest and most valuable pieces of furniture, of china, of jewelry, and of laces. It is as interesting to go through one of these shops as to spend an afternoon in a well stocked museum of art—which, in fact, they are Those Russians whose crash has not yet come, or whose fortune is so large as to preclude the possibility of it, are very fond of good *bric-à-brac*, and have excellent taste in it. They periodically visit these shops to pick up some rare *objet de luxe ou de vertu;* they ask the shopkeeper if he has anything new, and he answers that he has just received the remains of the entire establishment of Count this or Prince that. "Ah! yes, poor Count so-and-so, *le bon garçon!* Let me see his things." And then they proceed to search for some bronze or vase which they have long admired, and which they are so glad to secure for their own possession.

Whenever a number of Russian officers are seen in full dress, one is dazzled by the number of stars, decorations, and medals which cover their breasts. Some of these are of no value whatever, and others are records of the most signal feats in arms or state service, and confer great privileges. There are in Russia seven orders of knighthood for men and one for women. Three of these have but one class or degree, and are given only to persons of a certain grade in the "Tchin" or hierarchy, and the other four have various classes for various grades. The order of St. Andrew, founded by Peter the Great at the close of the seventeenth century, is conferred upon all princes of the imperial family at their birth, but is otherwise bestowed on only the highest dignitaries, such as chancellors, ambassadors, and full generals. Its insignia consist of a long collar of Russian double-headed eagles stamped in gold, which is worn around the shoulders. Next to this comes the order of St. Alexander Nevsky, also founded by Peter, whose insignia are a broad blue cordon, worn over the shoulder, and a star on the breast. Its bestowal is confined to the first three grades in the *Tchin*. The remaining order of this kind is the

White Eagle, which was founded by a Polish king in the fourteenth century. It is not much esteemed, and is usually conferred on some general who has done his duty in a battle but has not achieved success. Its insignia consist of a decoration worn at the neck.

The four remaining orders are the St. George and St. Vladimir, founded by Catherine, and both highly esteemed; the St. Anne, founded by Charles Frederick of Schleswig-Holstein, and the St. Stanislaus, founded by King Stanislaus of Poland.

The St. George is a purely military order, and is the most highly prized of all the Russian decorations. Any Russian will risk his life to obtain its little cross of white enamel and the ribbon of black and yellow, and no one ever does get it without his life having been in the greatest danger. It has four classes, each of which is bestowed only for certain services specified in the statute with great minuteness. The name of every knight of the order and the date of his knighthood are inscribed in gold on white marble columns in the hall of St. George at the Kremlin palace in Moscow. The first class is bestowed only upon commanding generals who, while in command of an army, have achieved some great feat, such as the capture or signal defeat of a hostile army. There have been but twenty-two knights of the first class since the order was founded, and their names all occupy a prominent place on the page of history. Among them are Potemkin, Suwarof, Kutusoff, Barclay de Tolly, Bernadotte, Blucher, Wellington, Paskevitch, Diebitch, and the Emperor William of Germany. It was conferred during the last war only on the two commanders-in-chief in Europe and Asia respectively—one on the fall of Plevna and the other on the fall of Kars.

The second class is conferred on chiefs of staff or commanders of large fractions of an army which gain an important battle. Von Moltke, the Crown Prince of Germany, and Prince Frederick Charles are knights of this class; and in the last war but eight were created, among them, Loris-Melikoff, Todleben, and Radetsky.

The third class is conferred upon generals having command of a corps or an independent detachment, who either capture a fortress, a considerable detachment of the enemy, or contribute in a vital degree to a victory. Thirty-seven of these were conferred in the last war; Gourko, for instance, receiving it for the first passage of the Balkans, Krudener for the capture of Nikopolis, etc.

The fourth class is conferred upon a commanding officer or chief of staff for valuable service in battle, or upon an officer of any grade for extraordinary heroism; thus it was bestowed on the two lieutenants who blew up the Turkish monitor *Se-ife* on the Danube by means of torpedoes from an open boat. Two hundred and eighty-eight in all of this class were conferred in the last war.

Every cross of this order is received, therefore, only as a reward for some act of conspicuous gallantry or distinguished service in battle. It is not bestowed by the Emperor directly, but only in accordance with the unanimous recommendation of a chapter of the order, stating the service in detail and the clause in the statute which authorizes it. It confers all the rights of hereditary nobility upon every knight, in addition to a specific pension and certain other privileges, such as that of having his children educated at the expense of the state in any of the military schools.

The order of St. Vladimir, which ranks next to that of St. George, is conferred for both civil and military services. Its cross is of brown enamel, and has crossed sabers on it when given for service in battle; the ribbon is black and red. It has four classes, the insignia of the first being the cordon and star; of the second and third, crosses of different size worn at the neck; and of the fourth, a smaller cross worn on the breast. The classes, however, are distinguished, not by the nature of the service, but by the grade of the person on whom conferred; the first and second for generals, the third for field officers, and the fourth for company officers. The order is conferred directly by the Emperor on the recommendation or "presentation" of the recipient's services by his commanding officers.

The orders of St. Anne and St. Stanislaus are the lowest of all. They are of three classes, according to the rank of the recipient when received, and are conferred for gallantry, but also as favors at autumn manœuvers, for several years' good service, etc. Not much consideration is attached to them.

In addition to these orders and their classes, every campaign against the enemy, whether a great war like that in Turkey, or a small expedition in Central Asia, has its own medal, which is worn alike by every officer and soldier who took honorable part in it. In full dress an officer wears all his decorations, in undress only the one which is highest; but the possessor of the St. George wears it on his coat and the ribbon on his overcoat on every and all occasions.

As an officer of fifteen or twenty years' experience is sure to have received a few of the minor crosses for faithful service, as he invariably receives one or two foreign decorations when sent abroad on a military mission, and as he has a medal for every campaign, and probably one or two decorations received during it in addition, it is evident that when he has seen active and varied service, and attained the grade of colonel or general, he has a good many decorations; and if in addition he has specially distinguished himself by gallantry, he has hardly room on his coat for all of them. Some officers of distinction who have passed through four or five campaigns, and have served forty years or more, have as many as twenty or thirty various crosses and medals.

The higher classes of the order of St. George correspond to the thanks of Congress or the presentation of a sword by that body; the other orders correspond to brevets. They have precisely the same value as brevets, some of them being the records of great deeds, and others the record of nothing but favor and influence, like so many of the two thousand or more brevets dating from the bloody 13th of March, 1865. With us the reward is a title higher than that of the actual rank; with the Russians it is a bit of ribbon and jewelry on the breast.

The "Tchin" or hierarchy, to which I have just referred, is one of the most peculiar institutions of Russia. All the servants of the government, including those of the church, have a relative rank by which their social, and, in a certain sense also, their political status, is absolutely fixed. There are fourteen grades in this "Tchin." The first or most exalted grade comprises only the Chancellor of the Empire, a field-marshal in the army, the Lord

High Admiral of the navy, and a metropolitan in the church. The second grade comprises an actual privy councillor in the civil service, a full general in the army, a full admiral in the navy, a grand chamberlain at the court, and an archbishop in the church. The next grade comprises a privy councillor, a lieutenant-general, a vice-admiral, a chamberlain, a bishop. Next come actual state councillors, major-generals, rear admirals, and archimandrites, and so on through the various classes. The ninth grade, for instance, is that of titular councillor, captain in the army, lieutenant in the navy, grand furrier at court, surveyor in the Public Works Department, master of arts of a university, and deacon in the church.

There are four distinct titles for the various grades, by which they are always addressed by their inferiors. The highest two are called "High Excellency;" the next two, "Excellency;" the next four, "High Nobility;" and the remaining five, "Nobility." These titles do not apply to princes and counts. A prince of the Empire is always addressed as "Most Serene Highness," and a count as "Illustriousness," no matter what his position.

All the servants of the crown above a certain grade belong ex-officio to the nobility, and for those of the sixth class (colonel) and above in the army, and fourth class and above in the civil service, the nobility is hereditary. By this it is not meant that they are noblemen, such as barons, marquises, and dukes, but simply that they belong to the *noblesse*, or noble class. The "*Zemstvo*," *i. e.*, the form of local self-government instituted by the present Emperor in 1864, whose duties are similar to those of our county commissioners, is composed of deputies elected in certain proportions by the landed proprietors, the municipal corporations, and the village communes or "*Mirs.*" The landed proprietors are the *noblesse*, and they have certain privileges besides that of electing deputies in more than their numerical proportion. To belong to the nobility, is simply to be one of this class of landed proprietors, and to have all its rights and privileges. The class is very large, being estimated, I think, to number about nine hundred thousand persons, or more than one per cent. of the whole population. The word nobility, in its ordinary acceptation as we derive it from the English customs, is evidently misleading; there are vast numbers of the nobility who have neither wealth nor social position, and who are never admitted to court; but the social customs of Russia being so different from those of other countries, there is no English word which correctly expresses the Russian meaning of the term *noblesse* (*dvorianstvo*).

The military class in St. Petersburg is the principal element in society; and society, as in all great capitals, is largely occupied with a gay life of pleasure. Those who criticise the Russians, and most of all the Russian critics themselves (particularly those of German origin), are never tired of expatiating upon the Russian *lieni* or idleness— "the genuine Slav love of indolence and pleasure."

This criticism seems to me to be unfounded. While the Russians have not much of that plodding character peculiar to the Germans, and are fond of pleasure when not urged to work, yet whenever there has been any necessity for long-continued and patient labor, the Tsar, the noble, and the peasant have proved themselves equally unremitting and faithful to their respective tasks.

But there is in the Russian character a certain volatile element which partially justifies Bismarck's criticism—as reported by Dr. Busch—that the Russians, like the French, are essentially feminine in character. They are very fond of criticism and of abstract discussions, and their criticism is frequently of the most illogical, not to say hysterical, order. It is a mistake to suppose that there is no public opinion in Russia; there is at all times a very strong public opinion, though it is very variable; it finds its expression in the press until checked by the warnings of the censorship bureau, when it becomes all the more violent in private conversation from its attempted repression in public. This public opinion is also far from being without influence; the late war, for instance, was almost wholly due to it.

The course of public opinion in the various stages of this war illustrates this femininity of character very forcibly. The declaration of war against the Turks was received with the liveliest pleasure by the whole Russian nation; whether or not the Emperor was personally opposed to the war, and only put himself at the head of the Moscow "national" movement because he could not stay it—as certain English papers have always represented—there are no data for stating; the Emperor's personal opinions are not so publicly stated as some correspondents would have us believe. But there is no question whatever that his celebrated Moscow speech in the spring of 1877, in which he declared his intention to act independently in case he could not obtain justice for the Christians in Turkey by means of the European concert, was hailed by Russians of every shade of opinion as the embodiment of their own feelings, and that the declaration of war was extremely popular with all classes. It is equally true that the public at large had very little idea of what war meant, or of the caliber and resources of their adversary, even unaided. They talked glibly of a military promenade to Constantinople, of "the mission of Holy Russia," and of "the regeneration of all Slavonic races;" they dictated the appointment of Prince Tcherkasski, one of the chiefs of the "national" party, as Civil High Commissioner, and provided him with a complete set of civil officials to govern the provinces of Bulgaria as they should be successively liberated, at the same time that they insisted that two hundred thousand men were enough to complete the war succesfully in a few months. Boundless confidence and enthusiasm were the order of the day.

After the war had begun there was some impatience at the delay in crossing the Danube, but this was soon forgotten in the brilliant success of the passage of the river, and in Gourko's daring advance over the Balkans. Then came the first check at Plevna, followed ten days later by a bloody repulse at the same place. Gourko was forced to retreat behind the Balkans, the Bulgarian refugees were abandoned to the fury of the Turks, one hundred and twenty thousand additional men were ordered to be mobilized and sent at once to the front, and the first ban of the militia was called out for service at the depots. The Turks, it seemed, were an enemy not to be despised.

The mercury of public opinion now fell in a day from the boiling point to far below zero. The papers advanced charges against the army far exceeding in virulence anything that had ever appeared in the English prints. The generals were incompetent, the whole commissariat system was a mass of stupidity and corruption, the chief of staff and his principal assistant were traitorous Poles engaged in a conspiracy to destroy the army; the Cesarevitch had openly shown his contempt for his uncle, the Commander-in-Chief, who was absolutely devoid of military capacity or even physical courage; the Emperor was represented as having lost all dignity by the compromised position he occupied in the army; Gortchakoff and Jomini were elaborating a new system of constitutional government, and national bankruptcy was the inevitable result of the war. While the people in Moscow proclaimed that the war must go on at all hazards—" The dynasty began the war, but the nation alone can and will terminate it "—they at the same time were unsparing in their criticisms of the government for having called out re-enforcements at once, instead of waiting till four weeks later, when "the crops would all be in!" Every college student was a strategist, who could tell you exactly just what principle of war had been violated, and thus brought disaster on the Russian arms; and the national party actually proposed that the whole system of supply for the army should be turned over to a committee of provincial organizations in Southern

Russia. In short, it was the genuine Gallic cry, "*Nous sommes trahis*," all over again.

This spirit of pessimism (from which even Anglo-Saxons are not altogether exempt, as was shown in the Crimean war) became so widespread and deep-seated by the long delay at Plevna, that the brilliant successes of the winter hardly sufficed to dissipate it. There was more or less a feverish exultation at the final capture of Plevna and the destruction of the remaining Turkish armies within a few weeks afterward, but every one's mind was now occupied with expectancy concerning the terms of peace. On this question they took very high ground indeed, and those who a few weeks before had predicted bankruptcy if the war should continue against Turkey alone, now demanded such a treaty as would unquestionably have brought them to war with the whole of Western Europe. They cared nothing for the wishes of Europe, but demanded that the "inmost aspirations of the Slavonic people" should be satisfied.

The treaty of San Stefano was finally concluded, mainly on the basis of the terms which had been proposed to Turkey by Europe collectively at the Constantinople conference of 1876. From one end of the land to the other there went up a howl of anger that Russia should have proposed any such moderate treaty, though, except that they desired an occupation of Constantinople, their criticism never indicated distinctly what they would have proposed. A few weeks later it was seen that Europe would not accept even this treaty, which the advanced Russians considered too moderate. They were at first bewildered and stunned by this idea, which seemed never to have occurred to them; but when, in the beginning of June, Russia decided to go into the Berlin Congress, they were fairly beside themselves with rage. Ivan Aksakoff, the President of the Slav Committee and one of the principal mouth-pieces of the national party, held forth in such language as the following: "Thou victorious Power, and yet so befooled! In the face of such folly in the diplomatic heads of Russia, in the face of such grandiose attempts to temporize, the power of language ceases, and thoughts can find no utterance. Even the most malevolent enemy of Russia and her dynasty could not have invented anything more destructive to her internal peace and tranquillity. There you see the true nihilists—the men for whom there exists neither a Russia nor Russian tradition, no Russian nationality, no orthodox church. . . . No—whatever may take place at the Congress, however much the honor of Russia may be degraded, there yet lives our crowned protector, and he will be our avenger. . . . Our hopes in our Tsar cannot be shipwrecked. His word has gone forth that the holy work shall be carried to the end, and his word cannot be broken."

I have referred mainly to the feelings and opinions of the national or Slavonic party; but the opinions of all classes of society were of the same nature, and only slightly moderated in tone. The current talk in St. Petersburg society during the six months succeeding the Berlin treaty was of the same character as that of Aksakoff. The Tsar and a few responsible statesmen at the head of affairs kept their heads cool, and accepted so much of what was forced upon them by Europe as was inevitable; but society in general completely lost its head, and in the general confusion of ideas and senseless criticism of the whole course of the war, the aggressive revolutionary party or nihilists, who aim at the destruction of all the present forms of social order, found their opportunity, and have taken advantage of it steadily for the last two years.

Nothing could explain more clearly than these few sentences of Aksakoff, the irresponsible and unpractical nature of Russian criticism and public opinion, the proneness for discussion of abstract rather than concrete ideas, and the feverish alternations of joy and despondency into which they are plunged by the course of events. Perhaps it can hardly be otherwise so long as the nation is in its tutelage, and forced to be always critics, and never actors responsible for putting their ideas into practical effect; but it is probable that it is also largely due to inherent traits of national character.

Much has been written concerning the differences of opinion between the Emperor and his heir on fundamental questions of internal as well as foreign policy. All attempts to trace these rumors to any tangible foundation only result in showing that it is one of those cases where the wish is father to the thought. The Cesarevitch is intensely popular with all classes, the nationals of Moscow no less than the cosmopolitan nobility of St. Petersburg; he has given some evidences of hostility to the "foreign" provinces of the Baltic and the Vistula; he has been less effusive than his father in his affection for his kinsmen in the German dynasty; he is intensely Russian in feeling; he has shown a decided will and strong character in all the public duties that have been committed to him; has been, up to the present, strictly pure in his domestic life (which is not the rule in his family), and by his founding the volunteer fleet, and other similar acts, has given rise to the idea that he sympathizes largely with the aspirations of the national party. In a word, while his father's uprightness of character, and the really great deeds which are associated with his name, will always insure him the love and veneration of his subjects, yet there is a vague, ill-defined feeling that he has in a measure out-lived his time, while his son is considered the embodiment of the Russian spirit of to-day. Every one believes, though no one can give the exact grounds of his belief, that the Cesarevitch will signalize his accession to the throne by a reform hardly less great than the abolition of serfdom, viz.: by granting some sort of constitution or charter of rights, of which the principal feature will be a national elective assembly. The longing for this is shared by great masses of people who have nothing whatever in common with nihilism, and nothing but abhorrence of its methods and principles. They care but little as to the share which this assembly shall have in practical legislation. Always basing their ideas on the same thought as that of the private soldier, "If the Tsar only knew, all would be well," they are anxious for the formation of a responsible chamber, through which the Emperor may know what his subjects' feelings are, and what are the doings of his government. At present, although the Tsar moves and talks freely and constantly among all the grades of his army, yet no other class of his people can have access to him except through his regularly constituted ministers. Every bit of information which he receives must be filtered through these, and it only too frequently happens that the unsavory portions never pass the filters. Could the Emperor know with certainty of the abuses which are perpetrated in his name by the subordinate officials in the "Third Section" or political police, in the press censorship, in the collection of taxes, in the disbursement of public moneys, they feel sure that these abuses would quickly cease. But how can he know of these things, they argue, when he is surrounded at all hours by an impenetrable veil of courtiers and ministers, interested in maintaining the present order of things, and tempted only too often beyond the limit of human resistance, knowing that their acts are secure from publicity? The Emperor Nicholas spent his life in attempting to stamp out the corruption of his public servants, but he failed utterly; and when his system of severity crashed to pieces during the Crimean war, he died of a broken heart. People reason that no one man can do any better than he did, unless assisted by a public opinion which shall be based upon responsible utterances and proofs of incontrovertible fact made in a public assembly.

No man can tell what will be the result of the crisis through which Russia is now passing; but that the crisis is a profound one in her history, it would be idle to deny. Few men, indeed, are able to form a clear idea of the depth or the shallowness of the seething ebullition of feeling which is the outcome of the liberal reforms and vast economic changes of the present reign, of the rise and growth of national and Slavonic aspirations, and of the events of the late war.

In the last ten years we have had three great books—those of Dixon and Wallace, and the long series of articles by Leroy-Beaulieu in the *Revue des deux Mondes*—which have revealed Russia to the western world as she has never before been revealed. All three have dealt mainly with the results of the recent changes in the internal government of the country. Within the present year they have been aptly supplemented by the work of one who is either a Russian of the Baltic Provinces, or else some one who faithfully represents the feelings of those provinces. In "Russia Before and After the War" we have a vivid portrayal of the current of Russian thought in the last few years, which is no less clear than the unconscious exhibition which it makes of that femininity of character which Bismarck speaks of. It abounds in sweeping and confused criticism of precisely the same kind that you will hear from any Russian who admits you to his confidence sufficiently to talk of the affairs of his own country. Wallace and Leroy-Beaulieu gave wonderfully plain accounts of the condition of Russia as it appears to a foreigner. The anonymous Germano-Russian reveals the confused and struggling current of thought which is running through Russian minds at this moment. What will be the outcome of it, it would be idle to attempt to predict. Whether another French revolution is impending; whether the present form of government will weather the storm; whether concessions can be made without the appearance of yielding to fear; whether these concessions will achieve the ends for which they are made, or whether they will only add fuel to the present flame of vague discontent; how much real sympathy, in fact, exists for this desire of change—all these are questions upon which it is almost impossible for any one to give conclusive answers. We can only see that, in the short period of twenty years, the most vast and fundamental changes have been made in the social economy of a great state; that these changes have more or less unsettled people's elementary beliefs, and have brought about a widespread commotion in the world of ideas; and that the more visionary and desperate class of the community have supplemented their ideas with deeds of foul and loathsome crime. Whether these people will succeed in imparting their own views to the nation at large, and bring about a vast uprising to be followed by anarchy and misrule, out of which eventually a stable but different form of government will arise, or whether the better and conservative sense of the community will assert itself to crush out lawlessness, and gradually accustom itself, to the new order of things, the future alone can determine. It is a great and in many ways a unique phase of national development, the progress of which we may be sure the world will watch with intense interest.

CHAPTER X.

THE EASTERN QUESTION.

IT may seem strange that, in a book intended to tell something of the habits and characteristics of the officers and men of the Russian army, I should have anything to say on a political question, concerning which volumes, and pages, and columns have already been written, particularly in the last few years. Yet it must be remembered that the Russian army exists, in a large measure, by reason of the Eastern question; that many thousands of Russian soldiers have died fighting in defense of their view of it, and that many more will probably meet the same fate before the question is decided. But for the Eastern question, the Russian army would only be a small fraction numerically of what it is now; the lives of its officers and men would be passed otherwise; their character, and feelings, and thoughts would be different from what they actually are.

The Eastern question overshadows and penetrates everything connected with the Russian army. During the year and a half that I was with it in the field, or at St. Petersburg, I breathed the atmosphere of this question at all hours; it filled a large portion of every newspaper that I received, whether from St. Petersburg, Paris, or London; it entered into every conversation of any length which I held with Russian officers; it was the all-absorbing topic in the diplomatic society of Constantinople and St. Petersburg. While one of its most important crises —that between the treaties of San Stefano and Berlin—was being developed, the whole army waited, expectant and anxious, but otherwise unoccupied, and watched its progress from day to day; for on the result depended the movements of the army and the lives of many of its officers and men. So far, then, from being foreign to the subject of these sketches, the Eastern question forms a large part of the thoughts and daily life of Russian military men, fully as much so as their marches and battles, and for this reason I have thought it not inappropriate to refer to it. While I cannot hope to say much, if anything, that is new on a subject that has been so thoroughly discussed, yet I have endeavored to bring together within a single chapter the salient features of this unique phase of history. I have also attempted to give prominence to the Russian views of the question—which, in the main, I believe to be the correct ones—because Americans are in the habit of hearing only the other side. Our language being the same as that of England, and the opinions of the Continent being transmitted to us principally through the English press, we receive constantly the most prejudiced, unfair, and at times false statements about Eastern affairs. It is true that the parties in England are sharply divided on this question, and we hear from both; but the arguments of the Liberal party are directed less to prove that Russia is following the cause of right, in waging war on the Ottoman government, than to show that the blustering course of the Conservatives has played into the hands of Russia. When in power, the Liberals have seldom acted fairly and openly with Russia, and it was a Liberal administration which framed tne treaty of Paris—the most false step in the whole history of Eastern affairs.

For the facts given in the earlier period of the following sketch I have drawn largely on Sir Edward Creary's "History of the Ottoman Turks," which, in turn, is founded on Von Hammer, who is the standard authority on the subject. For the later period I have relied on the voluminous Parliamentary papers referring to Turkey.

In 1356 the Ottoman Turks entered Europe by crossing the Dardanelles and seizing Gallipoli. The Eastern question then arose, and it has been a burning question for the greater part of Europe from that day to this. It arises from the irreconcilability of opposing religions, and is complicated in its later periods by the jealousies of the different nationalities professing that religion which has proved to be the stronger. But intrinsically it is a question of religion: the question whether the Turks —professing the religion which they do, carrying its precepts into every transaction of daily life, and possessing the character which springs from it— whether these Turks shall be suffered to remain in Europe, and to govern other races of a different creed in accordance with the prejudice founded on the Koran, and having almost the force of common law, that unbelievers are mere dogs, possessed of no rights, entitled to no justice, to oppress whom is a virtue, and to kill whom is a religious privilege.*

---

* There is not a chapter of the Koran which does not breathe forth hatred against all those who do not believe in it, and for the sole ground of this lack of belief. In one place it is commanded, "O true believers, wage war against such of the infidels as are near you;" in another it is said, "Hell shall surely encompass the unbelievers;" and again, "Mohammed is the apostle of God; and those who are with him are fierce against the unbelievers, but compassionate towards one another;" and finally, "The unbeliever is contemptible in the sight of the Lord." Quotations of a similar character might be taken from nearly every page, and in fact, next to the cardinal principles of the unity of God and the divine inspiration of Mohammed, the doctrine which the Koran most strenuously teaches, is the right and duty of waging unending war upon all those who do not acknowledge its divine origin and validity.

There is no cause which so deeply stirs men's souls, or prompts them to wage war so fiercely, as a dispute concerning the attributes of God, or concerning the merits of those who claim to be his prophets; and the difference between the Christian and Mohammedan creeds is so radical and fundamental, the statute and common laws based on them respectively are so utterly antagonistic in principle, and the feelings with which they are supported by their respective partisans are so intense, that there can never be lasting peace between contiguous nations, one professing one creed and the other professing the other; even were each nation composed only of members of its own faith. But if, in addition to this, one of the nations, and the one whose creed and practice are the most intolerant of opposition, the most regardless of ordinary justice, and the most reckless of human life, has in its power several millions of people belonging to the other faith, then we may be sure that the conflict will never end so long as both of them continue to exist. It will terminate only with the death of the weaker.

At the time the Turks entered Europe, the Eastern Empire of Rome had proceeded so far in its course of disintegration that nothing remained of it but Constantinople, Trebizond, and Salonica, and a small amount of territory around each, as well as the lower portion of the Peloponnesus. The kingdoms of Bulgaria and Servia comprised the lands south of the Danube; to the north of them was the extensive kingdom of Hungary, and to the east of this was Moldavia. The islands of the Ægean and the eastern Mediterranean were colonies of Venice or other Frank powers.

Every one of these countries was overrun and reduced to complete subjugation by the Turks in the course of the next two centuries. In 1361 they captured Adrianople, and made it, temporarily, their European capital. In 1363 they captured Philippopolis, in 1371 Tirnova, and in 1382 Sophia. In 1389 they destroyed in the battle of Kossova the last confederated army of Bulgarians, Servians, Wallachians, and Bosnians, and completed their conquests as far as the borders of Hungary. It was only in the next century, however, and nearly a hundred years after their entry into Europe, that, after repeated failures, they finally succeeded, on May 29th, 1453, in capturing Constantinople; and thus extinguished forever the Eastern Empire, and made themselves one of the most powerful nations of Europe.

For nearly seventy years after the taking of Constantinople the Turks were busy in consolidating their power in Europe, and in extending their dominion through Syria to Egypt. Then, with the accession of Suleiman the Magnificent in 1520, the tide of conquest turned northward again. In the next year Belgrade was taken, and, in a series of wars which followed, the kingdom of Hungary was destroyed, and passed under the direct or tributary power of the Turks. At the close of Suleiman's reign in 1566, the Turkish dominions included all the lands as far north as Buda-Pesth, and their tributary states comprised Transylvania, Wallachia, Moldavia, the Crimea, and the shores of the Sea of Azov; thus completing the circuit of the Black Sea, save a small portion inhabited by the mountain tribes of the Caucasus. Their territorial possessions in Europe were then far greater than those of any other nation, save only Russia, which was at that time more Asiatic than European. The Sultan ruled nearly fifty millions of people; he could put a well-equipped army of three hundred thousand men in the field; and he received a tribute of thirty thousand ducats a year from the proud house of Hapsburg. His fleet under Barbarossa was mistress of the Mediterranean, and was able to cope with and defeat the combined navies of Venice, the Pope, and the German Emperor.

Turkey was the first of the "Great Powers" of that day, equally feared and hated by all its rivals.

The wave of conquest had now reached its farthest limit; it remained nearly stationary for about a hundred years, and then the tide turned, and has ever since been slowly but surely receding whence it came, until now but little more remains to the Turks in Europe than did to the Eastern Empire at the time of their arrival.

This retrocession did not begin suddenly, however. The first decisive check was received by the Turks early in Suleiman's reign (1529), when an army of over two hundred thousand men was defeated under the walls of Vienna; and the second occurred later in the same reign, when the naval expedition against Malta resulted in total failure. In 1571 a fleet of two hundred and sixty ships and thirty thousand men was destroyed at Lepanto by the combined navies of Venice, Spain and the Pope; and about the same time the first encounter took place between the Russian and Turkish arms, arising from an expedition sent by the Turks to cut a channel from the Don to the Volga, and thus give the Turkish fleets an entrance to the Caspian.

But although all these expeditions resulted in defeat, the Turks were then in the full vigor of their youthful vitality, and they quickly recovered from them, without loss of prestige or territory. This vitality nevertheless soon came to be sapped in the succession of weak and sensual sultans who followed the great Suleiman, and in the general corruption of the ruling class, the beginning of which dates from this period—the close of the sixteenth and beginning of the seventeenth century. Constant revolts in Hungary also tended to weaken the strength of the Porte, and several years later the decisive defeat by John Sobieski, in 1683, of another great Turkish army at Vienna was hailed throughout Christendom as the beginning of the downfall of the Ottoman power.

It was not, however, until the end of the seventeenth century that the Turks ever formally ratified any cession of territory. The treaty of Carlowitz, which was signed January 26, 1699, at the close of a disastrous campaign against the Austrians under Prince Eugene, and the Russians under Peter the Great, is the great turning-point in Turkish history. Austria, Russia, Poland and Venice, took part in a congress, at which England and Holland appeared also as mediators, and all four nations signed treaties with Turkey, by which Transylvania, Hungary, and a part of Servia were ceded to Austria, Podolia to Poland, the shores of the Sea of Azov and the Crimea to Russia, the Morea and part of Dalmatia to Venice.

The ancient Turkish saying that "Every place where the hoof of the Sultan's horse has once trod becomes at once, and forever, part of the Sultan's dominions," was belied by the logic of events, and was henceforth but a vain and empty boast.

The wars of Austria and Russia against Turkey

continued at short intervals, and with varying success, throughout the whole of the eighteenth century. Venice disappeared from the scene at the peace of Passarowitz, in 1718, in which, although an ally of Austria, she was obliged to give back the Morea to Turkey.

Austria at first gained another large piece of Servia, but after Eugene's death was unable to retain it; while Peter was obliged in 1711 to sue for peace and to give back Azov and the Crimea, although they were recovered again by Münnich for the Empress Anne in 1739.

The Empress Catherine, the most ambitious of all the rulers of Russia, prosecuted the wars against the Turks to the full extent of her power during her entire reign. She permanently won back the Crimea and the Black Sea coast; and she also made a treaty, known as that of Kainardji, in 1774, which contained the following clause, which subsequently gave rise to much contention as to its true meaning, viz.: "The sublime Porte promises to protect constantly the Christian religion and its churches," and it also allows the Russian ambassador to make representations in behalf of the Greek church in Constantinople and its ministers.

A dozen years later Catherine embarked in another war against the Turks, this time in alliance with Austria; but the latter power withdrew, and

Russia prosecuted the war alone and with great success, thanks to Suwarof. By the treaty of Yassy, made in 1791, Russia advanced her frontiers to the Dniester, and compelled the Turks to acknowledge her authority over the tribes on the northern side of the Caucasus. Catherine was again preparing for another struggle, which she hoped might be final, when death put an end to all her plans in 1796.

An entirely new aspect was now given to affairs in the East by the rise of Napoleon in France, and for the next twenty years the Eastern question was diverted from its usual course and made subservient to the policies brought about by Napoleon's plans of conquest. His Egyptian campaign first brought England into the field, as an ally of Russia and Turkey against France. Subsequently, when Napoleon courted the friendship of the Sultan, England joined Russia against the Turks. But England's attention being soon occupied elsewhere, Russia continued the war alone, and in 1812 made a treaty by which her frontier was advanced to the Pruth.

After the fall of Napoleon Eastern affairs drifted back into their natural channel, and now the three principal nations interested—Russia, Turkey, and England—began gradually to assume the positions which they have maintained to the present day: Russia, the protector of the misgoverned Christians; Turkey, their oppressor; and England sustaining

Turkey in behalf of her own interests in the East. From this time Austria has remained in the background, except at decisive diplomatic moments.

The subjugated provinces also began to strike blows for their independence; Servia had been fighting since 1808, Moldavia and Wallachia since 1820, and Greece since 1821. The Emperor Nicholas, immediately after his accession, took all these people under his protection, and forced on the Turks without a war the treaty of Akerman in 1826, by which Servia became semi-independent, and the Hospodars, or governors of Moldavia and Wallachia, who were elected by the Boyars or lords of the land from among their own number, were not to be removed by the Porte except with the permission of Russia. In 1827, England, under the leadership of Canning, joined Russia and France in a treaty of mediation between Turkey and the Greeks, by which the independence of a portion of Greece was demanded. The Sultan declining to accede to this, the combined fleets of the allies destroyed the Turkish navy at Navarino in October, 1827. But Canning died, the battle of Navarino was spoken of by his successor as an "untoward event," and England and France withdrew from the position they had assumed. The Emperor Nicholas, however, determined to make his word good, and promptly waged war to accomplish it; Russian troops for the first time crossed the Balkans, and in 1829 dictated at Adrianople a treaty of which the essential feature was the erection of Greece into an independent kingdom. In addition to this, more guaranties were provided to secure the semi-independence of Servia, and it was stipulated that no Mussulman should reside in Moldavia or Wallachia.

This cursory review of the principal facts in Turkish history, from the time of their entry into Europe, is a necessary introduction to a study of the events of the last fifty years. We see that the Turks, after overrunning the weak nations south of the Danube, were finally stopped by Austria, and that it was Austria who held them in check and first began to drive them backward. Russia joined her in this work, and then finally took nearly all of it upon herself, while the western nations took no very active part in the matter until they became by accident, rather than design, involved in it during the wars of Napoleon.

It was but a few years after the treaty of Adrianople when, in 1833, the Turkish Empire was threatened with destruction by the great rebellion of Ibrahim, Pasha of Egypt. Such a fate promised no good to the Christians, and nothing but anarchy for Turkey, and the Emperor Nicholas at once came to the Sultan's aid by landing troops for the defense of Constantinople. In 1839, another war broke out with Egypt, and this time the great powers *all* united to suppress the rebellion, and to regulate the relations between the Sultan and his Viceroy. The treaty of 1841 which arranged these matters was signed by Austria, France, England, Prussia, Russia, and Turkey; and since that time the great powers have all taken cognizance of everything relating to Turkey.

That power which, after Russia, has assumed to have the most interest in the matter, is England. Her modern position on this question was first enunciated by Mr. Pitt in 1792; he argued that " the true principle by which the foreign policy of England should be directed, was the fundamental principle of preserving the balance of power in Europe; and that the true doctrine of the balance of power required that the Russian Empire should not, if possible, be allowed to increase, nor that of Turkey to diminish." This was the first enunciation of that theorem of the " integrity and independence of the Ottoman Empire " on which the Treaty of Paris was founded, seventy-four years later; it asserted that, no matter how hideous might be the misgovernment of the Turks, their empire must be propped up and maintained, that Russia must always remain a semi-Asiatic power, and that the wheels of progress must stand still. It assumed that it was possible " to dam up the waters of the

Nile with bulrushes;" and it was singularly opposed in principle to the views which Mr. Pitt's father had held in regard to the American colonies.

But Pitt was unable to enforce his views by any practical measures; England could not afford to wage war for them unsupported; France was in the throes of the Revolution, and the other nations could not be induced to support them actively. Not long afterward all Europe was distracted by the wars of Napoleon.

But meanwhile the English possessions in India were rapidly developing into a vast empire. When the wars of Napoleon were over and Europe had returned to its normal condition, Englishmen began to turn their thoughts to the East, and to make preparations to secure their eastern possessions against all possible rivals. Although Russia did not begin her advances in Central Asia till several years later, yet, in view of the possibility of a Suez canal or an overland route along the Euphrates, a certain class of Englishmen began to reason that the security of their eastern possessions depended on keeping Russia out of the Mediterranean at any cost. When, therefore, these same views of Pitt were repeated in a slightly different form by Palmerston and others, in the second third of this century, they found ready listeners; and hatred of Russia became an article of faith with a large portion of the English public.

We have seen that, in 1829, the Emperor Nicholas established the independence of Greece and the semi-independence of Moldavia, Wallachia, and Servia. The Ottoman Empire then began to totter, but the Sultan of the day, Mahmoud II., was a man of no small force of character, and he made a desperate struggle to put his house in order and prevent its fall. Early in his reign he had had the courage to attempt a reform of the most vital character, viz., the suppression of the rebellious and turbulent Janissaries. This body of soldiers was originally recruited by the system of "blood-tax;" *i. e.*, a certain number of Christian children were abducted every year from the conquered provinces, forcibly brought up in the Moslem faith, and incorporated in the army. They were for a long series of years the finest soldiers in the Turkish service, but eventually they became its most intolerable scourge. By their insubordination and rebellion at critical periods they caused more than one campaign to be lost; and it is a fine instance of retributive justice, that a system originally designed to exact the most hideous form of tribute should finally have come home to curse its authors, and been instrumental in hastening their downfall. Mahmoud saw that he could never hope for success in the field with a mutinous army, and he suppressed the Janissaries in 1826, by massacreing nearly twenty-five thousand of them at their barracks in Constantinople and elsewhere throughout the empire. After 1829 Mahmoud turned his attention to the internal condition of his country, with a view to make such reforms as might preserve it from destruction; but he died in 1839, before much progress had been made in formulating his projects, and far less in executing them.

His successor, however, had been carefully educated in his own ideas, and before he had been six months on the throne he promulgated the first of that long series of proclamations and edicts which have been so greatly in vogue with the Turkish rulers of the last forty years, and which, under the form of glittering generalities concerning right and justice, and imperial commands that the life and property of their subjects shall be respected, have in reality been addressed to Europe as an evidence of repentance on the part of the Turkish rulers, and a cause why judgment should not now be pronounced against them for their many and terrible crimes.

This remarkable document, the *Hatti-Scheriff* of Gulhané (where it was signed), bearing the date of November 3, 1839, begins by reciting that "all the world knows that in the first days of the Ottoman monarchy, the glorious precepts of the Koran and the laws of the Empire were always honored. The Empire, in consequence, increased in strength and greatness, and all her subjects, without exception, had risen in the highest degree to ease and prosperity. In the last hundred and fifty years a succession of accidents and divers causes have arisen, which have brought about a disregard for the sacred code of laws and the regulations flowing therefrom, and the former strength and prosperity have turned into weakness and poverty; an empire, in fact, loses all its stability so soon as it ceases to observe its laws."

The Sultan therefore prescribes and orders the following:

" 1st. Guarantees insuring to our subjects perfect security for life, honor, and fortune. 2d. A regular system of assessing and levying the taxes. 3d. An equally regular system for the levy of troops and the duration of service."

In order to carry out these projects it is ordered that "henceforth the cause of every accused person shall be publicly judged in accordance with the divine law," and "no one can be put to death by poison or otherwise," except after such public judgment. "No one shall be allowed to attack the honor of another." "Each one shall possess his property of every kind, and shall dispose of it in all freedom, without let or hindrance from any person whatever."

"We therefore grant perfect security to the inhabitants of our Empire, in their lives, their honor, and their fortunes, as they are secured to them by the sacred text of our law."

The document significantly concludes by commanding not only that this imperial rescript shall be published throughout the empire, but also that it "shall be officially communicated to all the ambassadors of friendly Powers, resident at Constantinople, that they may be witnesses of these institutions, which, should it please God, shall last forever." *

But this proclamation produced no practical result beyond deceiving Europe for a short time with its promises. Whether the Sultan was sincere in his intentions or not is a matter of no practical importance, for the Koran everywhere speaks of unbelievers in such terms of scorn and hatred, that the idea of their being treated with the same justice as Mussulmans is repugnant to the very fundamental doctrines of the Moslem faith. Were any such general edicts to be followed by detailed laws for their enforcement, and were any serious effort made to give them practical effect, the Sultan could not remain on his throne a minute. A grand mufti † would immediately be found, to whom would be pre-

---

* The text of this edict is given at length in Herstlet's "Map of Europe by Treaty," from which the above extracts are taken, as well as all other extracts and references throughout this chapter to treaties since 1815.

† Chief interpreter of Moslem law.

sented, as in the case of Sultan Selim in 1807, and Abdul Aziz in 1876, and several of their predecessors, a series of questions asking whether a Sultan who had done so and so had not violated the organic law, and made himself liable to deposition and death. The mufti, as in the other cases, would answer Yes, and cite a verse of the Koran; and a few hours later a salute of a hundred guns from Seraglio Point would announce the accession of a new ruler. This form of proceeding has been carried out too often to leave any doubt that it would be promptly repeated were any Sultan to offer such violence to Moslem traditions and feelings as to attempt really to enforce a law granting equal justice to the faithful and to the unbelievers.

The Emperor Nicholas, seeing that this proclamation was merely a grand farce, that the oppression of the Christians was becoming more and more intolerable, that the corruption and degradation of the ruling class were ever increasing, that the authority of the government was being weakened and its dissolution approaching, and that the Eastern question, so long as it remained in that condition, was a standing menace to the peace of Europe —resolved upon a course of action which certainly went to the root of the whole matter. He proposed that Russia and England should come to a distinct understanding concerning the Eastern question, and that the Ottoman government should then be driven out of Europe.

He first sounded several English statesmen on the subject, during a visit to England in 1844; but meeting with but little response, he deferred the subject for nearly ten years. In 1853 he brought it forward again in those memorable and much-quoted conversations with the British ambassador, Sir Hamilton Seymour, in which the Turk was first spoken of as a "sick man."

The Emperor disclaimed any desire for territorial aggrandizement, but said, "The affairs of Turkey are in a very disorganized condition; the country itself seems to be falling to pieces; the fall will be a great misfortune, and it is very important that England and Russia should come to a perfectly good understanding upon these affairs, and that neither should take any decisive step of which the other is not apprised."

In the next conversation he repeated the statement that the Turk was a very sick man, "liable to die on our hands at any moment," and suggested whether it would not be well to agree beforehand what should be done in such a contingency, rather than to leave everything to the chances of a European war, which would otherwise be unavoidable.

Subsequently he became more definite in his proposals and stated positively that he would never permit England to take Constantinople, nor would he take it permanently for himself. He suggested that Servia and Bulgaria should receive the same form of independence as that already enjoyed by the principalities of Wallachia and Moldavia, and that he had no objection to England taking Egypt and Crete if she desired. But these were mere suggestions, and he intimated his desire to hear what England had to propose, the great object being that England and Russia should come to an agreement about this never-ending Eastern question, and thus remove the greatest source of European wars. He also referred to the several millions of Christian subjects in Turkey, whose interests he was called upon to watch over, while the right of doing so was secured to him by treaty.

The English ambassador was far more than a match for the Emperor in diplomatic craft and astuteness; he succeeded in drawing him out very fully without in the least committing himself, or answering anything but the vaguest generalities, as a prelude to further questions. He then sent home a verbatim account of the whole series of conversations, which was published to the world about a year later, accompanying it with the remark that they proved that the Emperor considered that the time "not *of* the dissolution, but *for* the dissolution of Turkey had arrived."

To these frank proposals, uttered with so much of almost naïveness, the cabinet of Lord Aberdeen replied in a haughty tone, that it was not usual to make arrangements for dismembering an ally, and that England did not covet any of the Turkish possessions. The Emperor Nicholas was deeply mortified at the manner in which his confidences had been received, and this naturally inspired in him an intense hatred of England, which he bore to the day of his death, and transmitted to his successors; while England, on the other hand, looked upon him as a secret conspirator, who had shown his hand, but in whom no confidence was henceforth to be placed. In this state of affairs a war was only a question of time and opportunity.

A pretext for it was, in fact, already at hand in a triangular quarrel between the Roman and Greek churches and the Turks, concerning the holy places at Jerusalem. This quarrel was actively fomented by the French Emperor, who eagerly sought for anything to distract the attention of his subjects from his own usurpation. The Emperor Nicholas also fomented it, and went even further, by sending a special ambassador to Constantinople to demand a formal and more explicit acknowledgment from the Porte of his authority to protect the Christians in Turkey, as laid down in the treaty of Kainardji. This was demanded in eight days, and being refused, the Emperor Nicholas marched his troops into the principalities and began the war. England and France came to the aid of Turkey on the ground that "its integrity and independence had been recognized as essential to the peace of Europe;" later on Sardinia, anxious to attract the attention of Europe upon herself, and to lay the foundations of a great state by a war in which she incurred little or no danger, joined the allies in a struggle in which she had not the remotest concern.

The events of the Crimean war are too recent and well known to call for any recapitulation. It would be hard to say on which side there was the greater mismanagement and corruption in military administration; by common consent there was but one man —Todleben—of any military genius on either side. But Russia was overmatched, not so much by the numbers or resources of her opponents as by her own backwardness in civilization, her lack of railroads or other means of communication—in short, by the very hugeness and primitiveness of her Empire. The Emperor Nicholas died of grief as one after another of his life-long and cherished hopes, and plans, and beliefs crumbled to pieces and disappeared, and his successor was obliged to acknowledge himself beaten, and sign a treaty full of carefully devised humiliation, in order to devote himself and his people to the work of internal regeneration.

Englishmen came home as victors, well pleased with themselves, some asserting that they had set back the march of Russian conquest for a hundred years, while others claimed more modestly that they had prevented war between Russia and Turkey for twenty-five years to come. What Englishmen now think of the wisdom of the Crimean war may be judged from the fact that two years ago they could not be induced to repeat the experiment, although urged on to it by the most crafty and unscrupulous leader that England has had for many generations.

The treaty of Paris, which ended this war, was based upon two fundamental ideas: first, the maintenance of the integrity and independence of the Ottoman Empire, and its admission as an integral part of the European system of states; and second, humiliation of Russia.

To accomplish the latter it was provided that the natural frontier line of the Pruth and Danube, conquered by Russia in 1812, should be abolished, and in place of it an irregular line should be established a few miles back across the marshes of Bessarabia. By this means the frontiers of Russia and Turkey would not be contiguous, but would be separated by a narrow strip of territory belonging to the principalities. It was further stipulated that the Black Sea should be "neutralized;" *i.e.*, while remaining open to the commerce of all nations, no man-of-war should float upon it, and no arsenals should be maintained on its shores. Moreover, it was stipulated in a separate treaty between England, France, and Sweden, that the former Powers would guarantee the latter against encroachments by Russia. The Swedish territories were in no way threatened, but they afforded a convenient pretext for a gratuitous insult to Russia.

Concerning the maintenance of the Ottoman Empire, the seventh article of the Treaty of Paris admitted the Sublime Porte "to participate in the advantages of the public law and system (*concert*) of Europe," and declared that each of the Powers would "respect the independence and territorial integrity of the Ottoman Empire." The eighth article declared that each Power would resort to mediation before having recourse to force in case of a misunderstanding. By a separate convention, England, France, and Austria agreed to guarantee this integrity and independence, and to consider any infraction of the Treaty of Paris a *casus belli*.

The semi-independence of Wallachia, Moldavia, and Servia were confirmed, and these principalities were placed under the protection of the Great Powers, each of whom was forbidden to interfere in their internal affairs.

On its part, Turkey laid before the congress the edict of the Sultan, known as the *Hatti-Huma-*

youm, which had been formulated a few days before the treaty was signed, and "which, while ameliorating the condition of the Sultan's subjects without distinction of religion or of race, records his generous intentions toward the Christian population of his empire." This edict, however, was not to give the Powers, either collectively or separately, the right to interfere between the Sultan and his subjects.

Finally, the treaty reaffirmed the previous treaties by which the Bosphorus and Dardanelles were closed to foreign ships of war.

Such were the provisions of the instrument by which England flattered herself that she had curbed the ambition and dwarfed the power of the "Colossus of the North," had extinguished the aspirations of the races struggling to free themselves from the Turkish misrule, and had propped up and invigorated the decaying members of the most corrupt, intolerable, cruel, and tyrannical government that has ever existed in Europe. France, in general, cared little or nothing for the merits of the Eastern question, and had entered the war only for "glory," at the instance of a political adventurer who had placed himself on the throne and sought by foreign war to make his subjects forget how foully he had betrayed them.

What was the result of it all, this treaty that was

to put Eastern affairs on a new and permanent basis? Less than twenty-five years later, the French usurper had been disposed of ignominiously and forever in the fourth and last of his foreign adventures in quest of "glory;" Russia had torn up the clause relating to the Black Sea, and had reestablished her Bessarabian frontier; the territory whose integrity had been guaranteed had been reduced to one-third of its former proportions; the condition of its subject races was more intolerable than ever; their hatred of their oppressors more intense; the Turkish Empire was still more infirm, and its existence was more than ever a source of danger to the tranquillity of Europe.

Russia, indeed, was worsted physically, but not morally, in the contest in the Crimea. The principles for which she fought are living principles, and they have triumphed in this generation though defeated in the last. Even at this time, before a generous, sentimental sympathy for their co-religionists had taken deep hold upon the masses of the Russian people, her motives may well bear comparison with those of England. No one pretends that these motives were wholly devoid of self-interest; but what gives Russia the moral ascendancy over England in this long contest, is the fate which has made her material interests lie on the side of right and justice, while those of England—

as Englishmen see fit to interpret them—are on the side of oppression and wrong. It was in the interest of developing the resources of his country that Peter strove to push the Turks away from the northern shore of the Black Sea and plant his own people there; it was doubtless an imperial ambition which prompted all of Catherine's plans for southern conquest; it was probably for the benefit of the material interests of his country that Nicholas strove to arrange with England for the funeral of the Turk. But while Russia was all this time waging war for material benefits—as all strong nations have ever done—she was at the same time conferring a benefit on the whole Christian world by gradually breaking down a government under which no Christian could live in safety or comfort, and successively emancipating one race after another from the insufferable Turkish rule. It was by the aid of Russia that Wallachia, Moldavia, Servia, and Greece were all in turn set on their feet, and allowed to work out their own salvation, and achieve such measure of prosperity and happiness for themselves as their capabilities would permit.

England, on the other hand, has been the perpetual objecter and obstructionist throughout the whole of this natural development of history, which, however, she has not succeeded in greatly retarding, though her action has engendered many hatreds and prolonged much misery. And to justify her in this course, she has only the argument that by sustaining Turkey she puts a barrier to Russian ambition. She has never ventured to openly defend the Turkish system of government. Candid and uncandid Englishmen of all parties have time and again condemned the extortion, the cruelty, the injustice, and the utter barbarity of the Turkish rule, but they have always maintained, in the same breath, that still greater evils would follow were Turkey supplanted by Russia; for in that case English trade and commerce would suffer on the one hand, while, on the other, Russia would become so strong that the liberties of Europe would be endangered! The insufficiency of England's policy to accomplish its purpose of maintaining intact the Turkish Empire is no less remarkable than its injustice. When Nicholas proposed to come to terms about this long-standing nuisance of the Turk, it might have been expected that England—if she deemed his proposition to be dictated by selfish interest and a desire for aggrandizement—would have advanced some positive solution of her own, which had the elements of stability about it, but would not redound to the advantage of Russia; and then, if necessary, have fought for it, and established it. But she proposed nothing of the kind; she only demanded that the shaky, tottering *status quo* should be maintained. If any one believed, in 1853, that there were any elements of vitality in the Ottoman Empire, that any justice was to be found in its government of the Christians, that any faith was to be placed in its promises of reform, surely the events of the succeeding twenty-five years must have been enough to undeceive him. Nobody really did believe it then, any more than now; but in 1878, as in 1856, England is still insisting on the maintenance of the *status quo* (what is left of it), still accepting Turkish promises, still refusing to face the inevitable and frame some plan for the regeneration of the East which shall insure justice to the governed, protect her own interests, and prevent those of Russia from having undue prominence. Before this great problem, English statesmanship has seemed to be powerless; no one has ever proposed any scheme which could secure the support of even a respectable minority of his countrymen. As Russia advances and Turkey totters, England puts another prop under her—loans her more money, fights her battles, secretly aids her, gives her advice, and not infrequently illusory promises; but the only plan she has heretofore had, with which to oppose Russia, is Turkey as it is.* With every generation, in spite of England's aid, this Turkey becomes less: in 1829, it was Greece and the Danubian principalities that dropped off; in 1878, it was Bulgaria; in another generation it will be Roumelia and Constantinople itself.

If the English policy remains unchanged, the sick man, as Nicholas warned them, will die on their hands while they are still making plans for his "integrity and independence." The most that can be said of England's policy in the East, is that it has been an obstinate effort to stave off the inevitable, and to throw the solution of a great problem ever upon the shoulders of the next succeeding generation.

England vastly underestimated the pride of her antagonist if she imagined that she would remain quiet under such a humiliating treaty more than long enough to gather strength to destroy it. England, therefore, took the responsibility of standing ready to defend her treaty at all times by force of arms—as Germany stands ready to defend the settlement she made in 1870—or else she would inevitably be obliged to withdraw from the position she had assumed. It has never been possible to bring the majority of Englishmen up to the point of making war in defense of the Treaty of Paris, and England has therefore had perforce to accept the alternative of allowing the treaty and its principles to be destroyed.

The treaty was but four years old when, in the spring of 1860, Prince Gortschakoff, after consultation with the ambassadors in St. Petersburg, addressed a circular note to the signatory Powers, in which he called attention to the reports of Russian consuls in Turkey, showing that the grossest misgovernment and injustice were practised by the local governors in Bosnia, Herzegovnia, and Bulgaria; far from the Treaty of Paris being carried out by putting into effect the promises of the *Hatti-Humayoum*, these reports showed that the condition of the subject races in those provinces was becoming worse and worse. The circular, therefore, invited the Great Powers to take the matter into serious consideration, to verify the reports of the Russian consuls, and to exercise the powers of mediation provided for in the treaty in case any of its provisions should be disregarded. . The circular went on to say that Europe having decided that the maintenance of the Ottoman Empire was necessary for its tranquillity, it was of the highest importance to the Porte, no less than to Europe, that a "real, serious, and durable amelioration" of the condition of the Christians should be effected.

The reports of the Russian consuls were fully verified by those of England and the other Powers, but no further steps were taken under this call, for, before the year was ended, still more serious disturbances broke out in Syria. Something over fifteen thousand people having been massacred, the Great

Powers for once agreed to take the matter firmly in hand, and dispatched an English and a French commissioner, backed with a French land force and an English fleet, to restore order. The Pasha who was the ringleader in the massacres was hanged, a constitution was drawn up by Lord Dufferin for the government of the Lebanon, and the Porte, upon objecting to it on the ground of its independence being encroached upon, was simply informed that the French troops would remain in Syria until it was accepted. This small show of force and of united action was all that was needed to compel the Porte to submit. The constitution was adopted, the French troops remained long enough for it to get in working order, and there has been tranquillity in Syria ever since.

Six years later occurred another of the chronic insurrections against the insufferable tyranny of the Ottoman government. This time it was in Crete. The Powers immediately took note of it—Austria proposing that the Treaty of Paris should be revised, and the Christian populations be taken under the united protection of Europe, and endowed with a certain measure of local self-government; France seconded this, and proposed that Crete should be ceded to Greece; Russia was of the same opinion, and advised that the only escape from the series of makeshifts which had been so long and ineffectually tried, was in "the gradual development of autonomous states" out of the subject races of Turkey. All the Great Powers were united in the advisability of such joint action as had been taken in Syria, excepting only England. She refused to take part in any such plan, and in its place succeeded in imposing on the Cretans a new constitution, and a new series of promises, devised by the Turks. This has proved as ineffectual as might have been anticipated, and under it the Cretans have continued in a more or less chronic state of revolt to this day.

In 1870 two of the Powers that had forced the Treaty of Paris upon Russia were engaged in a great war. Russia then did what any other great nation would do which had been similarly humiliated and felt herself strong enough to resent it: she took advantage of the condition of affairs to nullify the most humiliating feature of the treaty. In a circular-note dated October 31, 1870, Prince Gortschakoff informed the Powers that Russia would no longer consider herself bound by that article of the treaty which "neutralized" the Black Sea. England, as her Prime Minister announced in Parliment, found herself without an ally to support this article by force. She was therefore compelled to yield, and on March 13, 1871, a convention was signed at London which provided that the article (No. xiv.) relating to the Black Sea "is abrogated."

The most essential of the safeguards provided by the Treaty of Paris against Russian ambition, and the most humiliating of all the insults contained in that treaty, were thus formally renounced and withdrawn by their authors just fifteen years after they had been formulated.

Four years later, in 1875, the insurrections broke out in Bosnia and Herzegovina, and ushered in the series of events which brought about the late war and all its attendant consequences.

When these disturbances broke out, Austria, as being the nation most nearly interested, took the lead in proposing to the Great Powers to initiate certain steps which would lead to a pacification of the locality, substantially on the same principle as that adopted in the Lebanon in 1861. The proposals were drawn up in what is known as the "Andrassy note," which was addressed to the various Powers on December 30, 1875.

The terms of this document are well known; they were summarized as follows:

" 1. Complete liberty of worship.

" 2. Reform in the system of taxation.

" 3. Sale of waste lands to needy inhabitants.

" 4. Mixed commissions in Bosnia and Herzegovina to supervise the reforms.

" 5. Granting of funds for works of public utility."

All the Great Powers gave their assent to this

note in principle, and all of them except England showed that they meant what they said by proposing to have the Porte enter into a definite and explicit agreement to carry out the remedies which they suggested. But Lord Derby, then Secretary for Foreign Affairs, wrote a long dispatch to the English ambassador, criticising and condemning every proposition in the note, and then authorizing the ambassador to give "a general support to Count Andrassy's proposals, but confine himself to oral communications."

Under these circumstances, the Porte accepted the note with great pleasure, promised to follow the advice it contained, and issued the customary proclamation. It thanked England with considerable effusiveness for its kindness, and then let the whole matter drop at once. But the other Powers were by no means satisfied to have their purpose so completely frustrated. The insurrection continued in Bosnia, and early in May the Consuls of France and Germany were murdered in Salonica. A few days later the Chancellors of the three empires met in Berlin, and after exchanging their ideas, they drafted a second document known as the Berlin Memorandum. This recited that such outrages as those at Salonica could only be prevented by sending men-of-war to the threatened localities, and providing their commanding officers with identical instructions as to the manner in which they should use their force. But this would only be a temporary expedient, unless the cause of all these agitations should be removed by the prompt pacification of Bosnia and Herzegovnia. By accepting the Andrassy note, the Porte had incurred an obligation to Europe to carry out its provisions; this note, however, had failed to accomplish any purpose, because the insurgents refused to trust the unendorsed promises of the Porte, and the Porte had failed to carry its provisions into effect. The Powers should therefore come to an agreement as to the guaranties necessary to insure the fulfillment of the promises made by the Porte to Europe. The first essential should be an armistice of two months; during this time, negotiations could be conducted between the Porte and the Bosnian delegates, on the basis of furnishing the refugees with materials for rebuilding their houses, under the supervision of a mixed commission; the Turkish troops to be concentrated at a few specified points; the Christians as well as the Mussulmans to retain their arms, and the foreign consuls to "watch over the application of the reforms in general, and the steps relative to repatriation in particular." If, with the aid of the Great Powers, a definite agreement could be made between the Porte and the insurgents on this basis, and put immediately into effect, a great step would be made toward pacification. But if these efforts should fail to accomplish their purpose, then it would be necessary for the Powers to "supplement their diplomatic action by the sanction of an agreement, looking to such efficacious measures as might appear to be demanded in the interest of a general peace." In other words, if advice failed, then more forcible measures must be employed, as they had been in 1860.

This memorandum certainly contained a positive plan of action, which would, for the time being, have put an end to the insurrection, and have prevented the outbreak of a war, which otherwise seemed inevitable, and in which Turkey was surely doomed to suffer, unless she found strong allies. France and Italy hastened to agree to it, but, to the surprise and regret of every one, England positively refused to assent to it in any manner whatever. What were her motives, is a mere matter of speculation, for her cabinet declined to explain them further than to denounce every article of the memorandum as being either an infringement on Turkish independence, or a sacrifice which it was unable to bear. Austria, Germany, France, and Italy all in turn pressed England to accept the memorandum, or to suggest any modifications she might desire in its language. She declined to do either. They then asked Lord Derby if he had any proposition of his own to make, and he replied none. "Her Majesty's

Government deprecated the diplomatic action of the other Powers in the affairs of the Ottoman Empire." Russia then asked what was the drift of England's policy; what were her ideas in the matter? To which Lord Derby replied, that he thought nothing remained but to let the struggle continue until success should declare itself on one side or the other. In other words, in British phrase, form a ring and let 'em fight it out with the usual result of indiscriminate slaughter and pillage which ever follows a case of fighting out an insurrection in Turkey. But the other five Powers were really desirous to bring about some permanent solution of the matter. They determined to leave England alone, and to present their views to the Porte without her concurrence. Their representatives, therefore, met at the German Embassy in Constantinople on the afternoon of May 29, 1876, and drafted a form of communication which contained the terms of the Berlin memorandum, and which, in identically the same language, was to be presented by each of them to the Porte on the following morning. During that very night, however, the Sultan was deposed; in the morning there was a new Sultan, and no diplomatic intercourse could be carried on until he had been recognized, and other formalities gone through with. The new Sultan only remained on the throne about three months, but before he was fairly installed the massacres had occurred in Bulgaria, and Servia had declared war; the problem had attained far greater proportions than the mere question of the Bosnian refugees, and the Berlin memorandum was entirely inadequate to meet it. So it was never presented to the Porte.

It is quite needless to recount the savage manner in which the feeble insurrection in Bulgaria was put down by the Bashi-Bazouks under Chefket Pasha. The horrible tale of the human heads piled up among the smoldering ruins of Batak is too fresh to have been forgotten by even the most casual reader. Its political bearing is stated with remarkable accuracy by Sir Henry Elliot in his well-known letter, in which he says "that the interests of England are deeply engaged in preventing a disruption of the Turkish Empire, is a conviction which I share in common with the most eminent statesmen who have directed our foreign policy, but which appears now to be abandoned by shallow politicians or persons who have allowed their feelings of revolted humanity to make them forget the capital interests involved in the question.

"We may and must feel indignant at the needless and monstrous severity with which the Bulgarian insurrection was put down; but the necessity which exists for England to prevent changes from occurring here which would be most detrimental to ourselves, is not affected by the question whether it was ten thousand or twenty thousand persons who perished in its suppression.

"We have been upholding what we know to be a semi-civilized nation, liable under certain circumstances to be carried into fearful excesses; but the fact of this having just now been strikingly brought home to us all, cannot be a sufficient reason for abandoning a policy which is the only one that can be followed with due regard to our interests."

These words may seem cruel and cold-blooded; but if the premises are granted—that English interests demand the maintenance of the Turkish Empire—their logical sequence cannot be refuted. It is true that many people in England still hugged the delusion that misrule, extortion, and massacre were not the necessary accompaniments of the Turk's rule; but they cherished this delusion in the very face of all the facts of Turkish history. In 1825 the massacres in Greece had been no less revolting and extensive than those in Bulgaria in 1876. In 1860 it had been the same in Syria. The whole course of Turkish history, from the time when Bajazet had all the prisoners taken at Nicopolis in 1396 massacred before his eyes, has been full of just such incidents; but in the last fifty years they have been so notorious and well authenticated that there has been no excuse for not knowing and believing them. Yet England, having all these facts before her, has, ever since the battle of Navarino, been engaged in maintaining and assuring the integrity of that very government under which alone they are possible, and all this time has been accepting promise after promise of reform in the treatment of the Christians, not one of which has been kept.

On the other hand, Sir Henry Elliot—and he represents a large class in England, though none of them have been so candid or so incautious as to express their views so clearly as himself—has no delusions about the nature of Turkish government; he knows it thoroughly, and fully appreciates its wickedness, but he considers it necessary to uphold that government in spite of its sins; he weighs the interests of British trade against the lives of the Christian subjects of the Porte, and declares the former to have the greater value. His policy is harsh; compared with it, the much-talked-of rule of "blood and iron" is mildness itself; but it is consistent, and he rightly says that if any questions of humanity are to become mingled with it, it at once loses all its force, and becomes the mere makeshift of shallow politicians.

But the English public was by no means so coolheaded and consistent as Sir Henry. A storm of indignant wrath went from one end of England to the other, crying out that such damnable outrages should cease, with the destruction of the government which permitted them if no other means were efficacious. The cabinet were powerless before this storm. Though England was the author of the treaty which upheld this atrocious government, yet the indignation was none the less great. The policy of active support, which there is good ground for believing the head of the cabinet desired to follow, and the policy of do nothing but let them fight it out, which the Foreign Secretary openly advocated, were both paralyzed. It was necessary to do something, and that shortly.

Nor was England the only country which was indignant on the subject. In Russia the whole mass of the people, from the highest to the lowest grades, were stirred to the very depths of their souls by the murder of their fellow-Slavs and co-religionists. They cried out for vengeance at once; but as their Tsar insisted on trying all the peaceful methods before resorting to war, they could do nothing to show their sympathy but send volunteers to join the Servians, who had just declared war against the Porte, in behalf of their Bulgarian fellow-subjects. Other nations were only less indignant, but feeling less immediate interest in the subject than Russia and England, they limited themselves to seconding the proposals of those countries. Austria, indeed, which had taken the lead in all the diplomatic steps of the past year, now had her hand stayed by the Magyar portion of her population, and was obliged to remain in the background. But there was practical unanimity among all the great nations, and a universal desire that measures should be taken which would afford an *effective* guaranty for good government, or at least common justice, in Turkey.

A great and unique opportunity was then offered to England to depart from her past policy, which had certainly failed to accomplish its purpose, and to enter upon a new one which should have a more substantial basis than propping up the decayed members of an almost lifeless state. The enormity and authenticity of the crimes which had just been committed were ample warrant for any change of policy, or the abrogation of any treaty. Had a Liberal administration been in power, it is probable that it would have seized this opportunity to put into *practical* operation that principle of local self-government and the extension of the area of autonomous states which was formulated at the Conference a few months later. But there was one cardinal measure which must be employed, or else all steps would be useless and end in nothing. That measure was the use of force. All Turkish history shows that it is by the question of force alone that the Turks gauge the intentions of the people with whom they deal. Without force to make good their wishes, the Turks look upon treaties, promises, edicts, and diplomatic correspondence, as a mere *jeu d'esprit*, in which they have always been masters, very engaging for the moment, but having no relation to practical affairs. The advice which Europe was to give to Turkey must be accompanied with a concerted show of force, ready to be freely used if necessary, and sufficiently great to convince the Turks that the advice was seriously meant; otherwise the Turks would pay no more attention to it than to make polite answers, and issue fresh proclamations.

This statement is warranted by the history of the achievement of Greek independence, which the Turks laughed at in 1827, but acknowledged after the war of 1829, by the readiness with which they accepted the interference in the affairs of Syria in 1861, which was supported by armed power, and by their total disregard of the provisions of the *Hatti-Humayoum*, whose execution rested on their promise alone. It is also warranted by human nature itself, for no government, whether good or bad, yields to advice concerning its own internal affairs, unless compelled to do so by force.

But at this critical juncture England did not have a Liberal administration, but one led by a statesman whose imperial ambitions were far more vast than those of Catherine, and who never has been troubled by scruples of humanity, or any other scruples, in the employment of means to gain his end. This cabinet invited the other Powers to meet in a conference at Constantinople, believing that this was the surest method to defeat the wishes of Russia, who was anxious to march a force into Bulgaria to restore and maintain order; but at the same time it adopted a course which was sure to prevent the deliberations of this conference from having any practical result; that is, it opposed most strenuously that very idea of the use of force or a show of force which alone could give any effect to the advice of the conference. Throughout the whole series of Lord Derby's dispatches during 1876 and 1877, there ran this double idea: inform the Turks that England will not come to their aid if attacked, but inform them also at the same time, that England will not sanction any *coercive* measures against them.

The Turks expressed their thanks with a due sense of gratitude, and thenceforth knew how to shape their course with that diplomatic address in which they have few equals.

The conference met at Constantinople on the 11th of December; the Turks were not invited to be present until the other Powers had agreed upon what they had to offer. The presiding officer announced the object of the conference to be, to determine first the conditions of peace between Turkey and Servia and Montenegro, and second, "the nature and extent of the administrative systems which should be applied to Bosnia, Herzegovnia, and Bulgaria, and the guaranties necessary to insure their effectual execution."

Lord Salisbury and General Ignatief took the lead in the deliberations, and they soon agreed upon the terms of peace, and the extent of the provinces to be formed within which the new form of local self-government, the nature of which was given in considerable detail, was to be applied. Its most essential provisions were Christian governors, nominated for five years with the approval of foreign Powers, an international commission to supervise the introduction of the new system, and a small force of some disinterested Power, such as Belgium, to act as escort to the commission, and give effect to its opinion.

The representatives of the foreign Powers having agreed upon the proposals they would make to the Porte, the Turkish representatives were invited to be present, and the first full meeting of the Conference was held on the 23d of December under the presidency of the Turkish plenipotentiary. The session was short, and toward its close occurred an incident which is thus recorded in the minutes of the proceedings:

"At this moment salvoes of artillery are heard. The President of the Conference states that these salvoes announce the promulgation of the Ottoman Constitution. 'A great act,' he says, 'which is at this moment being accomplished, has just changed a form of government which had lasted six hundred years. The Constitution with which his Majesty the Sultan has endowed his empire, is promulgated. It inaugurates a new era for the happiness and prosperity of his people.'"

One cannot but admire the dexterity of this stroke, and the infinite resource of the Turks. It might have been supposed that in forty years they had exhausted their stock of proclamations and edicts, which contained promises and schemes of government enough to make Turkey the most prosperous and happy country in the world—had they been really carried out. Every conceivable principle of justice had in succession been announced in these various *Hatts* and *Firmans*, and it was difficult to see how anything new of that description could be offered. But the Turks were equal to the emergency. Knowing that they had no hope of influencing any of the nations except England, they devised a new proclamation, appealing peculiarly to her sensibilities as the author of representative government. Midhat Pasha had framed a whole Constitution of no less than one hundred and nineteen articles, the essential feature of which was a Parliament, consisting of a Senate whose members were appointed by the Sultan, and a House of Deputies whose members were to be elected by the people in secret ballot, the manner of the election to be determined by a subsequent special law.

The card was well played; though it had but little effect on the Conference, it took very well in England, where certain Tory papers were soon speaking of Turkey as that enlightened country which was endowed with representative government, and which was so far in advance in civilization of Russia, which was ruled by an Asiatic and barbarous despotism! So easy is it to confuse matters if only the names of things are used, and not the acts which are done in those names.

The history of this Constitution is soon told. Its author, Midhat Pasha, remained in power a little over a year, and was then overthrown and banished from his country as being its greatest enemy. The Parliament held two sessions, one beginning in March, and the other in December, 1877. It exercised its privilege of criticism with no little freedom, succeeded in overturning several ministries, alarmed the Sultan at one time so greatly as to cause him to cross into Asia, and was finally dissolved in February, 1878; several of the deputies being ordered to leave Constantinople forthwith, but forbidden to return to their own homes. Since that time neither the Parliament nor the Constitution has been heard of.

When the Turkish plenipotentiaries had carefully read the propositions which the Conference submitted to them, they replied in the next meeting that some of them, such as the appointment of the Governors by foreign advice, positively could not be accepted; but that the whole scheme was unnecessary, for the Sultan had now, by his own volition, granted a Constitution which secured the welfare of all his subjects in the most complete manner. But the Conference was not to be so easily entrapped as had been that of 1856, and Lord Salisbury remarked that it had not met to take cognizance of Turkish promises, but to frame some positive scheme of relief for the disturbed provinces. Foiled in their intentions to evade the whole subject by means of their new Constitution, the Turks now submitted a counter-project, and for the next three weeks the discussion went on in the hope of reconciling the two schemes. The foreign representatives constantly receded from one after another of their demands, until only the outline of them remained; but this outline contained two very essential features, viz., that the Governors should be chosen with the consent of the other Powers, and that an International Commission should supervise the execution of the reforms. To both of these propositions the Turks positively refused to accede, on the ground that they were fundamentally opposed to that independence of the Ottoman Empire which was guaranteed by treaty, and which the English instructions had named as the first and most essential of the bases for the deliberations of the Conference.

Having warned the Turks that the responsibility of their acts must rest on their own heads, the Conference broke up on the 20th of January, 1877, and its members as well as the regular ambassadors quitted Constantinople without delay.

It had all come to naught from just one cause—the refusal of England to join the other Powers in enforcing their demands by arms, or at least by a well-supported threat of war.

The Russian plenipotentiary had been instructed to propose to the Conference that the most effectual guaranties for the execution of the reforms would be found in the occupation of Bosnia by an Austrian force, of Bulgaria by a Russian force, and of the Bosphorus by the combined fleets of the six Powers; or in the naval demonstration alone, if the land occupation was objected to. The land occupation found no advocates, but the naval demonstration was acceptable to all the Powers except England.

But on this point Lord Derby's instructions were most explicit that "Her Majesty's government would not be prepared to employ measures of active coercion to extort the consent of Turkey to the proposals which had been drawn up at Constantinople."

With such intentions, it is difficult to understand what it was hoped to gain by the Conference. Any proposals of effective reform, coming from the representatives of other Powers assembled in their own capital, must necessarily be most distasteful to the Turks. To expect that they would accede to them for the mere asking, was to suppose them possessed of an angelic spirit of submission which no people have ever shown — least of all, a warlike race like the Turks. No nation ever has or ever will accept such outside interference except upon compulsion.

But Russia had already announced that she did not consider the mere offering of advice a satisfactory solution of the present condition of affairs. If the Porte declined to accept advice, then she was determined to bring about an amelioration of the fate of the Christians by force of arms, alone if need be, or in conjunction with other Powers if they desired to assist. In the previous month of November, the Tsar had announced his purpose to exhaust all the peaceful methods of diplomacy and concerted action, but to act alone and by war if these should fail; and to show that he meant what he said, he had mobilized a considerable portion of his army.

The Conference having ended in nothing, he made one last appeal. He sent General Ignatief to the various Courts of Europe to obtain their views of what further could be done, in view of the failure of the Conference; and finally, at London, on the 31st of March, there was signed a protocol, in which the Powers proposed to Turkey to execute the reforms in its own manner; but they would watch their progress by means of their representatives in Constantinople, and if they were not carried out, they would "consider such a state of affairs incompatible with their interests and those of Europe in general." In that case, they reserved to themselves to consider what means would be necessary to cause them to be carried out. The Porte made its answer on April 10th, declining, without reserve, to give its assent to the principles contained in the protocol, and insisting that the treaty of Paris explicitly denied to the Powers the right to interfere collectively or separately in the relations between the Sultan and his subjects.

There was nothing more to be done. All the Great Powers had insisted most urgently that the condition and government of the subject Christians must be radically changed; only one of them was disposed to make its wishes effective, but this one did not hesitate in its task. On the 24th of April, 1877, the Tsar announced that all the resources of diplomacy had been exhausted, and that the Porte absolutely refused to give any effective guaranties for those reforms to which it was solemnly bound by previous engagements, and by which alone the Christians in Turkey could be protected from the arbitrary measures of local authorities. The moment had therefore come for him to act independently, and impose his will on the Turks by force, and his armies had been ordered to cross the Turkish frontier.

Throughout the whole of the diplomatic campaign which had been carried on during the two years preceding the war, no mention had been made of anything but the affairs of Turkey; it was on its surface a question of providing for good government of the Christian subjects of the Sultan. But underlying all this was another great question—one of those jealousies between the various nations of the Christian religion which, as I have previously said, have complicated the later development of the Eastern question. This was the mutual rivalry of Russia and England arising from their Asiatic possessions.

The growth of the Indian possessions of the

British Crown is not only one of the most remarkable features of modern times, but it is one which has no rival in all history. Nothing in the history of Rome ever compared with it in vastness. From a few trading stations conquered by the "Governor and company of merchants of London trading to the East Indies," which was chartered by Elizabeth in 1600, it has grown to be an empire of well-nigh two hundred millions of souls, acknowledging allegiance to the British Crown, and pouring into the treasury of British India the sum of three hundred million dollars annually. And not only for itself is it valuable, but because it represents in a pre-eminent degree that trade and commerce which are the foundation of the present greatness and prosperity of England. Deprived of her colonies and her commerce, England would at once sink to the level of the smaller states of Europe, following in the wake of Holland and Venice and Spain, who in their days have been great and powerful, but who have declined with the loss of their foreign possessions and the commerce which they sustained. Fifteen of the thirty-three millions of people in the British isles to-day subsist on food brought from abroad, and probably twenty-five millions derive their livelihood from the various branches of her foreign trade. The variety and extent of her wealth and power are vast—Lord Beaconsfield truly says that history may be searched in vain for their like—but they rest on commercial credit, and not on the resources of the British isles; and from the moment that the commerce on which this credit is based receives a fatal blow, the days of England's greatness are past. No single event could strike so serious a blow as the loss of India. Of all the great possessions—it is hardly a colony—it is the most alien to the British race, and it is held as a mere money-making investment. Its people are ground with extortionate taxation, are allowed no voice in their own affairs, are treated with studied scorn, are made to pay for gigantic systems of public works for which their simple wants have no necessity, but which are of enormous advantage to their rulers in developing the wealth of the country for their own profit. It is held as a market in which to buy cheap and sell dear, and as a place in which younger sons and needy relations can amass fortunes to be subsequently enjoyed in England. Its loss would result in a financial crisis which would shake the whole fabric of England's commercial prosperity, and deal a blow at her political prestige from which she could hardly recover.

It is no wonder, then, that everything pertaining to India is guarded by England with the most jealous care. Moreover, her rule is detested from one end of the peninsula to the other, and would be thrown off at the first opportunity. This uncertainty of tenure makes her see many imaginary dangers, at which she would only laugh were she sure of the loyal support of the native populations.

The greatest of these imaginary dangers is the idea that Russia covets the possession of India for herself. This theory has arisen entirely within the last twenty-five years. The vast acquisitions of territory made by Russia since Peter the Great's time, and the suspicion (probably unfounded) that the mutiny of 1857 was in part due to Russian intrigue, have made Englishmen, ever nervous for the security of their distant and discontented Eastern possessions, imagine that Russia would not stop until her Asiatic territory reached the Indian Ocean.

There is every reason to believe that Russia has no such ambitions. Her frontier has gradually advanced—rapidly, indeed, in the last fifteen years—across the deserts beyond the Caspian and Aral seas, but only in obedience to that law of necessity arising from the impossibility of maintaining any frontier with nomadic and semi-civilized people, with which our Indian experience on the plains has made us perfectly familiar. So soon as the Russian and British frontiers in Asia are contiguous, this necessity will cease; and if the two nations will come to terms of friendship, Russia will have no more designs on India than she has on Germany or Austria. But although

Russia does not covet the possession of India, yet if England continues to pursue her with the same relentless hatred that she has shown in the past fifty years, then, undoubtedly, Russia, in accordance with that law of self-defense which allows any nation to strike its adversary in its weakest point, will strike England in India; not by attempting to take the country for itself, but by stirring up an insurrection which shall exterminate the English residents and the English power. Thus we may yet see the Eastern question settled on the banks of the Indus.

This I believe to be the whole of Russia's intentions on India—to use it as a leverage in case England should again attack her in defense of the intolerable Turkish misgovernment. It was on this principle that, when war with England seemed inevitable in the spring of 1878, Russia took steps to prepare a way for her troops across Afghanistan.

It was this anxiety about India that made England see a hidden purpose in every step that Russia took in regard to Turkey throughout the whole of the negotiations of 1875, '76, and '77, and made her refuse to believe that Russia was guided by any disinterested feeling for the oppressed Christians. At this critical period England was peculiarly sensitive on the subject, for she had then a Prime Minister of a truly oriental imagination, of boundless ambition, and intensely devoted to the idea of developing closer relations between England and her foreign possessions. He made the Queen Empress of India; he sent the Prince of Wales to see the country; he brought Indian troops into Europe. In his mind, everything else was of secondary importance to the necessity of strengthening the security of these possessions, and any means were justifiable to attain this end. He scoffed at the misery of the Christians in Bosnia and Bulgaria, and thwarted every proposition that might lead to their benefit, simply because they could not be really benefited except at the expense of the Turkish power; and the maintenance of the Turkish power was, in his opinion, essential to the security of India.

When, therefore, the last resources of diplomacy had been exhausted, and war followed, his cabinet promptly declared that Russia had deliberately violated the Treaty of Paris in attacking the integrity of the Ottoman Empire, but that England would remain neutral so long as British interests were not attacked. Being pressed for a definition of British interests, the cabinet enumerated specifically four propositions, a violation of any one of which would render it impossible for England to remain neutral. These were as follows:

First. The navigation of the Suez Canal must not be blockaded or interfered with.

Second. Egypt must not be attacked or occupied.

Third. Constantinople must not pass into any other hands than those of its present possessors.

Fourth. The existing arrangements concerning the navigation of the Bosphorus and the Dardanelles must not be changed.

To the first two propositions Russia gave her unqualified assent. To the third she replied that the course of the war could not be foretold, but Russia had no intention or desire to acquire Constantinople permanently. Concerning the fourth proposition, Russia replied that she always desired to have the navigation of the Straits governed by international agreement. In general, the British interests, as above defined, would be respected by Russia so long as England remained neutral.

These promises were rigidly kept.

To make these assurances still more complete, Prince Gortschakoff sent a dispatch in June announcing the Emperor's intentions concerning the war, and in August the Emperor requested Colonel Wellesley, the British military attaché at his headquarters, who had been summoned home on public business, to convey to the British cabinet a memorandum in which he stated, with the utmost frankness, for what he was waging war, and how he should conclude it. He should demand for himself the retrocession of the piece of Bessarabia taken away by the Treaty of Paris, and a small territory in Asia, but nothing more. If the Turks sued for peace without forcing him to cross the Balkans, the limits of the new Bulgaria would be fixed by those mountains; if he was forced to cross them, these limits would extend much further to the south. The events of the war might compel him to occupy Constantinople temporarily, but he had no intention to take permanent possession of it. He had no desire or intention to interfere with any of the British interests in the Mediterranean or in India. The war was waged to provide a good government for the Christians in Turkey, and he should insist on a treaty which accomplished this purpose.

The British cabinet sent back by Colonel Wellesley a memorandum in which they stated that "they received with satisfaction the statement made by His Majesty as to the object of the war in which he was engaged, his disclaimer of any extensive ideas of annexation, and his readiness to enter into negotiations for peace. They are grateful for the assurance which he has given of his intention to respect the interests of England." The cabinet raised no objection whatever to any of the terms and conditions of peace stated in Prince Gortschakoff's dispatch of June, or Colonel Wellesley's memorandum of August. Yet the Treaty of San Stefano was framed on these very terms and conditions, not one of which it violated; and when this treaty was made England prepared for war. Why did the cabinet take such different action on the same propositions? In all probability because, at the date of their answer to the Wellesley memorandum (August 14), Russia had just received her second great defeat at Plevna, and the war had come to a standstill pending the arrival of re-enforcements. Lord Beaconsfield shared the delusion then current with his party, that Russia would gain no substantial success over the Turks, and would never have the opportunity of dictating the terms which the Emperor suggested.

The war then took its course. The Turkish resistance proved to be greater than had been anticipated, and it had the effect of storing up the force of the Russian invasion, which broke forth with resistless momentum on the fall of Plevna. At the end of January, 1878, the Russian armies were at the gates of Constantinople, and Turkey lay, for the moment, helpless at their feet. England immediately ordered her fleet to proceed to Constantinople, without regard to any protest of the Turks based upon treaty stipulations in regard to the navigation of the Straits. She also began to make other preparations to be prepared for any emergency.

The Russians at once set to work to negotiate a preliminary treaty directly with the Turks. It was, perhaps, an unwise step, for no settlement, temporary or permanent, of the Eastern question can be made without the full consent of all the Great Powers. Perhaps it would have been better to call a general Congress at once, say that Russia had conquered from the Turks all that the Constantinople Conference had demanded, and then ask the Great Powers to put the propositions of this Conference forthwith into effect. But, on the other hand, it must be remembered that Russia had had a painful experience of the fruitlessness of conferences and diplomatic proceedings generally, and now too much blood and treasure had been expended to allow any risks to be run of their objects being defeated. Acting on this idea, Russia determined to first obtain the consent of the Turks, by means of a preliminary treaty, to new forms of government for the conquered provinces, and then to submit this to a future Congress as an accomplished fact, to be modified in its details, if necessary.

The bases of peace were agreed to before hostilities were suspended. They were—

1. Bulgaria, within limits not less than those indicated by the Conference, to become a self-governing tributary principality, with a Christian governor and a native militia. The Ottoman troops to no longer remain in it, and the Danubian fortresses to be destroyed.

2. Montenegro to be acknowledged independent, and receive an increase of territory.

3. Roumania and Servia to become independent, and to receive territorial indemnity.

4. Bosnia and Herzegovnia to be "endowed with an autonomous administration and sufficient guaranties."

5. Turkey to pay Russia for the expenses of the war, either in money or territory.

The Treaty of San Stefano was framed on this basis. It increased by a few hundred square miles those limits of Bulgaria which had been indicated by the Conference. The former limits had followed an irregular line about forty miles distant from the shores of the Ægean; the new limits gave the principality an outlet to the sea at Salonica, and along the coast for about sixty miles east of the Chalcidean peninsula.

It made Roumania completely independent, took back the small piece of Bessarabia which had been awarded to it by the Treaty of Paris, and gave in exchange a larger territory in the Dobrudja.

To Servia were given independence and a slight increase in territory.

In Bosnia and Herzegovnia were to be introduced those measures of reform which had been formulated at the first meeting of the Conference, subject to any changes that might be made by Austria, Russia, and Turkey in common.

The war indemnity was fixed at a little more than a thousand millions of dollars; but of this the territory in Bessarabia and the fortresses of Batoum, Kars, Ardahan, etc., in Asia, were valued at seven hundred and fifty millions, leaving two hundred and fifty millions to be paid in cash, the details of the payment to be subsequently arranged.

The Russians were to use the ports of the Black Sea and the Sea of Marmora to embark their troops, and the evacuation of Turkey was to commence at once, and be concluded within six months after the signature of a definite treaty of peace.

Such was the Treaty of San Stefano, signed on the 3d of March, 1878.

Before the treaty was signed Austria had already taken the lead in proposing a general Conference for the consideration of Eastern affairs; to this Russia and other Powers acceded. But on the signature of the treaty England proposed additional conditions on which alone she would enter the Conference; these were, that the treaty should be submitted entire to the Conference in order that it might judge what portions of it were of general concern and should be subject to modification. To this Russia replied, that there were no secret articles to the treaty; that the whole of it had been furnished to each of the Powers, and that each of them might raise any discussion that it chose; but Russia must decline to accept the discussion if it was not upon a matter of European interest. This answer was not satisfactory to England, and after considerable correspondence had passed on the subject, all hope of the meeting of the Conference was abandoned. England then called out her reserves, and there seemed every prospect of war. Lord Derby, who had so long tried to maintain the *status quo* by neither helping the Turks nor coercing them, now resigned. He was succeeded by Lord Salisbury, and on the 1st of April the latter sent out his famous circular dispatch to the Powers, announcing the position of England.

This dispatch rehearsed the argument, the practical importance of which it was hard for any but Englishmen to comprehend, about Russia *submitting* the entire treaty to the Conference, and then proceeded to criticise the whole bearing and intent of the San Stefano treaty. In Lord Salisbury's opinion, this treaty created "a strong Slav state under the auspices and control of Russia, possessing important harbors on the Black Sea and the Archipelago, and conferring upon that Power a preponderating influence over both political and commercial relations in those seas. . . ." This state would be "subjected to a ruler whom Russia will practically choose, its administration framed by a Russian commissary, and the first working of its institutions commenced under the control of a Russian army. . . ." Finally, "the general effect of this portion of the treaty will be to increase the power of the Russian Empire in the countries and on the shores where a Greek population dominates, not only to the prejudice of that nation, but also of every country having interests in the east of the Mediterranean Sea." As the Treaty of San Stefano had prescribed that the Prince of Bulgaria should be freely elected by the population and confirmed by the Porte, *with the consent of the Great Powers*, and that he should not belong to any of the ruling dynasties, it is hard to understand how he would be a "ruler whom Russia would practically choose." As for the size of Bulgaria, it was but slightly larger than that proposed by Lord Salisbury himself and the other members of the Conference; at that time he was as well aware as now of the number of Greeks inhabiting it. How Russia was to derive any more advantage from the small and poor harbors of the new principality in the Ægean than she had derived from the numerous ports of Greece which had been freed by her arms in 1829, was not explained; but even if she did, it required a most ardent prejudice to explain how Russia, by having a few harbors in the eastern end of the Mediterranean, was to be inimical to the interests of every other nation, any more than France, Italy, and Austria, which had abundant and good harbors on the same sea or its tributaries, and were possessed of stronger navies and greater naval aptitude than Russia.

The argument on all these points was by no means conclusive, and Lord Salisbury's position was singularly opposed to that which he had maintained at the Conference.

In view of this defiant and unreasonable attitude of England, Russia at once proceeded to send General Ignatieff to sound the intentions of Austria. For England single-handed she had no fears whatever. With great effort England could land ninety thousand raw troops at Gallipoli, to oppose the three hundred thousand veterans which Russia had south of the Balkans; the Russian ports could be protected by torpedoes against England's fleet, which could land but a few thousand marines at Constantinople. Russia could fit out cruisers to prey on English commerce, and could stir up insurrection in India. So long as her land communications were safe, Russia cared nothing for the navigation of the Black Sea, which had already been closed to her by the Turkish fleet.

These views were shared by all the Russian generals. But if Austria was to enter on the scene, the whole condition of affairs would be changed. A glance at the map will explain this at once. From the Carpathians to the Black Sea the distance is but one hundred and twenty miles. Through this narrow gap came all the supplies for the Russian army. Should the Austrian army, which was to be supported by English money, block this passage, and the English fleet occupy the Black Sea, Russia's position in Turkey was a checkmate; which could only be broken by crushing the Austrian army. To attempt to fight the Turks at Constantinople, the English at Gallipoli, and the Austrians in Bessarabia, would require sacrifices of the most onerous character.

The nature of the negotiations between General Ignatieff and the Austrian government has never been made public; but they undoubtedly ended in failure. Austria, as in the Crimean War, seized the diplomatic opportunity and used her strategic position to the utmost advantage. She declined to make any terms with Russia, and General Ignatieff returned without success. It was at once evident that Russia must make certain concessions or attempt the task of opposing a most formidable coalition in behalf of interests which were only remotely her own.

Under these circumstances Count Shouvaloff was summoned to St. Petersburg by the Emperor, and on his return to London he made a secret agreement with Lord Salisbury, specifying the conditions under which Russia would enter a Conference, the project of which had been revived by Germany.

The essence of this agreement was that Bulgaria should not extend to the Ægean; that it should be divided into two provinces, separated by the Balkans—the northern one to be a tributary principality, and the southern one to have a large measure of self-government, and no Turkish troops to be stationed in it; the war indemnity not to be converted into territorial cession, but Russia to insist on the return of the portion of Bessarabia and the acquisition of certain territory in Asia.

With this understanding the Powers convened in Congress on the 13th of June, 1878. The treaty which they signed just one month later, confirmed the provisions of this secret agreement, and added a provision that Austria should occupy and administer Bosnia and Herzegovnia. No term was fixed for this occupation, and it will in all probability be permanent. Thus Austria, which had taken no part in the war, was the only Great Power that received any considerable territory in Europe as the result of it. She resumed her ancient position as the legatee of the territory which the Turk was unable to hold and defend.

Before the treaty was signed or the Congress had met, England had concluded a secret alliance with Turkey by which she guaranteed to defend the Sultan's Asiatic possessions against further encroachments by Russia, provided he ceded to her the island of Cyprus as a base for her operations.

Though Russia lost nothing personally by the Treaty of Berlin, yet it was undoubtedly a heavy blow to her pride, in that she had been obliged by Europe to renounce the settlement which she had first made, in favor of one much less advantageous to the suffering people on whose behalf she had undertaken the war. Her own settlement contained far more elements of stability than that which Europe dictated, for nothing could be so fruitful of future dissensions and insurrections as the division of the lands occupied by the Bulgarians into two provinces, one of which enjoys a complete government of its own, and the other—as Lord Salisbury proudly boasted—is restored to the " direct military and political authority of the Sultan." Nothing could be more illusory than the theory that the Balkans form a strong line of military defense, which was the central feature of Lord Beaconsfield's arguments in the Congress. Nothing is so opposed to the teachings of history as the idea that Russia's influence with the subject races in the Balkan Peninsula would be diminished by the obstructions and restrictions which England offers to the freedom which these races have gained or aspire to.

On the conclusion of the Treaty of Berlin, many Englishmen cried out with joy—as they had in 1856

—that the Eastern question was now finally settled. It has required but two short years to prove to every one how far this is from being true. The boundary of Greece is still undefined, the boundary of Montenegro the same; not a step has been taken toward reforming the government in Armenia, and Cyprus turns out to be too unhealthy for British troops to inhabit it. Realizing how completely they have been deceived by the showy but unsubstantial foreign policy of Lord Beaconsfield's government, the British public has lately overturned it in the most complete manner.

But the Treaty of Berlin has this great advantage over the Treaty of Paris, that it is a step in advance and not in retreat. It says no word about the "integrity and independence of the Ottoman Empire," and it sanctions the diminution of that empire in favor of self-governing Christian states. That its settlement is only a temporary one, there is no doubt. The Turkish government is bankrupt, its officials, civil and military, are unpaid, the respect for its authority is everywhere diminishing, its decrepitude is rapidly increasing, and it has not the means of introducing reforms even if it had the will. Its dissolution is near at hand. Will England still try to galvanize its lifeless members and to prop it up, or will it come to terms with its neighbors and arrange for its exit?

Such is the Eastern question—the question whether the Turk shall live in Europe and misgovern Christian subjects; whether the teachings of the Koran or of the Bible shall have the ascendancy in Southeastern Europe. For five hundred and twenty-four years the Turk has occupied some of the fairest lands known to man—lands which in times past have been the seat of the first nations of the earth, and whose mineral and agricultural wealth, wonderful climate, and geographical situation would make them to-day the rivals in prosperity, wealth, and happiness, of any country in Europe, were they fairly governed. How has the Turk administered this rich heritage? Save a few of the earlier Sultans, who were possessed of strong characters and military skill, in these five hundred years Turkey has produced no great man; in art and in science Turkish history is an absolute blank, and its literature consists of little but dissertations on the Koran. The wonderful mechanical genius which during this century has so aided the development of wealth and of material prosperity and happiness throughout the civilized world, has never been allowed to enter Turkey. Its lands are tilled as they were two thousand years ago, its mines are unopened, and its highways of communication are such as were left by the Roman conquerors. You may search as you please through the records of these five hundred years, and you will find no evidence of the slightest advance in civilization. It is only a barren and sickening tale of wars and oppression and misrule, of grinding extortion and barbarous massacre, of personal corruption and the grossest immorality.

How to remedy this without allowing all the benefits to accrue to one nation, is the problem which now faces Europe, as it has for more than a century past. It is a problem of stupendous magnitude—the problem above all others of international politics in Europe. It involves every great nation in the world, save only ourselves, and absorbs the unceasing attention of the greatest minds in those nations. That it will end in the expulsion of the Turk from Europe at no distant day, may be confidently asserted, but, further than this, it is hazardous to attempt to predict the details of the solution. Certain fundamental principles, however, which have now been proved beyond a doubt, must form the basis of any permanent settlement; and the most essential of these are, first, that the existing Ottoman government is incapable of introducing reforms in the government of its subject races; and, second, that it is impossible for it to permanently maintain its existence either with or without foreign aid. The principles of the Treaty of Paris have been shown to be utterly untenable, and must be abandoned in favor of something more in accordance with facts and justice. In short, the *status quo*, which England has striven to maintain for so many years, has now proved itself an impossibility, and it is imperatively necessary to provide a substitute. Will England frankly join the other Great Powers in endeavoring to provide a substitute; will the Powers be able to agree, even if England joins them, or will the Ottoman government make its exit in the midst of a convulsion brought about by new rebellions of its own subjects? The time for the final solution of this long-pending Eastern question seems now to be at hand, but no man can tell how the solution will be made.

THE END.

The best Biography of the Greatest of the Romans.

CÆSAR: A SKETCH.

BY

JAMES ANTHONY FROUDE, M.A.

One vol., 8vo, cloth, with a Steel Portrait and a Map.
Price, $2.50.

There is no historical writer of our time who can rival Mr. Froude in vivid delineation of character, grace and clearness of style and elegant and solid scholarship. In his *Life of Cæsar*, all these qualities appear in their fullest perfection, resulting in a fascinating narrative which will be read with keen delight by a multitude of readers, and will enhance, if possible, Mr. Froude's brilliant reputation.

CRITICAL NOTICES.

"The book is charmingly written, and, on the whole, wisely written. There are many admirable, really noble, passages; there are hundreds of pages which few living men could match. * * * The political life of Cæsar is explained with singular lucidity, and with what seems to us remarkable fairness. The horrible condition of Roman society under the rule of the magnates is painted with startling power and brilliance of coloring.—*Atlantic Monthly.*

"Mr. Froude's latest work, "Cæsar," is affluent of his most distinctive traits. Nothing that he has written is more brilliant, more incisive, more interesting. * * * He combines into a compact and nervous narrative all that is known of the personal, social, political, and military life of Cæsar; and with his sketch of Cæsar, includes other brilliant sketches of the great men, his friends or rivals, who contemporaneously with him formed the principal figures in the Roman world."—*Harper's Monthly.*

"This book is a most fascinating biography, and is by far the best account of Julius Cæsar to be found in the English language."—*London Standard.*

"It is the best biography of the greatest of the Romans we have, and it is in some respects Mr. Froude's best piece of historical writing."—*Hartford Courant.*

Mr. Froude has given the public the best of all recent books on the life, character and career of Julius Cæsar."—*Phila. Eve. Bulletin.*

₊ For sale by all booksellers, or will be sent, prepaid, upon receipt of price, by

CHARLES SCRIBNER'S SONS,
743 AND 745 BROADWAY, NEW YORK.

"A work of strange power and poetry."—N. Y. WORLD.

THE COSSACKS.

TRANSLATED BY

EUGENE SCHUYLER, Ph.D.,

From the Russian of Count Tolstoy.

1 vol., small 12mo, cloth, ... $1.25

CRITICAL NOTICES.

"The translation is excellent, although the Russian flavor still remains. Yet this rather heightens than mars the fascination of the book."
—*Baltimore Gazette.*

"A story of high merit and well-sustained interest."—*Phila. Bulletin.*

"The Cossacks is a novel likely to please a much wider circle of readers in this country than anything that the more famous novelist (Turguénief) has done, than any other Russian novel which has been translated, indeed, including even the stories of Pushkin."
—*N. Y. Evening Post.*

"The characters are all sketched by a master hand, and the story, without being artistically woven, is full of living interest and warmth, and we thank Mr. Schuyler for breaking up this new ground, and hope he will follow up the lead, for he has what our appetites for more of this brilliant writer's work."—*New York Herald.*

"Its interest, besides the interest of the qualities we have mentioned, resides in its broad and firm, yet delicate and subtle portraiture; and apart from its novel characteristics, it should be welcome for the acquaintance it enables one to make of the different personages it so admirably sketches."
—*New York World.*

"The story is one that American readers will enjoy, not only because it is in many respects a masterpiece of literary work, but also because it takes them into scenes entirely new to them, and among characters as strange as the scenes in which they are placed."—*New Haven Palladium.*

*** *The above book for sale by all booksellers, or will be sent, post or express charges paid, upon receipt of the price by the publishers,*

CHARLES SCRIBNER'S SONS,

743 AND 745 BROADWAY, NEW YORK.

"A GREAT SUCCESS."—Pall Mall Gazette.

A NEW AND CHEAPER EDITION.

MR. EUGENE SCHUYLER'S

TURKISTAN:

Notes of a Journey in 1873, in the Russian Province of
Turkistan, the Khanates of Khokan and Bukhara,
and Provinces of Kuldja.

By EUGENE SCHUYLER, Ph.D.,

Formerly Secretary of the American Legation at St. Petersburg, now Consul-General at Constantinople.

OPINIONS OF THE PRESS.

From the London Times.

"Mr. Schuyler will be ranked among the most accomplished of living travelers. Many parts of his book will be found of interest, even by the most exacting of general readers; and, as a whole, it is incomparably the most valuable record of Central Asia which has been published in this country."

From the N. Y. Evening Post.

"The author's chief aim appears to have been to do all that he says he tried to do, and to do greatly more beside—namely, to study everything there was to study in the countries which he visited, and to tell the world all about it in a most interesting way. He is, indeed, a model traveler, and he has written a model book of travels, in which every line is interesting, and from which nothing that any reader can want to hear about has been excluded."

Mr. Gladstone in the "Contemporary Review."

"One of the most solid and painstaking works which have been published among us in recent years."

From the New York Times.

"Its descriptions of the country and of the people living in it are always interesting and frequently amusing; but it is easy to see that they have been written by one who is not only so thoroughly cosmopolitan as to know intuitively what is worth telling and what had better be omitted, but who is, also, so practiced a writer as to understand precisely how to set forth what he has to say in the most effective manner."

From the Atlantic Monthly.

"Undoubtedly the most thoroughly brilliant and entertaining work on Turkistan which has yet been given to the English-speaking world."

From the Independent.

"It is fortunate that a record of the sort appears at this time, and doubly fortunate that it comes from the hand of so wise, well-informed, and industrious a traveler and diplomat."

From the New York World.

"Its author has the eye and pen of a journalist, and sees at once what is worth seeing, and recites his impressions in the most graphic manner."

Two vols. 8vo. With three Maps, and numerous Illustrations, attractively bound in cloth, price reduced from $7.50 to $5.

*** *The above book for sale by all booksellers, or will be sent, post or express charges paid, upon receipt of the price by the publishers,*

CHARLES SCRIBNER'S SONS,

743 AND 745 BROADWAY, NEW YORK.

The Authorized Edition. Two Vols. in One.

The most Famous Book of the Day.

Bismarck

IN THE FRANCO-GERMAN WAR.

AN AUTHORIZED TRANSLATION FROM THE GERMAN

OF

Dr. MORITZ BUSCH.

Two Vols. in One, black and gold, ... $1.50

American readers now have an opportunity to make acquaintance with the most widely-discussed book of the day, and those whose expectation has been aroused by the reviews and correspondents will be able fully to understand the excitement it has called forth in Europe.

Covering the whole period of the war, the book gives an account—as vivid as only the smallest details can make it—of Bismarck's daily life, habits, and methods of work, his comments on everything and every one about him; his opinions, epigrams, and smallest table-talk.

"*It is a ravishing book, we have said, and one who takes it up does not lay it down again until he has read its last page, and has turned back to read again and again some of its most entertaining paragraphs. It is a wonderful book, too, considered merely as a piece of faithful reporting.*—N. Y. EVENING POST."

"*The publication of Bismarck's after-dinner talk, whether discreet or not, will be of priceless biographical value, and Englishmen, at least, will not be disposed to quarrel with Dr. Busch for giving a picture as true to life as Boswell's 'Johnson' of the foremost practical genius that Germany has produced since Frederic the Great.*"—LONDON TIMES.

"*Nobody can understand the political history of the Franco-German war, nor the man Bismarck, its chief maker, who has not read the diary of the Reichskanzler's Boswell. . . . . The English version is far more readable than the German.*" —LONDON ATHENÆUM.

*** *The above book for sale by all booksellers, or will be sent, prepaid, upon receipt of price, by*

CHARLES SCRIBNER'S SONS, PUBLISHERS,

743 AND 745 BROADWAY, NEW YORK.

The Standard Edition of Gladstone's Essays.

Gleanings of Past Years.

BY

The Right Hon. W. E. GLADSTONE.

Seven Volumes, 16mo, Cloth, per volume, $1.00.

The extraordinary scope of Mr. Gladstone's learning—the wonder of his friends and enemies alike—and his firm grasp of every subject he discusses, make his essays much more than transient literature. Their collection and publication in permanent shape were of course certain to be undertaken sooner or later; and now that they are so published with the benefit of his own revision, they will need little heralding in England or America.

What Mr. Gladstone has written in the last thirty-six years—the period covered by this collection—has probably had the attention of as large an English-speaking public as any writer on political and social topics ever reached in his own life-time. The papers which he has chosen as of lasting value, and included here under the title of *Gleanings of Past Years*, will form the standard edition of his miscellanies, both for his present multitude of readers, and for those who will study his writings later.

Vol. I. **The Throne, and the Prince Consort; The Cabinet, and Constitution.**

Vol. II.—**Personal and Literary.**

Vol. III.—**Historical and Speculative.**

Vol. IV.—**Foreign.**

Vol. V.
Vol. VI. } **Ecclesiastical.**

Vol. VII.—**Miscellaneous.**

*** The above books for sale by all booksellers, or will be sent, prepaid, upon receipt of price, by

CHARLES SCRIBNER'S SONS, PUBLISHERS,

743 AND 745 BROADWAY, NEW YORK.

"A book abounding in matter of solid interest."—London Spectator.

The Government of M. Thiers.
By JULES SIMON.
Translated from the French.

Two vols. 8vo,　・　・　・　・　・　・　・　・　$4.50.

The importance of this book among the materials for the history of the time is at once self-evident, and can hardly be exaggerated. Simon's part in the most intense action of the period he describes, his intimate relations with Thiers himself, and his position in the Republican party of France, unite to give a worth to his narrative such as could hardly attach to that of any other eye-witness of these events. Such records, by men writing of matters in the very crisis of their own activity, generally have to wait for the future historian to put them into their lasting form, and give them their greatest interest as parts of the whole story. But the most remarkable feature of M. Simon's book is that it does not need this treatment, and is not so much a personal memoir—a contribution to history—as a completed picture of the period. There is a justice of proportion and truth of historical perspective about it that is very unusual in the work of one recording the politics of his own day. Parts are not unduly magnified because they were subjects of the author's special personal observation and interest; but the relative weight of different events is as carefully given as though by a philosophical looker-on rather than an actor. There is a strong probability that a century hence the book will still be looked upon as among the first authorities, in impartiality and full appreciation of the time it treats.

Simon's pen-pictures of contemporaries—even of adversaries—are very striking, in the fact that they are generally just without losing any of their vigor. They are as interesting from another point of view—if not as "ruthless"—as those of the great German chancellor, whose comments on the characters of those engaged in the same scenes are often supplemented by these sketches. The future historian of the last ten years can hardly complain that he lacks knowledge of their leading men, when he has at hand this history and Dr. Busch's memoirs of Prince Bismarck.

From the "London Spectator."

"The special interest connected with these volumes is to be found in striking and vivid notices scattered through them of points which only one intimately connected with the transactions under review could have known. With the single exception of M. Barthélemy St. Hilaire, no person was so closely associated with M. Thiers during the course of his administration as Jules Simon. * * * The various chapters are devoted to so many episodes—many of them stirring episodes—that are told with striking force. Of course the spirit of the narrative is strongly biased, but it cannot be said that M. Jules Simon writes with want of candour. * * * The history of the constant and patient struggle of M. Thiers against turbulent and factious combinations, though not unfrequently attended by sallies on his own part of seeming impatience and querulousness, is narrated in graphic chapters. Two especially must command attention—those in which M. Simon tells the tale of the Commune and of the negotiations which M. Thiers carried on with so much skill and pertinacity for the liberation of France from the invader at a term earlier than that fixed by the original treaty."

** *The above book for sale by all booksellers, or will be sent, prepaid, upon receipt of price, by*

CHARLES SCRIBNER'S SONS, PUBLISHERS,
743 AND 745 BROADWAY, NEW YORK.

"Two as interesting and valuable books of travel as have been published in this country." NEW YORK EXPRESS.

DR. FIELD'S TRAVELS ROUND THE WORLD.

I.
FROM THE LAKES OF KILLARNEY TO THE GOLDEN HORN.

II.
FROM EGYPT TO JAPAN.

By **HENRY M. FIELD, D.D.,** Editor of the N. Y. Evangelist.

Each 1 vol. 12mo. Cloth, gilt top, uniform in style, $2.

CRITICAL NOTICES.

By George Ripley, LL.D., in the New York Tribune.

Few recent travellers combine so many qualities that are adapted to command the interest and sympathy of the public. While he indulges, to its fullest extent, the characteristic American curiosity with regard to foreign lands, insisting on seeing every object of interest with his own eyes, shrinking from no peril or difficulty in pursuit of information—climbing mountains, descending mines, exploring pyramids, with no sense of satiety or weariness, he has also made a faithful study of the highest authorities on the different subjects of his narrative, thus giving solidity and depth to his descriptions, without sacrificing their facility or grace.

From the New York Observer.

The present volume comprises by far the most novel, romantic, and interesting part of the Journey [Round the World], and the story of it is told and the scenes are painted by the hand of a master of the pen. Dr. Field is a veteran traveller; he knows well what to see, and (which is still more important to the reader) he knows well what to describe and how to do it.

By Chas. Dudley Warner, in the Hartford Courant.

It is thoroughly entertaining; the reader's interest is never allowed to flag; the author carries us forward from land to land with uncommon vivacity, enlivens the way with a good humor, a careful observation, and treats all peoples with a refreshing liberality.

From Rev. Dr. R. S. Storrs.

It is indeed a charming book—full of fresh information, picturesque description, and thoughtful studies of men, countries, and civilizations.

From Prof. Roswell D. Hitchcock, D.D.

In this second volume, Dr. Field, I think, has surpassed himself in the first, and this is saying a good deal. In both volumes the editorial instinct and habit are conspicuous. Dr. Prime has said that an editor should have six senses, the sixth being "a sense of the *interesting.*" Dr. Field has this to perfection. * * *

From the New York Herald.

It would be impossible by extracts to convey an adequate idea of the variety, abundance, or picturesque freshness of these sketches of travel, without copying a great part of the book.

Rev. Wm. M. Taylor, D.D., in the Christian at Work.

Dr. Field has an eye, if we may use a photographic illustration, with a great deal of collodion in it, so that he sees very clearly. He knows also how to describe just those things in the different places visited by him which an intelligent man wants to know about.

⁎ *The above books for sale by all booksellers, or will be sent, post or express charges paid, upon receipt of the price by the publishers.*

CHARLES SCRIBNER'S SONS,
743 AND 745 BROADWAY, NEW YORK.

A FASCINATING BOOK.

Prince Bismarck's Letters

TO

HIS SISTER, WIFE, AND OTHERS,

From 1844 to 1870.

TRANSLATED FROM THE GERMAN,

By FITZH. MAXSE.

One Vol. 16mo, cloth, ... $1.00

These select letters of Prince Bismarck, which have been collected, translated, and published with his express consent, illustrate, and perhaps as forcibly as ever before, the wide separation there may be between the public and private life of a great statesman. No matter how familiar the reader may be with Bismarck's political career, this volume will contain for him a revelation as remarkable as it is intensely interesting. For in them we see not the diplomatist but the man.

From the "New-York Evening Post."

"The careful reader will see on nearly every page some sentence which reveals the character of this remarkable man as it has never been revealed in his public acts or words."

From the "Boston Transcript."

"Even the most confirmed Bismarck-hater cannot help feeling his prejudices softened, and his respect for this wonderful man increased in reading these revelations of his inner life. The work which contains them will have the effect of changing in no small degree the popular estimate of his character in this country, and will form an important volume in autobiographic literature."

From the "Nation."

"The impression conveyed throughout these letters is that Bismarck, in respect to his political life, is a Diogenes, who, in an hour of weakness, has been persuaded out of his tub, and who regrets the emergence as an error. But in its humor, its melancholy, its self-consciousness, Bismarck's is a thoroughly modern mind; in his lack of intellectual subtilty, and in his downright religious convictions, he is less evidently of our time. orthodoxy being now in Germany, for the most part—at least among the *Hofwelt*—an anachronism. * * * Complete vigor and genuineness of nature, combined with rare patience and good humor, rather than a profound insight, have given Prince von Bismarck his position in European affairs. These letters alone are enough to show that their writer was never destined to an inferior place."

*** *The above book for sale by all booksellers, or will be sent, prepaid, upon receipt of price, by*

CHARLES SCRIBNER'S SONS, PUBLISHERS,

743 AND 745 BROADWAY, NEW YORK.

AN INVALUABLE ADDITION TO ARCHÆOLOGICAL DISCOVERY.

DR. SCHLIEMANN'S GREAT WORK.

DISCOVERIES AND RESEARCHES
ON THE SITES OF
ANCIENT MYCENÆ AND TIRYNS.

By DR. HENRY SCHLIEMANN, Author of "Troy and its Remains."

With Preface by the HON. W. E. GLADSTONE.

With Maps, Colored Plates, Views and Cuts, representing several Hundred Objects of Antiquity discovered on the Sites.

[IN ALL, FIVE HUNDRED ILLUSTRATIONS.]

CRITICAL NOTICES.

"In this magnificent volume we have finally the story of Dr. Schliemann's last and most important discoveries. He has been the most fortunate of archæological explorers; for even a greater luck than rewarded him in the Troad has fallen to his portion in Argolis. * * * We suspect that the final verdict of scholars will be that Dr. Schliemann has actually discovered the remains of the man, some part of whose history, at least, is preserved in the Agamemnon of Homer and Æschylus."—*The N. Y. Tribune.*

"Dr. Schliemann's book is worth all the prolegomens and commentaries upon Homer that have been written since the revival of learning."—*The Boston Globe.*

"The interest of the work is not confined to either England or America. Every enlightened nation will welcome it, for it opens up a new world to the modern generation. No work of the time has attracted wider attention."—*Boston Post.*

"This splendid volume is a museum of itself which every lover of history and classical literature will feel that he must possess, and which any intelligent reader is competent to understand and enjoy by means of its abundant and truly splendid illustrations."—*Buffalo Commercial Advertiser.*

"Dr. Schliemann has made the most important contribution of the present century to Greek archæology."—*The Nation.*

"We commend the volume, with its admirable typography and multitudinous illustrations, to the attention of our readers, assuring them that they will find it possessed of a rare and enduring interest."—*Boston Journal.*

"We add our testimony in saying that a copy of Mycenæ is necessary to the library of every scholar, and—which is no mean praise—that the printing and illustrations of this work are worthy of the matter."—*Baltimore Gazette.*

One vol. quarto, superbly printed on superfine paper, cloth extra, $12.00.

⁎ *The above books for sale by all booksellers, or will be sent, post or express charges paid, upon receipt of the price by the publishers,*

CHARLES SCRIBNER'S SONS,
743 AND 745 BROADWAY, NEW YORK.

"The world has waited for this publication, and now that it has appeared, it will be diligently read by all men."

THE AUTOBIOGRAPHY
—OF—
PRINCE METTERNICH.

Edited by his Son, PRINCE METTERNICH. Translated by Robina Napier.

With a minute index prepared especially for this edition.

2 vols., 8vo.   With Portrait and Fac-similes   -   - $5.00.

For twenty years—since it became known at his death that the great diplomatist of the Napoleonic period had left his memoirs—the publication of this book has been looked for with such interest as perhaps no other personal revelations could have aroused. Prince Metternich's own directions kept it back during this time; and this fact, with the complete secresy preserved as to the contents of the manuscript, rightly led to the belief that he had treated the events and persons of his day with an unsparing candor.

The simultaneous publication of the memoirs in Germany, France, England and America is therefore something more than a literary event. Metternich alone held the keys of the most secret history of the most important epoch in modern times, and in this book he gives them up—an impossibility during his life. Even to especial students, who know what problems these disclosures have been expected to solve, the value of what they open will be as surprising as the extraordinary care with which they have been guarded.

The announcement alone is of sufficient interest, that we are at last in possession of the autobiography of the statesman who from the French Revolution to Waterloo, took part in the making of nearly every great treaty, and was himself the negotiator of the greatest; and who from 1806 to 1815, was the guiding mind of the vast combinations which defeated Napoleon and decided the form of modern Europe.

EXTRACTS FROM REVIEWS OF THE METTERNICH MEMOIRS.

"The great chancellor writes with an exceedingly easy pen. It is indeed interesting to follow his narration, so clear that one never loses the thread of his story, and so graphic that we get a glimpse of the scenes as with our own eyes. The work is intensely interesting to read, and of the greatest value to the historical student."—*N. Y. Independent.*

"Of the great value of the work we have already spoken. It not only enables the world for the first time to understand clearly the objects for which Prince Metternich contended throughout his long public life, but casts fresh light on some of the most obscure historical incidents of his day."—*The Athenæum.*

"The Memoirs of Metternich are to be heartily welcomed by all who are interested either in the serious facts or the lighter gossip of history. There is no period, indeed, in recent history, more important or attractive than that covered by the first volume of these memoirs."—*Boston Literary World.*

** *For sale by all booksellers, or will be sent, prepaid, upon receipt of price, by*

CHARLES SCRIBNER'S SONS, PUBLISHERS,
743 AND 745 BROADWAY, NEW YORK.

www.ingramcontent.com/pod-product-compliance
Lightning Source LLC
Chambersburg PA
CBHW031853220426
43663CB00006B/601